THE SEVEN WIVES
OF
HARALD FAIRHAIR

FIRST KING OF ALL NORWAY

CIRCA 850-933 A.D.

A VIKING SAGA

MARCIA LEE LIAKLEV
mnelson@alumni.uidaho.edu

"Harald Harfagre was remarkably handsome, great and strong, and very generous to his men. He was a great warrior, and his large posterity spread over the whole land; for of his race, ever after, have come the Kings of Norway."

Heimskringla

INTRODUCTION

Harald was not inherently romantic, but he did envy the look of love he saw in the eyes of his powerful father whenever his lovely mother was near. Their influence was key to the remarkable man he would become.

Enter Odin, the Allfather who ruled the mortals under his charge. Would the god actually ask Harald to marry at the age of eleven, regardless of the stunning red-haired beauty chosen for his mate? But she was only the bait--- the bait that would set the young prince on his quest to fulfill the destiny requested and required of him by Odin in the pre-mortal world.

Little did this Viking lad know that Asa would be just the first of the wives Odin would choose for him to wed. After countless successful battles and many years as the powerful ruler, Harald began to feel proud of his great accomplishments and neglected to pay homage to the god who had protected and guided the events of his life.

Then came the witch. The confident king was helpless under her power and she used him as she pleased. Only after he had sired four sons while hidden in the dark, filthy cave did Odin allow him to be rescued.

Some lessons are hard to learn, but those are the kind one never forgets. Fortunately for Harald, he had yet more women to love and more sons to be brought into the world. The noble blood that ran through the veins of these sons would insure the longevity of his royal line.

The Seven Wives of Harald Fairhair, First King of All Norway brings to life a superhero of the Viking Age whose story needs to be told. He shall take his place among the great leaders of the Norsemen. It is a saga of love and war, but mostly love.

This is a work of fiction, based on facts as found in the ***Heimskringla, A History of the Kings of Norway,*** an ancient text written in the Old Norse language. It was compiled by Snorre Sturluson from documents, now lost, that were recorded during the 9th to the 12th century.

TABLE OF CONTENTS

LIST OF MAIN CHARACTERS

1. Aasa Haraldsdatter...Harald Fairhair's grandmother
2. Gudrod the Hunter...Harald Fairhair's grandfather
3. Halvdan the Black Gudrodson...Harald's father
4. Ragnhild Sigurdsdatter...Harald's mother
5. Guttorm Sigurdson...Harald's uncle
6. Asa Hakonsdatter...Harald's 1st wife
7. Harald and Asa's sons...Guttorm, Halvdan the Black and Halvdan the White, and Sigrod Haraldson
8. Svanhild Eysteinsdatter...Harald's 2nd wife
9. Harald and Svanhild's sons...Olaf, Bjorn, and Ragnar Haraldson
10. Gyda Eiriksdatter...Harald's 3rd wife
11. Harald and Gyda's children...Alov Arbot, Rorek, Sigtrygg, Frode, and Torgils Haraldson
12. Snofrid Svasesdatter...Harald's 4th wife
13. Harald and Snofrid's sons...Halvdan, Gudrod, Sigurd and Ragnvald Haraldson
14. Ragnvald, Jarl of More...Harald's uncle
15. Hrolf Ganger Ragnvaldson...Haralds' distant cousin
16. Ragnild Eriksdatter...Harald's 5th wife
17. Harald and Ragnild's son...Erik Bloodaxe Haraldson
18. Ashild Ringsdatter...Harald's 6th wife
19. Harald and Ashild's children...Ring, Dag, Gudrod, and Ragnhild Haraldsdatter
20. Tora Mosterstrong...Harald's concubine
21. Harald and Tora's son...Haakon the Good Haraldson
22. Odin...the Allfather and God to the Vikings

CHAPTER 1

THE GRANDPARENTS

King Gudrod was called the Hunter and he lived up to his name. Not only did he need to prove his power by hunting down animals, but he took the same actions when dealing with people. Gudrod was accustomed to getting his own way and he did what he needed to make that happen. When his first wife died, he decided he would have Aasa from the neighboring kingdom of Agder for his next wife.

Aasa was a young woman of exceeding great beauty. She was tall of stature with long, flaming red hair and piercing green eyes. Her beauty was only exceeded by her strong will and her sharp intellect, and Gudrod had desired her for a long while. He sent his men west to Agder to ask Aasa's father, King Harald Redbeard, to give his daughter to him.

"There will be no match between Gudrod the Hunter and my daughter," exclaimed Harald Redbeard, "Take your request and go elsewhere! Aasa would never consider a man like Gudrod to wed."

The ambassadors returned to their master and told him the result of their errand.

"Harald Redbeard refused my offer?" shouted Gudrod. "We shall see how he likes my next offer! Gather the men and ready the ships. We sail for Agder tonight!"

A great force of ships and men landed before dawn near the estate of King Harald and crept, with stealth, up the hill to the longhouse.

After his men had completely surrounded the building, King Gudrod shouted at the door, "Harald Redbeard, you shall pay dearly for refusing to give your daughter Aasa to me. Tonight, she shall be in my bed and you shall be dead!"

Then Gudrod made good on that threat, for though Harald summoned all the forces he had at the manor, it was not enough. The Hunter had told his men beforehand that none should slay Harald but him. He alone would claim revenge for the offense given.

Harald and his men fought valiantly, but they were severely outnumbered. Gudrod watched the King as he would his prey, waited until the man's energy was spent, and then went in for the kill. A swift stroke with the broad axe and off went Harald's head.

Aasa's brother Gyrd, fighting at his father's side, saw the bloody head roll by just before losing his own. When Harald Redbeard's men realized that their leader was dead, along with most of their comrades, they beat a hasty retreat into the woods.

Her father had told Aasa to escape to the woods when he realized the armed men at his door belonged to Gudrod. She tried to flee from a back door, but saw that the longhouse was completely surrounded by the Hunter's men. Aasa went to hide in her bedchamber, but soon she heard the shouts of Gudrod, searching for her inside the house.

"There is no escaping me, Aasa," cried Gudrod. "Your father is dead and your brother with him. There is no one left to protect you. You belong to me now!"

Gudrod chopped down the door to each bedchamber until he came to Aasa's. There she sat, on the bed platform, her back straight, her head up, her green eyes defiant.

"You may think you own me, Gudrod, now that you have murdered my family, but I tell you, you will never own me. You may treat me like one of your animals, but you will get no pleasure from me. My body may be in your bed, but my mind will never surrender!"

Gudrod only laughed at Aasa's proud words. He did not care. It was all about power and possession with him. He scooped her up and carried her stiff body to his dragon ship and sailed for his home in Vestfold. It had been a very successful night. He enjoyed a prey that made him work for it. He liked the challenge as well as the reward.

Aasa spoke not a word at the wedding feast. If Gudrod's friends felt sorry for her, they did not say so. Everyone seemed to be enjoying themselves, except for her. They would eat, drink and be merry, and then fall into a stupor of sleep. Not so for her. She would endure the wedding bed and never give Gudrod the satisfaction of knowing how much he hurt her.

Nine months later, a son was born to the miserable captive. Gudrod poured water on the boy and named him Halvdan, after his father. It was a proud name, but Aasa had wished her son could bear the name of her dead father Harald. However, she would not give Gudrod the satisfaction of asking him. Aasa never spoke to her husband unless she had to. He was her enemy and she could never forget that.

It was wonderful to have a son, despite the loathing she felt for the father. There was finally a small feeling of happiness in the horrible existence that had come to be Aasa's life. Having Halvdan allowed her to sleep in a separate bedchamber from Gudrod and kept her from having to endure his drunken advances.

Gudrod was drunk much of the time these days. Aasa hoped that he was as miserable as she was. Maybe the joy for him was only in the hunting, and once the prey was captured or killed, the joy vanished. That would explain the sullen look on Gudrod's face each time they had to be near each other.

Halvdan was such a joy. Despite the fact that he had black hair versus the red hair that would have shown her family resemblance, Aasa loved him dearly. He grew strong and straight and gave her life new meaning. Life at Vestfold became bearable with the birth of her son.

Shortly after Halvdan turned one year old, Gudrod made an announcement that caused Aasa's heart to stand still.

"Prepare Halvdan's things for a journey. I am taking him to the home of my father's brother. He will foster him and you will be rejoining me in my bedchamber."

Aasa wanted to scream. She wanted to shout that she would kill Gudrod before she would let him take away her one and only possession. Her good sense stopped her before she could give vent to her feelings.

"Halvdan has been waking much in the night of late and needs some more training before he will be ready for fostering by your father's brother. You would not want him to be a burden on their family. I will work with him while you are gone and he shall be ready for your next trip."

Gudrod was undecided if he should agree with his arrogant wife on this matter, or if he should insist on following his plan. His uncle's wife was older, and would not want a crying child added to their household. He decided that a few months wait would not make much difference. He was anxious to have a woman back in his bedchamber at night, but he was also looking forward to the round of feasts at Stiflesund.

"I will leave Halvdan for now. Make sure he will be ready when I return," growled Gudrod with an angry frown on his face..

Aasa was so relieved she almost answered pleasantly, but she knew that would make Gudrod suspicious. She had not said a pleasant word to him in the two years she had spent as a captive in his longhouse at Vestfold.

As Aasa watched Gudrod and his men push off in their dragon ships, she wondered how she could find a way to see that he never returned. Just then, one of her servants spoke behind her.

"I think it will be a sad day for you when Gudrod takes Halvdan away, My Lady."

Aasa turned to see Thorn, her thrall, standing there. Thorn admired Aasa greatly and he also loved little Halvdan.

"Would that I could keep Halvdan with me always," said Aasa, "but Gudrod will have his way."

She knew that Gudrod had beat Thorn several times for looking too kindly at her.

"I would help, My Lady, if I could," replied Thorn. Aasa decided that was the answer to her problem. She would just have to trust him to carry out her plan.

Gudrod was enjoying the feasts at Stiflesund and drinking heavily every night, but this evening would prove to be different from all the rest. As he was walking from his ship, in a drunken stupor, a man came out of the darkness and ran him through with a spear. Gudrod clutched at the weapon and looked up in surprise to see Thorn standing there...a smile of satisfaction on his face.

An animal like growl escaped the lips of the great hunter. He could never have imagined he would meet his end in such a humiliating way. Several men came running when they heard Gudrod's cry. Thorn was still standing by the dying man, enjoying the scene. He told them he was of Gudrod's household, but the other men knew he was Aasa's servant.

Thorn was hung the next day and offered as a sacrifice to the Gods for the death of the mighty hunter. Gudrod's men traveled back to tell Aasa that her husband was dead. If any of them expected to see tears from her eyes, they were disappointed. No one accused her of plotting her husband's death and she never denied it. Her hell was over and she had finally gotten revenge.

Thus tells Thjodolf of it: --

"Gudrod is gone to his long rest,
Despite of all his haughty pride --
A traitor's spear has pierced his side:
For Aasa cherished in her breast
Revenge; and as, by wine opprest,
The hero staggered from his ship,
The cruel queen her thrall let slip
To do the deed of which I sing:
And now the far-descended king,
At Stiflesund, in the old bed
Of the old Gudrod race, lies dead."

Heimskringla

Aasa, as his wife, was the last person to look on the dead body of once proud Gudrod as he lay in his large dragon ship. He was dressed in his kingly robes with his battle axe on the right side and his sword on the left side of his body. His men had placed them with him in his burial mound so that he might use them in the next life. Aasa seethed with anger when she thought about the fact that this was the very battle axe that had been used to sever the head of both her father and her brother.

The one possession of Gudrod's that Aasa wanted was his sword. She was glad that he had not used this beautiful weapon in the death of her loved ones, for then it would have been tainted in her mind. This sword had been passed down from father to son for many generations in Gudrod's royal family and Aasa wanted to pass it on to Halvdan when he was old enough to use it.

Glancing from the corner of her eye, Aasa saw that the men who were guarding Gudrod's mound had their backs to her. She lifted the heavy sword and placed it under her thick cape. With that final action, she turned her back on the man who had been her captor and her enemy. She hoped she would never have to see him again...even in the next life.

Aasa left Vestfold and moved back to her ancestral home in Agder and raised her son to be as much like her father, Harald Redbeard, as was possible. Despite the fact that he carried the blood of Gudrod the Hunter in his veins, he grew up to be a kind and considerate boy. Halvdan's hair was black like his father's, but that was the only resemblance he bore to the ruthless man who had sired him. He came to be called Halvdan the Black.

When Halvdan was ten, Aasa told him the story of his father. She was finally able to express the hate that still burned within her breast when she thought of Gudrod. She wanted Halvdan to know that his father had murdered his grandfather Harald and his uncle Gyrd. She wanted him to hate Gudrod as much as she did.

Aasa had also decided that this was the time she would present Halvdan with Gudrod's sword. It was a beautiful weapon with a hilt of silver and gold. The long, broad two-edged blade was inlaid with gold and contained rune inscriptions naming the warriors who had carried it in battle. There were interlaced horses on both sides of the sword pommel and horses ornamented the scabbard.

"I haven't given you this sword before, Halvdan, because any mention of your father gives me pain. Now that you are old enough to have heard the story of your father, you are old enough to receive his sword. I stole it from his burial mound because I wanted you to have it. It is said to have magical powers that will protect its owner from death in battle."

"Frey is the name inscribed on the sword. You know that is the name of Odin's son and is probably the source of the sword's magic," Aasa told him. "There will come a time when you will want to reclaim Gudrod's kingdoms that were lost at his death...and I want you protected. You must always watch carefully that you do not let an enemy steal this sword from you."

"I vow to always keep Frey by my side and guard it with my life. Then it will protect my life, won't it mother?"

"Yes, son, that is right. You are so much like your grandfather Harald and I love you even more for it. I would wish you to name your first son Harald...and please never give any child the hated name of Gudrod."

"Of course, Mother, I will do whatever pleases you."

Aasa also told Halvdan about her abduction and rape. She wanted him to know how horrible life had been for her with his father, so that he would never commit that kind of crime toward a woman. Halvdan's body was mature for his age, and Aasa knew that he could soon be looking for the woman who would become his wife. She hoped he would choose someone for love and not just for lust.

Halvdan developed a keen sense of the role of just and unjust practices and how they could affect a person's life. He felt shame for his father whenever he thought about the actions Gudrod had taken to secure his mother Aasa for his wife.

Neither the murder of his grandfather, Harald Redbeard and his uncle, Gyrd, nor the abduction and rape of his mother had ever been judged or punished. He felt his mother was totally justified by the action she had taken in the murder of his father. Halvdan determined to see that these crimes were not allowed to go unpunished when he became ruler of his kingdoms.

Having just one child to care for gave Aasa the time and determination to raise her son to be a man she could be proud of. She had grown up with a strong faith in the Gods who ruled her world. Odin had been revered in her home and she taught Halvdan to feel the same. The yearly sacrifices were always practiced and the boy was obedient to the wishes of his mother and his God.

Halvdan was content to grow into manhood while helping his mother rule. On his eighteenth birthday, Aasa gave him total control of the kingdom of Agder. Then he traveled to Vestfold to claim his half of Gudrod's estate that had been under the control of his half brother, Olaf. Many kingdoms that had belonged to Gudrod had been taken over by other kings, and Halvdan was determined to regain possession of them.

There were petty kings ruling over small kingdoms who did not like to see a young, aggressive man seeking power and influence. It was the way that when kings desired more land and possessions, they gathered their army and tried to win a victory over a neighboring kingdom. This is what had happened to most of Gudrod's kingdoms when he died.

As it was, Halvdan spent the next few years fighting battles to regain those kingdoms. He was stout and strong and gained the victory over all who came against him. With his sword Frey in his hand, he found great success. After a matter of time, he had subdued Raumarike, south Hedmark, Toten and Hadeland. These kingdoms were added to Agder, Vestfold, and Vingulmark that were already in subjection to him.

This was the time Halvdan received the inspiration from Odin that would determine his destiny. He was given the direction and purpose for his life. He had been angered by the injustices practiced on his mother and her family, which made him the perfect vehicle to help Odin re-establish the Code of Laws that would bless his people.

In Halvdan's veins ran the blood of noblemen, even the bloodline of Odin. The principles of justice and fairness he had learned from his mother had given him the foundation to make him the ruler Odin knew could begin to implement his just plan.

Odin came to him in a dream and gave him instruction. "Halvdan, my son, you have been chosen to begin to establish a Code of Laws in your kingdoms, that it may spread in time to other kingdoms and help mankind to become better. A just law must be given and a just punishment affixed. If there be no law, man must act according to his passions. How can there be a law, save there be a punishment? The plan allows for vengeance in the face of wickedness to appease the demands of justice."

"These same principles have been in place in Asaheim and even before, but man has not always followed them. You, Halvdan, were born to a raped woman who would teach you about the injustices that man has wrought on his neighbor...since the beginning of time. I say to you, it is enough! You must tread another path...you who are the product of just such a crime. It is for this purpose you have come to be born at this time."

"You must make laws and enforce them, and live by them yourself and then justice will begin to be practiced in all of your kingdoms. It is not in the nature of man to change, and change will come slowly, but it will come as you continue to be fair and enforce the law with just punishments. You shall see my will carried out in your life time and beyond. It is enough for you now to make a beginning."

Halvdan shared Odin's message to him with his mother the next morning. She was thrilled to know that she had raised a son who was deemed worthy to be chosen by their God for such an important work. It made all the suffering she had gone through worth the sacrifice.

He was a great warrior and an able man, very large of stature and remarkably handsome. As he was traveling in the kingdom of Sogn, he met a woman named Ragnhild, daughter of Harald Goldbeard. Halvdan was very impressed with the independent, yet compassionate nature of this woman. Despite the fact that her hair was golden versus red, she reminded him of his amazing mother.

When Halvdan asked Harald Goldbeard for permission to marry his daughter, he was reluctant to give his consent. Ragnhild was his only child and he hoped she would find a husband among the Jarls of Sogn. He hadn't counted on the immediate attraction she felt for this striking, black haired king. She readily accepted his proposal and a wedding feast was planned.

Aasa was both glad and sad to hear about Halvdan's proposal. She did want her son to have a happy marriage, but she also knew that bringing another woman into their home would mean she would have to share her son's affection.

However, she was pleased that the woman of Halvdan's choice was named Ragnhild. That had been her mother's name and it made her feel that her ancestors may have had a hand in choosing a woman that would bring her son happiness.

Her mother's marriage ring had been left to Aasa. It was an elaborate gold ring that was marked with rune inscriptions of her mother's name. She chose to give the ring to Halvdan for his bride. It pleased her to think that another Ragnhild would wear the precious ring.

The wedding feast was held in Sogn and attended by all the close neighbors and friends. They were glad to witness the joining of such a fine young couple. There was only one person at the marriage who did not share in the feeling of joy...the father of the bride...who had just given away his only child.

Soon a son was born to this union. He was named Harald, after Halvdan's grandfather and Ragnhild's father. Harald Goldbeard was old and sickly and pleaded with Halvdan to allow his daughter and her son to stay with him in Sogn until his death. This was agreed upon and Halvdan divided his time between Sogn and Agder and the other six kingdoms that he had conquered.

After a time, Harald Goldbeard died and left his kingdom to his daughter. Within a short time, Ragnhild became ill and also died. This was a sad time for Halvdan, but at least he still had his son. Harald was brought from Sogn to Agder so Aasa could care for him.

The sickness that had already claimed the life of his wife also infected young Harald. Soon he died and the kingdom of Sogn became part of Halvdan's empire. This same illness was the cause of many deaths in the area. Harald's body was burned so that his disease would be destroyed with him.

It was too late to save Aasa, however. She had contracted the disease as she cared for young Harald. On her death bed, she gave her last words of counsel to her dearly loved son.

"Do not despair, my son. You will yet be rewarded for your goodness. My mother's ring will find another Ragnhild's finger to grace and another Harald will come of your seed."

With those words, she breathed her last. She had devoted her whole life to raising a son who would fight for justice and she had instilled in his nature a determination to deal fairly and honestly with his subjects.

Halvdan wanted to honor his mother in death as he had honored her in life. He had a great mound built at Oseberg in Vestfold and laid his wife and his mother together in Aasa's masterfully carved ship. The things they would need in the next life were placed with them.

The bodies of the two women he loved were dressed in their beautiful gowns and adorned with gold necklaces, earrings, brooches, bracelets and rings as befitted women of their stature. They were placed on eiderdown cushions atop magnificent beds and covered with costly silks and then the finest of furs. A large tent was placed over their bodies to protect them from the soil of their mound.

Standing looms, stools, wooden pressing irons, scissors, sewing awls, whetstones, and boxes of linen, hemp, and woad dye were placed in the ship so that the women could enjoy the use of them in the next life. Wheat, oats, apples and hazel nuts along with plates, bowls, knives and cooking equipment were also included.

Leather covered chests filled with their best gowns and jewels were placed at their feet. Only the Ragnhild ring and three heirloom brooches were kept out of the burial goods. They had been placed in a small carved wooden box so Halvdan could save them for his next wife...Aasa had been adamant about that.

The most beautiful wall hangings were added to their goods so the women could adorn their heavenly home. Each had a decorated sleigh and wagon, as well as their favorite horse, to carry them swiftly into the next life. Even Aasa's pet peacock was sacrificed to spend eternity with its mistress.

Now Halvdan had much land but had lost most of his family. He tried not to be overcome with the sorrow that filled his heart. His time was spent traveling throughout his kingdoms, maintaining the laws he had set up to allow his people to live under a fair system of justice. He wanted his mother to look down and be proud of the son she had reared.

The year was 849 and Halvdan had decided to spend the Yule season at his great estate in the Ringsaker area of Hedmark. The manor house there was in a very good place, situated on a slight hill overlooking Lake Mjosa. There were barns large enough to stable many horses. The beautiful lake was frozen and the ground was completely covered by a layer of white snow.

A feast had been prepared for Halvdan and his men. They were about to partake when there was a loud pounding on the outer door. A servant opened the heavy door to a man, cold and breathless, who said he had a request to make of King Halvdan. The request was for aid on behalf of his master and mistress who had been taken captive by Hake the Berserker.

Halvdan knew Hake. He had been involved in several battles where Halvdan was the victor. Hake was a bad sort...the kind of man who killed for the sport of it. Despite the fact that he was the owner of many large farms across the lake in Toten, none of his neighbors trusted him.

Now Hake had attacked Sigurd Hjort, King of Ringerike, and kidnapped the daughter, Ragnhild, and the son, Guttorm. In addition, he was bragging that he would force Ragnhild to marry him as soon as his wounds healed. He had already set the wedding feast day and invited his friends and neighbors.

Everyone knew Halvdan to be a fair and respected King who was determined to see justice carried out in his kingdoms. Whenever he heard about men who treated a women like an animal, with no feelings and no rights, he would think of his mother and the trials she had endured with his father.

Hake's neighbor had told the servant to seek help from King Halvdan the Black in Ringsaker and he had hurried to Tande Manor. He ordered his hundred men to dress, ready for battle, and prepare to cross the frozen Lake Mjosa to rescue Ragnhild and Guttorm. The men gathered their weapons, mounted their horses and made their way to Toten. A sleigh followed to carry the prince and princess back across the ice covered lake.

By the time they arrived in Toten, it was almost dawn, but there was still a mist of darkness over the land. Halvdan and his men broke into the longhouse and found the bedchamber where Hake was keeping Ragnhild and Guttorm captive. Once they were safely back outside, one of the soldiers started the house on fire.

As the longhouse began to fill with smoke, Hake came running out of the house, brandishing his sword. He chased the men and the sleigh all the way to the lake. When Hake realized that it was King Halvdan who had rescued the prisoners, he stopped. There, on the ice packed snow, Hake the Berserker turned his sword-hilt to the ground and let himself fall upon the point. The sword went through his heart and blood made red the ice of Lake Mjosa. He had chosen to end his own life rather than be further humiliated by Halvdan the Black.

CHAPTER 2

THE PARENTS

There was great rejoicing in the manor house at Tande Manor, Halvdan's residence in Ringsaker, during that Yule season. Ragnhild was twenty years old when she was rescued by Halvdan. She would be eternally grateful that he had saved her from a fate worse than death.

Halvdan was surprised by the strength of feelings he had for this rescued damsel. Was it just that she kept thanking him and telling him how wonderful he was for the brave act he had performed? No, he had done other brave acts in the past without this strong feeling in his heart. Halvdan began to realize how lonely he had been since the death of his wife. Was this the other Ragnhild who would wear the beautiful gold ring that had belonged to his grandmother?

"I seem to have a fondness for women named Ragnhild," he told her as they sat before the glowing fire. "You and my dead wife have the same distinguished name."

"She must have been a very fortunate woman to have had such a strong and able husband as you," replied Ragnhild. "Do you think you will ever marry again?" she asked with a shy smile.

"Only if I find another Ragnhild that can love me as deeply as I was loved before," responded Halvdan.

At that statement, Ragnhild turned her face to Halvdan's and looked into his eyes with longing. "Would that I could be that Ragnhild," she whispered.

Halvdan touched her cheek gently and thought he could hear his mother's voice of approval. "Do you think you could grow to love me?" he asked.

"After days spent contemplating the horror of having my brideshead broken by that horrible Hake, I am ready to give myself to a man I can respect and even love."

"That would please me greatly. May I ask your brother Guttorm for your hand this very night?"

"Yes, you may," answered Ragnhild with a timid, but eager look on her face.

"If I proposed a wedding feast be prepared while my friends are gathered here for the Yuletide festivities, would I seem too anxious?" he asked.

Ragnhild gave him a shy smile. "It would be better for you to seem too anxious than me!"

Halvdan gave her a swift kiss on the lips and turned to go and find Guttorm. He thought he could feel the rapid beating of his heart beneath his festival robes. How good it would be to have a wife again. He had not realized, until now, how lonely life had become with just his men for company.

Guttorm was not only happy, but relieved that Ragnhild had agreed to be married to Halvdan. He was the younger brother, and now that their father was dead, it would have fallen to him to act as the protector of his sister's virtue until she married. Those terrible days they spent as a captive at Hake's farm had given him plenty of time to berate himself for not being strong enough to free them from the evil clutches of the berserker.

Halvdan was a noble and respected king and would be a very good match for his beautiful, spiritual sister.

"You may marry Ragnhild with my blessing," answered Guttorm with an expression of relief in his voice.

There was much excitement in the air as the wedding feast was prepared. The servants at Tande had deep respect for their master. He was fair and generous and they were happy to see him marrying the lovely Ragnhild. It would certainly be a Yuletide to remember.

A large boar was roasting over the open fire and a delicious aroma filled the great manor house. Sweetmeats had been prepared and there was a joyous atmosphere among the guests. Everyone was happy for Halvdan and glad that he was marrying such a gracious woman. They were also happy for Ragnhild...that she had been spared the ultimate assault by Hake.

A beautiful gown of deep blue had been a gift from the wife of a jarl who lived on a neighboring estate. Ragnhild's hair, plaited with blue ribbon, was as golden as Halvdan's was black. They made a handsome couple. Halvdan wore his king's robes with great dignity and there was a gleam in his eye that had been absent for some time.

He presented his future wife with the prized gold ring that had already been worn by two other special Ragnhilds. A brooch of silver and gold was also given her to fasten the heavy cape on her narrow shoulders. The brooch had belonged to Aasa and he was sure she approved of his marriage to this Ragnhild.

The wedding night of his second marriage was much better for Halvdan than his first one had been. He was more practiced and relaxed. He was also more concerned for the feelings of his bride than he had been last time. He was almost thirty years old and had much worldly experience.

Ragnhild was not as young at twenty as his first wife had been, but she had spent her sheltered childhood in Ringerike with just her father and brother as companions. Ragnhild's mother had died at the birth of her brother Guttorm, so there had been no one to teach her the ways of a woman.

The king's bed chamber at Tande Manor was large and lavish. It was hung with thick drapes and tapestries that glowed in the warm candlelight. Ragnhild was nervous. She knew that Halvdan had a kind nature, but she wasn't sure what she could expect him to be like in the bridal bed. She was not disappointed, however, for he was both gentle and loving.

"How does it feel to be a married woman, sharing a bed with a man?" asked Halvdan when they awoke the next morning.

"It is much better than I expected," she answered with a blush. They lay in each other's arms thinking their own private thoughts.

"I have already had one son, you know, but he became sick and died an early death. I should like to have many sons," mused Halvdan.

"And what of daughters," asked Ragnhild.

"Oh, you can have as many of those as you would like," he answered, "but the sons must come first."

"I was the first child of my mother and father and they weren't disappointed," she bantered.

"Well, that is because they were overwhelmed by your beauty and charms," Halvdan teased as he turned to face her.

"Guttorm is a good brother," Ragnhild was suddenly serious, "I hope I will be able to still have a close relationship with him."

"Of course, you will!" he exclaimed. "Do you think I am such a tyrant that I will demand all of your time and attention?"

"As this is my first time at being a married woman, I am not sure what to expect!" she responded as she smiled at her new husband.

After the days of feasting, Guttorm returned to Stein Manor in Ringerike. Life would never be the same there with their father dead and Ragnhild married, but the couple planned to spend some time visiting with him. They would also be gathering clothes, jewels and household items that Ragnhild planned to take to her new home.

Many of their possessions had been stolen by Hake when he and his men had attacked their home and kidnapped them. But they had escaped with the most important things...Ragnhild's virtue and their very lives. Guttorm would always be grateful to have the friendship and protection of Halvdan and his men.

The newly wed couple found much joy as they came to know each other better. As spring arrived and the roads became passable, Halvdan prepared to make the rounds of his many kingdoms from Agder in the south to Hedmark and Sogn in the north.

"I hate the thought of being parted from you for such a long while, Halvdan. Can't you take me with you?" pleaded Ragnhild.

"I would like to have your company as well, but I think the journey will be long and hard for you. Why not just stay here in the comfort of Tande Manor, and we will make a trip to see Guttorm in Ringerike when I return."

"The manor will be empty and lonely when you are gone. Please take me with you. I would like to see all of the kingdoms ruled by the great King Halvdan the Black."

"If you think I am going to take you with me just because you flatter me, you are mistaken," he said with a smile.

"Well, just take me with you because you want to make me happy then," pleaded Ragnhild.

"Alright, have a trunk packed today for we shall depart on the morrow as the sun begins to rise," Halvdan relented.

The horses were standing in their harness in front of the packed wagon when Ragnhild walked out of the house. There was a certain unease in her stomach this morning, but she did not want to say anything to Halvdan, lest he change his mind and have her stay home. Perhaps it was some bad meat she had eaten at last night's meal that was causing this stomach problem.

Just as she was about to step into the wagon, the smell of horse dung assailed her and she threw up her breakfast. The foul smelling mess covered the fur pelts that were piled on the floor of the wagon, waiting to provide her with warmth.

Halvdan came riding up on his black stallion, Sleipni, in time to see Ragnhild bending over in pain. She looked up at him as he quickly dismounted and rushed to her side.

"I am sorry to cause this delay," she cried, "There must have been some spoiled food in my stomach."

With his arm protectively around her waist, Halvdan turned her face toward him. "I think My Lady has something more valuable in her stomach than spoiled food. Did no one teach you what to expect when a child begins to grow within you?"

"What? A child? Oh, Halvdan, do you think so?" beamed Ragnhild.

"I think so!" he replied, "You forget, I have lived before with a woman who was with child!"

Ragnhild was so excited she wrapped her arms around his neck and kissed him over and over.

"Not such tender embraces in front of my men, please," he whispered in her ear.

"I am sorry, but I am too excited to care," she cried.

"Let us get you back in the house before there is another accident," Halvdan smiled. "Now there will be no question of your coming with me."

Ragnhild was about to argue, but she was too happy about the thought of a new life growing inside her to worry about anything else.

"When you start to feel better, I will have some of my men escort you to

Ringerike and you can visit with Guttorm until I return."

"That sounds wonderful. I can not wait to tell him that he is going to be an uncle," she replied.

And so it was that Ragnhild spent her days of waiting for the child to be born while sleeping in her own bed at her ancestral home, Stein Manor. Perhaps it was this setting, plus her hopes and plans for this new life, that prompted the dream.

Ragnhild had always been a person who dreamed great dreams. But the dream she had that summer in Ringerike seemed to be the most important of all.

"Ragnhild dreamed that she was standing out in her herb garden. She took a thorn out of her apron, but while she was holding the thorn in her hand it grew and became a great tree, one end of which struck itself down into the earth. It became firmly rooted and the other end of the tree raised itself so high in the air that she could scarcely see over it, and it also became wonderfully thick. The under part of the tree was red with blood, but the stem upwards was beautifully green and the branches were white as snow. There were a great many limbs on the tree, some high up and others down low. So vast were the tree's branches that they seemed to her to cover all Norway, and even much more."

Heimskringla

She could hardly wait until Halvdan returned so she could share her dream with him. She had told Guttorm about it and he felt it was definitely a sign telling about the greatness of the baby she was carrying. The warmth of the summer sun not only caused the herbs in her garden to grow, but gave strength to her ever expanding body as well.

By the end of summer, Halvdan was back and Ragnhild was so happy to have him there. Still, she wished for a mother's presence as her time drew near. The memories she had of her mother were vague, but at times Ragnhild thought she could hear the echoes of her mother's laughter as she spent time walking the same floors her mother had walked so long ago.

Her father, Sigurd, had discovered his future wife, Princess Thorny, while he was traveling through Jutland in Denmark. Ragnhild had never thought about it before, but now she realized that her mother had come to Ringerike to live in her husband's kingdom and left her own parents behind. She must have found happiness with her little family in Norway, because Ragnhild remembered her mother's laughter, but not her tears.

Here she was sitting...feeling sorry for herself because she did not have a mother to help her through the difficult time that childbirth could bring. Then she thought about her mother. She must have had these same thoughts and concerns, as she looked forward to the birth of her first child, with her own mother far away in Denmark.

These thoughts made Ragnhild determined to follow in her mother's footsteps. She would be brave and fill her days with laughter and not tears. She hoped she could live up to the lofty goal.

Her husband watched her carefully these days, looking for the signs that meant this baby was ready to be born. He tried to remember the signs from the birth time with his other Ragnhild, but it had been many years in the past.

Some of the women's maids that had been a part of caring for Ragnhild and Guttorm after their mother died were still serving at Stein Manor. It was an honor for them to be asked to care for their mistress during her birthing time. They were kept busy putting all in readiness for the day this child should come into the world. They told the King not to worry, but he still felt uneasy.

Halvdan knew that the time of childbirth could be dangerous for a woman. Many times the baby died, immediately or later. Many times the mother died also. Sometimes the mother died and the baby lived. Sometimes they both lived. As much as he wanted a son, he would not want to lose another wife...especially this one.

There were times when he almost felt grateful to Hake for his foul deeds. Without Hake's kidnapping of Ragnhild and Guttorm and bringing them to Toten, just across Lake Mjosa from Ringsaker, he may never have met Ragnhild. When he thought about his good fortune, he decided the Gods must be watching over him.

Ragnhild had told him every detail about her dream. It was very interesting. Halvdan did not realize he had married a woman of dreams. That part of her nature made her even more special. Maybe that was what Guttorm meant when he always referred to her as his beautiful and spiritual sister.

Halvdan was awakened by a scream. It was Ragnhild lying in the bed next to him.

"It must be time," Halvdan said as he tried to comfort her. "Just lie here and I will go and get the women. You know Gerd was there to help at your birth, and she is prepared to help you with this birth."

Is this really the way children are supposed to come into the world, thought Ragnhild. Why does there have to be so much pain?

Soon, faithful Gerd was at her side, wiping her forehead and telling her to push. Push, she thought, if I push any harder I will push my insides right out onto the floor!

Ragnhild wanted to scream each time she tried to push, but then she thought of her mother and the happy laughter, and she was sure her mother had not knelt there screaming. How long could she endure this awful pain in silence?

For two days, Ragnhild suffered the pains of labor. By the second day she was too delirious to control herself and the screaming began. Halvdan had been sitting outside the birthing chamber on the first day, but when the screaming started, he had to leave the house.

On the evening of the second day, the servant Gerd came out to speak to Halvdan. "The baby is too large to be born," she told him. "Perhaps we should open the belly and take the baby out," was her suggestion.

"Then who would die?" asked Halvdan.

"The baby might die, but it might save Ragnhild," she answered.

"Then we must do it!"

Ragnhild hardly felt the knife pierce her skin for the splitting pain that was in her back. A large baby boy was removed from the cut opening and placed on the bed. The women paid little attention to him as they tried to tightly wrap Ragnhild's belly to soak up all the blood.

Gerd reached to cut the cord that still hung from the baby's belly and he cried lustily. Halvdan, waiting by the door, hastened into the room. The sight of blood was one he was used to from conflicts with his enemies, but to see his beloved Ragnhild laying in a pool of blood unnerved him.

He bent to kiss her forehead and she opened her eyes. "Where is my baby," she whispered. Halvdan looked questioningly across at Gerd.

"You have a fine baby boy, My Lady. Just let me wrap him up and you can hold him." Gerd placed the bundle on Ragnhild's arm and bade the women leave the room.

"I am so glad to see you still live," breathed Halvdan. "And you have given me a fine baby boy. He even has the light golden hair of his mother."

Halvdan knew that both the baby and Ragnhild could still die, but he did not want to think about that right now.

But they did not die. Ragnhild lay in bed for many months, trying to get her strength back. Halvdan poured water over the baby and named him Harald. He knew that Ragnhild wanted to name him Sigurd after her father, but he had promised his mother Aasa, before she died, that he would name his next son Harald after her father. He thought about his first son Harald...who had died...and prayed that would not be the fate of this second Harald.

"We will name our next son Sigurd," Halvdan promised, and she nodded in agreement. But there was never to be another son, nor any daughters. Ragnhild's body was too damaged by the birth of Harald and she could conceive no more children. That made baby Harald just that much more precious.

One night, as they lay in bed talking, with baby Harald lying between them, Halvdan told Ragnhild how worried he had been that either she or the baby would not live.

She responded, "Do you remember my dream about the large tree growing up in my herb garden?"

"Yes, I remember you telling me about the dream," he answered.

"Well, if we are to have posterity whose branches will reach out and cover all of Norway, then baby Harald will be the one to make that dream come true," she said.

"So you think he will conquer even more kingdoms than I can give him?" Halvdan asked with a smile.

"I am not saying he will be better than you, I am just saying what the dream said," Ragnhild answered softly.

"Well, I am content to try and control the eight kingdoms I am ruling now, so you will have to be the one to teach baby Harald to try and overtake his father!"

The new mother just lay there smiling into the face of her precious child. She was sure there had never been another baby quite like him. She was going to try and raise him to be the best and noblest man in all of Norway.

Halvdan wondered why it was that he hadn't received the same message from Odin. He wanted a dream like Ragnhild's that would tell him the future of their son. He went to Thorleif the Wise and asked for his advice. He was told to sleep one night in a swine-sty and then he would have his revelation dream. The advice was strange, but Halvdan decided to try it. That night he did have a revelation dream.

> "Halvdan dreamed he had the most beautiful hair. The hair was all in ringlets...some so long that they fell to the ground, some reaching to the middle of his side, some to his neck and yet some were only as knots springing from his head. The ringlets were of various colors of black and gold, red and brown. One golden ringlet surpassed all the others in beauty, luster and size."

> "This dream he told to Thorleif the Wise who interpreted it thus. There should be a large and great posterity from his loins and his descendants should rule over countries with great honor, but not all with equally great honor. One of his descendants, the golden ringlet that was longest, would be more celebrated than all the rest."

> **Heimskringla**

Halvdan went home and sought out Ragnhild. "I had a revelation dream last night, just as Thorleif said I would. He has also told me the meaning of my dream. It is very much like your dream and now I know that we shall have a great and honorable posterity. It will be our duty to raise Harald to be a man of truth and uprightness, for he will influence all the rest."

Baby Harald was a fortunate child. He had been sent to a mother who was both intelligent and kind. She had enough love in her heart to raise a son who could both love and be loved. She also had a spiritual strength that would shape his thoughts and actions and make him an obedient servant to the Gods that were revered as an ever present influence in their lives.

He had a father who was a wise man, who ruled with fairness and obeyed the laws himself. He required those in his charge, including his family, to know the laws and to follow them. If there was a dispute, he judged the matter fairly, for both servant as well as jarl. This made for peaceful times in Halvdan's kingdoms and his subjects loved him.

CHAPTER 3

HARALD, THE CHILD

Harald was a large boy at birth and continued to grow strong and sturdy. He was fine looking with a charming smile and thick golden ringlets. At first, Ragnhild was sad that she could not produce any more children for Halvdan. She remembered what he had told her on the morning after their wedding feast that he wanted to have many sons, and she could have as many daughters as she chose. Well, it hadn't turned out that way, but she had produced one amazing son, and that was enough for her.

Guttorm thought Harald to be very much like their father, Sigurd Hjort. He visited his sister at Tande Manor often and the uncle and nephew developed a close relationship. That relationship was destined to last to the end of Guttorm's life.

Harald loved spending time with Halvdan and his men. Whatever they were doing, he wanted to do also. One sunny afternoon when he was about two years old, Ragnhild had allowed Halvdan to take Harald with him down to Lake Mjosa where he and some of his men were working on their dragon ships.

The boy started to pick up little pieces of wood and throw them into the water. The sticks would not stay out in the water, but came floating back into shore. Harald walked a few steps into the water to get the bad sticks and throw them back into the water. He kept going out farther and farther until he tripped on a rock and fell head first into the deep lake water.

His father and the men were busy working and weren't watching the boy. Suddenly, there was loud barking coming from the King's big wolfdog, Thor. Halvdan hurried around the end of the ship to see why Thor was barking. He panicked when he saw his son's body floating face down in the water.

Halvdan raced to Harald and scooped him up in his arms. The boy's face looked white and he wasn't breathing. He tipped the little body upside down and slapped him on the back. A gurgling sound came from Harald's throat and out came water...followed by his morning meal.

The boy began to cry loudly as his father cradled him on his shoulder. "That's my big boy," he crooned, "That's my big boy."

If anything had happened to his only son, Halvdan would never have forgiven himself. He decided he would not tell Ragnhild about this brush with death...and he would watch Harald more closely in the future.

That night, Halvdan lay staring at the boards above their bed after his wife had fallen asleep. If it hadn't been for the barking of Thor, their son would be dead and Ragnhild would be lying here sobbing. He determined that he would give Harald his own pup out of their next litter.

The protective wolfdog had gone into battle with Halvdan and been at his back during fierce fighting, and Harald would also need such a dog. Halvdan would train Harald's dog to watch over him, just as Thor had done today.

At the end of harvest time, the new pups were born. Harald chose the biggest one for his own. It was a black and grey male and he named him Torda. It did not seem like a very distinguished name for a fighting wolfdog, but Harald could say it and it sounded a little like Thor.

Torda and Harald spent hours playing together on the floor in the warmth of the fire that winter season. Yuletide came and with it came Guttorm. He had not yet found a wife and wanted to spend Yule with Ragnhild and her family. The uncle was anxious to see his nephew grow to manhood and make his way in the world.

But before Harald could grow to manhood, he needed to get through childhood. That would prove difficult for an independent and adventurous boy. He was about five winters when he had his next brush with death. This time he was old enough to remember it vividly.

It was always exciting to walk in the woods up behind the buildings at Tande Manor. It was especially enjoyable in the spring when the snow began to melt and the pine sap was running. This was also the time when melted snow exposed pine cones under the fragrant trees. Harald was planning to fill a sack with pine cones to give to his mother. Ragnhild used them to hang from ribbon on the posts in the great hall. Their fragrance made the room smell as fresh as the woods.

Torda and Harald had just reached a tree with great numbers of pine cones beneath its branches. As the boy reached down for the cones, he saw some movement on the other side of the tree. When he went to investigate, he discovered a small bear cub coming toward him.

Next, he heard a snarl come from the throat of his protective wolfdog. When he turned to look, he saw that the hair on his dog's back was standing on end. Torda was growling at the large mother bear hurrying toward her cub. Harald wasn't sure what to do. He had his bow and arrows with him, but he did not think they would stop a bear.

He wondered if he should try to climb the tree or run. He chose to run. As he hurried down the path, he realized Torda was not behind him. He could hear growling and yelping and realized his wolfdog had attacked the bear to keep it from chasing after him. Harald wanted to go back and get Torda, but he knew he needed his father's help.

Halvdan heard the shouts before Harald emerged from the woods. "Help, Father, help," he cried. "A bear is killing Torda."

Within seconds, Halvdan grabbed his spear and ran for the woods. The sounds of growling and snarling and yelping made it easy to tell where the bear was. The five men Halvdan had been talking to were right behind him with spears in hand.

It took all six spears to kill the mother bear. Harald saw the bear fall and then noticed the body of his beloved Torda lying under the tree. Red blood was oozing out onto the grey fur and the dog was not moving.

"You men take care of the bears while I carry Torda to the house," commanded Halvdan. "Harald, you come with me."

It took many weeks of healing, but finally Torda was well enough to run outside with Harald again. The men had skinned the bear and given the meat to the other dogs. The bear skin had been prepared and was given as a gift to the boy.

"I hope this bear skin will always be a reminder to you to guard your life," Ragnhild said. "I am pleased that you were planning to surprise me with the pine cones, but you are not quite old enough to go walking in the woods alone."

"I wasn't alone," answered Harald. "Torda was with me."

"Yes, but would you have traded Torda's life for a sack of pine cones?" asked his mother.

"No, of course not," the boy replied as he remembered the bloody body of his dog. "I want Torda to stay with me always."

"May he always be there to protect you, my son," sighed Ragnhild.

In her private thoughts, she imagined the evil spirits that would like to see Harald die before he was able to accomplish that which he was destined to achieve in his life.

Halvdan had his own thoughts. A gold Thor's hammer amulet hung from his neck and acted as a protection for him when he was in battle. He had thought to have one made to give to his son when he was eight, to mark his transition from a boy to a young man. But Harald wasn't just an average boy. He was large for his age and too daring for his own good. Halvdan decided Harald would now get his Thor's hammer amulet for his sixth birth day... and hopefully he could stay out of trouble until then.

"Train up a child in the way he should go: and when he is old, he shall not depart from it." **Proverbs 22:6**

CHAPTER 4

THE GODS

Ragnhild was a very spiritual woman and tried to seek guidance as to how she should live her life. One of the things she felt strongly about was teaching young Harald about the Gods and how they could influence your life.

Harald knew that Odin was the most important of all the Gods that ruled over his people. He had once been human, but had become a divine personage with power over life and death. He was the Allfather to his people and had earned this title through great unselfish acts. He was both a God of wisdom and of war.

But this was not the beginning. Odin's earth life began in Asaheim, a land washed by the Volga River. His people had come there from lands to the west, bordering the great sea. There had been a time of captivity when they were ruled by the ungodly...but after an era of struggle, their tribes had been set free.

They cast lots to decide whether to return south and west to their former homeland or to strike out for new lands to the north. The lot fell to the north, so the tribes gathered their families, together with their flocks and herds, and began their journey north and east. They moved with the land, following the river valleys until they came to an area that was far out of the reach of their former captors.

Life was peaceful for a time and flocks and herds increased. Children were born and elders died...but the peace was not to last. A new enemy began searching out the tribes farther abroad than just those along the great inland sea. They were conquerors and fancied themselves as rulers of all the lands in the known world.

Many people fled before them. Odin's father, Fridleif, had foreknowledge of this enemy. He did not want his son to live and raise his sons in captivity, so he sent him to settle the lands farther north. He counseled him to go far enough away so that they could not be found by their enemies.

Odin had many strong sons and an equally strong wife named Frigg. The patriarch instructed each of his sons to choose a wife from among their people who would not only be willing to move to a new land and bear many children, but who possessed a spiritual nature. This strong spirit would be important to the many generations that followed.

Finally, all was in readiness for the journey to begin. Fridleif called the group together and gave them instructions. He laid hands on the head of his oldest son, Odin, and pronounced a blessing.

"The God of Heaven hath charged me to send you and your family--together with your horses and cattle and sheep and man servants and maid servants---to inhabit the Land of the North---for a purpose of his own---to establish a mighty kingdom and rule in righteousness---as a patriarch and high priest unto thy people---to grow in power and strength--and in due time, to spread thy blood and thy influence far and wide, beyond thy borders. And a just law will come down from thee---through thy loins---and it shall spread throughout the world---and be a power for good unto the people of God. And in the last days, thy descendants shall turn their hearts to the God of Heaven---and then he shall bring them forth, at the last, to accomplish His great work."

Thus, Odin traveled forth to settle in the northern part of the world, along with a great number of his people. They left their home in the eastern country of Asia and their great city of Asgard, which had been a notable place for sacrifice. They carried with them the hope for a better life and prayed that they could fulfill the promises set forth in their blessing.

"Odin had second sight and his wife also; and from their foreknowledge, he found that his name should be exalted in the northern part of the world and glorified above the fame of all the other kings. As the immense army journeyed northward, the land of Gardariki was the first area conquered. Next, they traveled to the west until they came to a large region called Saxland. Here the warriors did battle with and overcame the people living there. As the victors, Odin gave his three sons, Vegdeg, Baldr and Sigi full charge over all of Saxland."

Prologue, Prose Edda

His three youngest sons continued on with the family. Following a lengthy journey, they arrived at a large sea in the North. After some exploring of the area, and praying for inspiration, Odin called his sons and their families together and told about the lands they had seen.

Then he laid hands on the head of his son, Seaming, and said, "I bless you to settle and rule in the land of Norway. You are being sent to the kingdom that is the most mountainous with the least amount of pasture land. You are given this area, not just because you are the oldest, but because you are the strongest in body and spirit. You also possess great courage and determination, which will be needed in your new land. Your powerful descendants shall travel far and wide."

Next, he laid hands on the head of his second son, Yngvi, and said, "I bless you to settle and rule in the land of Sweden. You are being sent to a kingdom that has great grass lands and also great forests. I pray that the mountain lands that run between your kingdom and Seaming's will not keep you so divided that you will forget that you came from the same womb. You shall have a mighty posterity and they shall make you proud."

Last, he laid hands on the head of his youngest son, Skjold, and said, "I bless you to settle and rule in the land of Denmark. You are being sent to a land that is the smallest of the three kingdoms. This is not just because you are the youngest son, but because this land will be the easiest to grow food and raise animals. The rolling hills will provide pasture land for your animals and you shall be able to provide abundantly for your family. Brave and great men shall come from your seed."

For his home, Odin chose an island in the sea, within easy sail of both his two younger sons. His older son was the best with sailing vessels, so he knew he could sail to the island whenever he needed to. The large oak trees and tall spruce trees that grew abundantly in this new land would make great, strong sailing vessels. The knowledge of ship building they brought with them from their years of living along the great inland sea to the south.

Odin was a powerful chief and warrior who had conquered many kingdoms and was successful in every battle. It was his custom, when he sent men into battle, that he first laid hands upon their heads and called down a blessing upon them. Because of this, his people believed their undertaking would be successful.

They were also able to call on him whenever they needed comfort or were in danger, and he would hear them and help them. He called twelve priests to judge the people and direct the sacrifices. The people served and obeyed them. They presided over the Things and other meetings when Odin was not in attendance.

His twelve priests taught the people the principles and laws that he had taught to them. Odin possessed a beautiful countenance and all who heard him believed his words...yet he could strike terror in the heart of his foes. His enemies feared him but his friends put their trust in him.

The same laws that had been in force in Asaheim were enforced in the kingdoms of the north. Sacrifices were made three times each year. At the beginning of winter there would be a blood sacrifice for a good year and in the middle of winter, the sacrifice would be for a good crop. A third sacrifice would be in summer for victory in battle. All the people were required to pay a scat or tax to Odin and in return they would be defended against any enemies.

When asked by the Supreme God what his ultimate wish would be, Odin chose wisdom. His desire was so great that he was willing to give up his left eye in exchange for it. To prove his willingness to sacrifice, he hung suspended from the Ash Tree for nine days and nine nights until his offering was accepted.

Odin was a great patriarch and high priest even before his quest for wisdom. But after his ordeal, he gained a level of perfection that set him apart from other men. He lived a god-like life, and when he died, his spirit continued to lead and guide his people in the far northern kingdoms.

As he was near death, Odin had himself marked with the point of a spear and said he was going up to Godheim. He said he would be there to welcome all his people. Brave warriors were to be dedicated to him and should have a standing stone to mark their burial. Under his law, men of consequence were to have a mound raised to their memory. After his death, Odin became one of the main Gods in Godheim and had charge over his people on the earth.

Heimskringla

When many generations had passed away, the people of the northern kingdoms forgot that they had all descended from the three great brothers; Seaming, Yngvi and Skjold. Then, contention began to creep into the hearts of the children. When battles were fought, Odin was not just an innocent observer, but he played an active part while ruling from the world of spirits.

He was pleased to find that his earthly wife continued to be the wife of his heavenly life. He could see that having his earthly family continue on into the eternities was the great blessing of the next life. There he was blessed to associate with the ancestors who had died before him and he could see the generations of mankind stretching on...back to the beginning of time.

When Odin joined the ranks of the Gods in Godheim, his fame grew and many miraculous things were said to follow him. It was said he rode on an eight-legged horse named Sleipni, who carried him on journeys far and wide. He also had two black ravens that helped him watch over the earth and two pet wolves that traveled with him and protected him from evil spirits.

Odin lived in Valaskjalf, a large hall with a roof made of silver, where he sat in his special highseat and could watch the entire world at once. He had another hall, named Valhalla, where the spirits of warriors who had died in battle were taken for their reward. The third hall, named Gimli, had a roof of gold and it was where righteous men and women would go after death.

There were many Gods who also lived in Godheim. One of Odin's spirit sons was Thor. He was the God of Thunder and the strongest of all. Thor's great treasures were a hammer that could slay giants and shatter rocks, a belt of power which made him doubly strong, and iron gloves to help hold the powerful hammer.

Freyja was the Goddess of Love and had power over the affairs of the heart. She rode in a chariot drawn by cats and could turn into a falcon. As the leader of the Goddesses, she presided over fertility in both nature and humans.

Also in Godheim was a great ash tree that connected heaven and earth and its roots went down into the realm of the dead. The ash tree was called Yggdrasil or the World Tree because it was the guardian of the whole world. It was charged with linking the world of Asgard with the world of Midgard, where humans resided and the world of Hel, a land of darkness and freezing mist.

Heimskringla

Many, many generations would pass away from the time when Odin was a mortal until the time when Harald's spirit would be sent to the earth to obtain his mortal body. Odin knew of Harald's potential as a leader and knew that he had made promises, before he left the spirit world. Like other great leaders, he would strive to accomplish all he had been foreordained to do.

Harald's spirit realized that the earth life was a time of testing and that a veil would be drawn over his memory and he would be required to learn the earthly lessons...and live by faith. But he also knew that he would be sent to an earthly family that would teach him the truths he would need to know and give him the guidance to make the right choices.

There were these and many more stories that Harald would hear as he grew to manhood. Because of the dreams his parents had about him before he was born, he understood that there was a great deal expected of him. As he learned to know and understand the realm of the Gods, he knew how important it was to be obedient. He was very grateful to have been born of goodly parents, who taught him the nature of the Gods and the ways of the world.

Ragnhild explained to her son the ancestry that reached from her father, Sigurd Hjort, back through many generations to Odin through Skjold of Denmark. She explained that his father, Halvdan, was descended from Yngvi of Sweden through his father, Gudrod the Hunter. Also, Halvdan's mother, Aasa, was a descendant of Seaming of Norway through her father, Harald Redbeard, King of Agder. Hearing about his great ancestors made Harald realize the importance of the earthly mission that had been given to him through Odin.

"Go thee out of thy country, and from thy kindred, and from thy father's house, into a land that I will show thee."   ***Genisis 12:1***

CHAPTER 5

HARALD, THE BOY

When Harald was eight years old he was already a great horseman. He loved to ride through the woods and feel the strong muscles of the horse beneath his legs. One day in early spring, Harald was riding far from home when his horse suddenly reared back on its hind legs. A large black snake was lying coiled in the path and startled his horse. The sharp rocks of the mountain path bruised Harald's skull as his head hit the ground.

He lay on the path in a state of unconsciousness. While in this state, a vision opened up to him. He saw Odin standing by a giant tree, motioning to him to come closer. When Harald got close, he could see that the tree was encircled at the bottom by a menacing serpent. Odin told him that the serpent represented the powers of death and evil.

"The mighty ash tree is the Tree of Life, reaching its branches up to the Heavens. The leaves are covered by dew which will allow the partaker to gain great wisdom." counseled the God.

Odin warned Harald to climb quickly up the tree before the serpent could grab him and crush him into its evil snare. Harald used his strong arm and leg muscles to climb to the highest branches. There he could see the world from the top of the remarkable tree. Odin instructed his two ravens, Huginn and Muninn, to tell Harald of his past and his future.

Huginn brought memories of the past, memories that were stored in the mind and out of reach until shown by command of Odin. In his mind, Harald saw his ancestors, from his parents back to the first parents that were born on the earth. He understood that they were watching over him and guiding him so that he could fulfill all the promises he made to them before he was born. His promises included following the guidance of Odin through all the important events in his life.

Muninn brought about an awareness of the events that lay in the future. Harald saw the branches of the tree reaching out to cover all of Norway, plus the islands of the sea. He began to understand that great deeds were to be performed by him in his life. He was told that he would be guided and protected if he would ask Odin for help and try always to follow his instructions.

"It is now time for you to descend from the tree, my young one. I will stand on the head of the serpent to protect you until you can get a safe distance away."

Odin stood before him and asked, "Will you take an oath to always do your best in all your actions and follow the counsel of your God?"

"I will," was Harald's solemn answer.

"Will you take an oath to fulfill all the promises you made before your spirit gained a body and came to this earth?"

"I will," promised Harald.

"That is enough," declared Odin. "You may now return to your body, but keep in remembrance the oaths you have made. An oath is a sacred promise and must not be broken...at the risk of your life."

"Yes, I will," was his humble reply.

"As you are obedient, you will be guided and protected," were Odin's parting words.

Suddenly, Harald's eyes opened to see his horse standing over him. There was no sign of the snake...and he was glad of that. But what about the snake wrapped around the base of the tree? Harald lay on the ground, looking up through the broad branches of the tree and remembering the vision that had came into his mind. He knew now, for himself, that the revelation dreams of both his father and his mother meant he had a great work to do in his life.

As they sat around the fire that night, Harald told his parents about the vision he had experienced while riding in the woods. Ragnhild and Halvdan looked at each other, and each was thinking about the dreams they had dreamed about this special son. It seemed to Halvdan that Harald was too young to be burdened by such heavy oaths, but it made him realize, anew, that this son had been chosen for a special mission during his sojourn on the earth.

One of Halvdan's prize mare's was about to foal. He worried that the foal would be born on May Eve, which would be a bad sign, and the foal would probably come forth dead. Halvdan watched with several of his men and Harald, as the mare struggled with this birth. The night was passing slowly, but it was almost midnight.

Halvdan did not want to lose this favorite mare, but more than that, he had promised this foal to Harald. The great stallion, Sleipni, was the sire and Halvdan knew it would be a special horse. If only it could wait to be born on May Day instead of May Eve.

May Eve was unlucky because it was the last day of nine that Odin had hung from the tree in his quest for wisdom. Odin had not died, but then he was a God. Anyone born on May Eve, animal or human, usually died.

Just at midnight, the mare pushed the foal out. The umbilical cord was wrapped around the foal's neck and it was dead.

"It can not be dead, Father. It can not be," cried Harald.

Seeing the anguish on his son's face, Halvdan took action. Quickly, he grabbed the dagger from his belt and slit the cord from the foal's neck. The foal shuddered and took a breath.

"He's not dead!" Harald shouted.

The mare nudged her wet foal and he stood on wobbly legs.

The boy wrapped his arms around the foal's neck and said, "You were born dead on May Eve, but you were brought back alive on May Day. You are my miracle horse! I shall call you May Day."

Harald spent the rest of the night in the barn, watching to make sure his May Day stayed alive. May Day's mother did not need any help, of course. She knew just what to do for him. Around dawn, Harald fell asleep lying in the fresh straw. In his dreams, he was riding into battle on his white stallion May Day with his grey wolfdog Torda by his side. The fight was long and hard, but he emerged victorious.

The boy was turning into a young man. He seemed mature for his age in some ways, yet too soft hearted to suit his father. He had an adventurous spirit, which always made his mother worry. She could not forget the times he had narrowly escaped from death and she was determined to keep him safe.

"You baby the boy to excess," Halvdan told Ragnhild.

"He is growing up too fast," she protested.

"We want him to be able to make good decisions on his own, do we not?" he asked.

"Yes," she replied reluctantly.

"Then you have to start trusting him with a little more freedom. He will need to fill the judge's seat in all of our kingdoms when I am gone, so he needs to be thinking on his own," Halvdan continued. "I plan to take him with me this summer as I make my rounds of the other seven kingdoms."

Ragnhild turned away quickly.

"Now, please do not cry. You know I am right. You can not make him stay as a young boy forever. What of all the great deeds our dreams have predicted? He needs to start preparing."

"You are right, Halvdan, I know you are, but it will be so lonesome here with both of you gone," Ragnhild answered softly.

"I would invite you to come also, but that would not be wise. I think Harald will always make the choice you would make if you are beside him. He needs to start thinking like a man. Remember how much more confidence Guttorm developed when I started taking him on my rounds? Now he holds the title of Duke and he has grown into a man of trust."

"I know you are right, Halvdan, but that doesn't make it any easier. I long for the days when my Harald was little and followed me around, or sat by the fire playing with his pup. He will soon be a grown man and he won't need his mother."

"He will always need his mother! If, for no other reason, to tell him of our dreams for him and to help him to live up to the challenges we know he will face in this life," said her husband reassuringly.

So Harald traveled with his father and his uncle on the rounds of the seven other kingdoms that summer. It was great to feel like a real man as he rode his horse up front between the two strong men of his family. The brown horse he rode was a trustworthy animal, but nothing like the big black stallion of his father's. Harald began to imagine how much more enjoyable this trip would be when his own stallion, May Day, was old enough to be ridden.

Ragnhild attempted to be brave as she said goodbye to the three men she loved most in the world. Harald tried to make her feel better by asking her to watch over May Day and Torda for him while he was gone. That had made her smile a little, but she still looked pretty sad.

Halvdan always traveled south to Vestfold first. Even though his half-brother Olaf ruled the southern half of the kingdom, a jarl had been placed to manage affairs in the northern half of Vestfold. A jarl was also chosen to take charge of each of Halvdan's other seven kingdoms during the time he and his family were in Hedmark. The King maintained a retinue of one hundred of his best soldiers at Tande Manor and they traveled with him on his rounds. His second hundred were put on alert to guard the area when the first hundred left Ringsaker.

Each jarl was responsible to train one hundred men, and these made up the first guard of each kingdom. These men were to be ready to assemble at a moments notice. Additional men made up the second guard and also the third guard. All Halvdan's men were equipped with sword, shield, battle axe, spear and dagger. The first guard had chain mail and metal helmets made for them. The second and third guard wore leather shirts and helmets for protection. They were all trained to fight, but they spent most of their time working the land as farmers.

The jarls collected scat or taxes from each farmer each year. The amount of tax was based on the amount of land that was farmed and the farmer paid on his increase. If there was a bad crop year, little or no scat was collected. The three hundred soldiers were paid from the scat collected in their own area. Everyone knew the benefit of having a trained guard to prevent trouble. The first guard got the most, and then the second and third. Halvdan paid half of his revenue back into the purses of the farmers in each kingdom.

The kingdoms were divided up into large farms, and every worthy and able man was responsible to utilize the land in the best way possible. The abundant forests provided wild game and trees for buildings and ships. Farm ground was precious in a land with so many mountains and every bit was used to grow crops and support families.

Each farm also raised animals. Horses were necessary for plowing and land travel. They were the most prized animals because the biggest, strongest and best horses carried their masters into battle. Cows provided milk, butter, cheese, meat and leather. Sheep and goats could graze even on the steepest hillsides and their wool was used for cloth. Pigs had large litters and provided some of the most favored meat. Life was good when the crops were good and all had plenty to eat.

Life was also good when there was peace in the kingdom and Halvdan had brought peace to the lands he ruled. He had enough show of strength in his armed men to discourage any other petty kings from trying to take over the lands he held. He had proven his strength when he first came into power as a man of eighteen. Now he was a seasoned ruler with twenty years of enforcing the law behind him. In addition, he had a young son that he was training to rule when the time would come for his spirit to leave his body behind in the earth.

Harald sat beside his father and listened to the problems that Halvdan was adjudicating. There were issues between neighbors, issues about land usage, issues of theft and even murder. Early on, Halvdan had set a penalty and compensation for every injury or problem. In each kingdom a lagman, or lawman was chosen. The lagman and the presiding jarl took care of minor issues during the time when Halvdan was with his family in Ringsaker.

When the King made his annual trip to each kingdom, he dealt with the major problems. Death was a major problem. Some deaths were accidental and some were the result of murder. Even though people knew there was going to be a penalty, murders were still committed.

A person who committed a murder was branded an outlaw and they would become a dishonored person. The guilty outlaw would have to pay heavy compensation to the family of the person they murdered. However, if someone murdered an outlaw, there was no compensation required. It was considered an act of revenge, and revenge was an acceptable action to take against an outlaw.

You could be branded an outlaw for a time period or an outlaw for life, depending on how serious the crime was that you committed. Often, the outlaw would just leave the area rather than face the penalty meted out when Halvdan came to sit in the judgement seat. A judgement was passed anyway, so the person would not try to come back. As the years passed and the trouble makers left the country, things became more and more peaceful in his eight kingdoms.

If these laws had been set and enforced when Halvdan's father Gudrod the Hunter had murdered his grandfather, Harald Redbeard and his uncle, Gyrd, Gudrod would have been branded as an outlaw. Aasa would then have been justified in seeing that he was killed for his actions. Halvdan was glad that he resembled his dead father only in appearance and not in temperament.

CHAPTER 6

THE HORSE FIGHT

While his father was sitting in judgement at the Haugathing in Tunsberg, a case came before him that made a great impression on Harald. It concerned the owners of two horses. Odd Vemundssen accused Gretti Thorgilssen of bringing his grey horse into the fighting ring right after Odd's red stallion had won a fight with Gaut Arnessen's stallion. Because the red stallion had just finished a severe and long fight, he slackened and was easily defeated by the grey. Gretti insisted he had thought the red was the fresh horse led forth as his grey's opponent.

Odd scoffed at that weak defense, saying that it was plain to see that his horse had just fought as it had many fresh bites that were red with blood. Gretti countered that he could not see the bites because of the red fur of Odd's horse. Odd could not remain quiet on account of his anger and shouted that Gretti had caused the death of his champion fighter. Gretti moved closer and began to shout in return. Halvdan asked Jarl Geir to stand between the two men, lest their tempers should flare out of control.

"You both know the rules for pleading your case at a Thing! Just one man may speak at a time and the man to speak first is the one making the accusation. Odd will state his case and only then will we hear from you, Gretti," stated Halvdan with his strong authoritarian voice.

Odd described the fight with great emotion in his voice. It was clear to all those present that he had loved his fighting horse.

"My stallion had just finished eleven rounds of fierce fighting and had caused Gaut's horse to retreat. I left him standing in the ring and went to find my trainer who was holding our heated mare just beyond the crowd. The next thing I knew, I heard my red scream and returned to see Gretti in the ring with his grey. His horse had taken hold of the jawbone of my horse and would not let go. I told Gretti to get his horse off of mine."

"He raised his pole and struck my horse instead of his. He kept striking blow after blow, but always missed his horse and injured mine. Finally, he succeeded in getting his grey to open its mouth and release its grip, but my horse fell down from exhaustion and never afterwards arose. I charge him with planning to let his horse attack mine because he was envious that my horse was the champion in all of Vestfold."

"What say you to answer these charges, Gretti?" demanded Halvdan.

"I deny the charge! I did neither plan to kill his horse, nor did I envy him his horse," replied Gretti with barely concealed anger.

"I do not believe you," responded Halvdan. "Has your grey stallion ever won a fight with Odd's red stallion before?"

"No," came the sullen reply.

"Have they fought before?"

"Yes."

"How many times?" the King questioned.

"Three."

"Has your grey ever come close to winning?"

"He won this time!" replied Gretti with a sneer.

"That was not my meaning. Has your grey ever come close to defeating Odd's red stallion in the past three fights?"

"Well..."

"The answer is no," shouted Odd.

Despite the fact that Odd spoke out of turn, Halvdan chose to ignore it.

"Were there any umpires watching this fight?" asked the King.

Gretti was silent, so Odd spoke up. "The umpires from the former fight had left the ring at the same time that I left. Gretti probably saw us leave and pushed his horse in for the kill while we were absent!" he shouted.

"It is not necessary for me to hear any more testimony. I will tell you the law as it applies to horse fighting. 'Whenever a man makes the horse of another fight without the owner's permission, he shall pay the loss that ensues and indemnity to the owner, according to lawful judgement. If the hurt is valued at half a mark, he shall pay full rett according to law, as if it were done from hatred or envy. Every man shall answer for himself at a horse fight, whoever may have the fight. If a man strikes a horse without necessity at a horse fight, he shall pay indemnity to the owner. And if the horse is damaged by it, he shall pay compensation for damages and rett-of-envy to the owner.'"

"Odd Vemundssen, what is the value of your dead fighting horse?" Halvdan asked.

"With the King's permission, I would ask the life of the grey stallion that took the life of my red," Odd answered.

"That is not just!" shouted Gretti.

"I am the man who decides what is just in my kingdom," countered Halvdan. "Odd shall have your grey stallion to do with as he wishes, and you will pay three marks of silver for accusing your King of being unjust!"

Gretti's face was red with anger, but he dared not say another word.

That night, as they were getting ready for bed, Harald asked his father why they never had horse fights on Tande Manor.

"We do not have horse fights because I do not like them. I love my horses too much to want to see them fighting each other and causing injury and often death. My father, Gudrod, loved horse fighting and kept many fighting stallions, but after his death, my mother never allowed another horse fight on our manor. She abhorred violence of any kind, except that which was necessary to make a right from a wrong."

"I have seen horse fights, but I do not enjoy them. Slepni could be the best fighting horse, but he is my warrior horse. A warrior horse is much more valuable than a fighting horse. A warrior horse can save your life in battle. Men often use their fighting horses to make them feel important. I have never needed that kind of praise and I hope you will not either."

"I would never want to see my May Day cut and bleeding...or killed just for someone's pleasure. I think I shall never attend another horse fight!" spoke Harald.

Halvdan smiled at the brave words of his son. He hoped that Harald was learning to have good judgement from his experience at the Things so he would grow into the kind of man he and Ragnhild would be proud of...and Odin also.

Guttorm, Halvdan and Harald stayed at the King's estate in each of the kingdom's they visited. The governing jarl lived on the estate in the King's absence. At most of the estates, there were sons of the jarl that were Harald's age or older. The young men enjoyed entertaining themselves with sword play and it was good practice. None of them had gone to war with their fathers, as none of the kingdoms were threatened at this time.

However, these young men often watched the jarl's one hundred men practice sword fighting. Usually, these fights were good spirited games, but occasionally, someone would get angry. There were some accidental wounds that were inflicted, but it was usually all in sport.

At Eidsvold, Jarl Torbjorn had a son of fourteen named Bjorn who fancied himself a champion with a sword. He was anxious to prove he was better that even the King's son at sword fighting. Harald had not done much sword fighting, except for an occasional duel with Guttorm. There had been some sword fight games with the jarl's sons in Vestfold and Vingulmark, but the boys in those kingdoms were careful to let Harald win. He was just eight years old, even though he was tall and broad for his age.

"How about a little duel, Prince Harald?" taunted Bjorn.

He wasn't usually called Prince Harald, but just Harald.

"That sounds like great fun," he answered enthusiastically.

"I assume you brought your sword," Bjorn countered.

"Yah, I have had some good sword fights with Herlof and Sigve."

"The rule here is you do not stop until someone draws blood," Bjorn stated.

Harald wasn't sure about that, but he did not want to seem like a baby. He just nodded his head in agreement.

Bjorn was really good at this, Harald thought. He tried to remember the things Guttorm had attempted to teach him. The older boy's look was serious and he was fast. The fight continued until Harald thought his arm too tired to even wield the heavy sword. Bjorn took a lunge and slit an opening in Harald's left arm.

Harald immediately reacted with a broad swing that severed Bjorn's small finger on his left hand. Bjorn screamed as he looked at the bloody finger lying on the ground.

"You should have stopped," he hollered. "It was all over because I drew the first blood."

The loud shouts brought Bjorn's father, Torbjorn, and Halvdan out into the yard.

"What is happening here?" demanded Halvdan.

Bjorn cried, "Harald cut off my finger. It was an unfair fight. He should have stopped when I sliced open his arm!"

Halvdan turned to see the blood running from his son's arm. All he could think about was Ragnhild's reaction when she found out that Harald had been cut while sword fighting. Torbjorn responded before Halvdan got a chance.

"Bjorn, you got what you deserved. Harald is just a boy and not practiced in the art of sword fighting as you are. Feed that finger to the dogs and let that empty place on your hand be a lesson to you!" he shouted.

Harald wasn't sure if he was ashamed of himself or proud of himself. Bjorn was a lot bigger that him, but he was glad he did not have to feed his finger to the dogs. Halvdan had an angry look on his face, but he decided Bjorn's punishment was just, so he said nothing about Harald's cut.

"Let's get something to wrap that arm before you lose too much blood," Halvdan spoke in a low voice to his son.

Harald searched his father's face for a sign that he had done bad or good, but all he saw was a frown. He decided it might be best to wait and talk with him about it after they left Raumarike.

"Guttorm, you need to get serious about teaching Harald to defend himself," Halvdan said with a note of concern in his voice.

"I agree. I did not think he was old enough to need serious training, but I guess the sword fight with Bjorn changed that," Guttorm responded. "Do you think that training might be better coming from you? After all, you are the King who subdued seven kingdoms as an eighteen year old warrior!"

"If someone is going to draw blood from Harald, I would rather it be you than me. Ragnhild would never forgive me, but maybe she would forgive you!" was Halvdan's reply.

From that day on, Harald and Guttorm could be seen sword fighting at every stop. No blood was drawn from Harald during those sword lessons, but Guttorm lost some blood and several shirts.

"I am sorry, Uncle Guttorm, I did not mean to draw your blood!" the boy cried.

"There will come a time when you will need to draw the blood of your opponent, Harald, and you need to get ready for that."

Guttorm's look was very serious and Harald wondered when that time would come. It seemed strange to think about actually killing someone. It probably would only feel good if they were also trying to kill you, he thought.

Harald knew that his father had a special sword that only he used. It was named Frey and was richly decorated with both gold and silver. Halvdan wore this sword whenever he traveled with his men, especially when he was making the yearly rounds of his kingdoms.

"Why do you not sword fight with me so I can show you all that Guttorm has taught me?" asked Harald.

Halvdan looked down at the sword hanging in the scabbard at his side. "This sword is for killing, not for playing!" was the serious reply.

"Why do you always wear it when you make the rounds of the kingdoms, then? Are you planning to kill someone?" Harald questioned.

"I did much killing with Frey when I was eighteen and just establishing my kingdoms. There were those who would have taken over what was mine by right, but I was victorious over all my foes. Now I have rule over eight kingdoms and have taken scat in land taxes from them all these many years. When I carry Frey it is a sign to all who see that I am ready to defend my kingdoms against every enemy."

Harald liked to hear his father talk about the days of conquest when he was but eighteen years old. He wondered if he would need to be using Frey to defend the eight kingdoms when he got to be eighteen winters. That seemed a long way away from his current age of nine. He would be content to sword fight with Guttorm using the small sword that had been made just for him in the blacksmith shop at Tande Manor.

Soon it was harvest time and they were back at Tande Manor. Ragnhild was overjoyed to see them, all three of them, but especially her son. His golden curls had turned almost white after riding for months in the warm summer sun. His face and arms were tanned and he had a healthy glow. She was sure he had grown a foot taller.

Before long, winter and Yuletide were upon them. It was always the happiest time of the year for Ragnhild. Occasionally, she thought about her father's death at this time, but she always believed he was in a better place, together with her lovely mother. The memory that filled her heart with extra love each year was the remembrance of Halvdan coming to save her from Hake the Berserker. She had been able to let go of the horrible parts of that memory, but held fast to the wonderful parts.

One of the things that Harald loved the most about the Yule celebration was listening to his mother sing the familiar songs while accompanying herself on the lyre. He would close his eyes and think of all the Yuletides he had spent in the shelter of his home. It made him feel safe and loved.

Halvdan had those same feelings as he watched his graceful wife sitting next to him, filling their home with beautiful music. He was indeed a fortunate man.

The winter was finally over and the May Day celebrations brought the beginning of summer. Halvdan was planning to bring Harald with him as he made his rounds of the kingdoms again. This time Ragnhild did not protest. She could see a new confidence and maturity in Harald's behavior after the months spent traveling with his father and uncle. As much as she would miss him, she wasn't selfish enough to keep him at Tande with her.

Harald's ninth summer passed without incidence. He no longer drew blood when he and Guttorm practiced sword fighting. He still enjoyed sword fights with the sons of the jarls, but they did not have to let him win...for he had become skilled beyond his years. Bjorn's father had forbid him from sword fighting with Harald, and so had Halvdan. They weren't sure who would come off victor if there was a return match, but neither wanted to risk it.

During Harald's tenth summer, something changed. Suddenly, the main enjoyment of visiting all the jarl's and their families living on the king's estates turned from sword fighting to girl watching. Harald was surprised to feel embarrassed when his friend's sisters wanted to watch the duels. Sometimes, he got distracted and wanted to impress them with his great abilities.

Where had all of these girls lived before? They must have been here, but he hadn't noticed them. Why did he want to spend time talking to them this year? He could not really explain it. He knew he must be younger than most of them, but he was bigger than all the rest, even Bjorn. Guttorm said he must take after his grandfather, Sigurd, who was said to be stouter and stronger than any other man.

Ragnhild had told Harald the stories of his grandfather and his feats of bravery. Twelve year old Sigurd had killed, in single combat, the berserker Hildebrand and eleven of his men in an effort to protect his family home in Ringerike. Harald was proud to have such a strong and brave grandfather. He wondered if he would be strong and brave enough to kill twelve men when he was just twelve years old.

CHAPTER 8

A TRIAL OF THEIR FAITH

An unusual thing happened at the Yuletide feast when Harald was ten winters old. A stranger named Svase the Finn had come to Tande Manor with a request from his master, Herse Herlaug. The request was that Halvdan travel to the Uplands in the spring with his one hundred men as a show of support and strength. This request was refused by Halvdan, who disliked the fact that Herlaug had sent the message with a Finn. Halvdan knew you could never trust a Finn.

Harald was in the barn feeding some apples from the storage bin to his colt, May Day, when the Finn came up behind him. There was a strange feeling on the back of his neck, and Harald turned around to see the man touching him with a willow wand.

"That is a mighty fine looking colt you have there," the Finn remarked.

"He's my magical horse," Harald replied.

"Do you believe in magic?" asked the stranger.

"Of course I do," answered Harald.

"Would you like me to show you some magic?"

"I would....," but Harald was interrupted by one of Halvdan's men who came into the barn.

"Leave the Prince alone," he shouted at the Finn.

"Oh...the Prince, you say?" smiled Svase.

"Harald, go into the house and report to your father...right now!" the soldier commanded.

Harald wondered what was wrong with talking to the man in the barn. His appearance was somewhat strange, but he had somehow attracted Harald by his eyes...and he had felt that tingling from the willow wand on his neck.

"What were you doing talking to that Finn?" Halvdan questioned, wearing a frown on his face that Harald rarely saw.

"He wanted to know about my colt, May Day. When I told him my horse was magical, he said he would show me some magic," responded Harald.

"You need to learn that a Finn is not to be trusted. Finns use magic alright, but they use it in an evil way. They always cause trouble and I do not want you near him again."

"Do you not want me to learn to make my own judgements Father? Is not that what I have been learning by watching you on the judgement seat the last three summers?"

"There are no Finns in any of my kingdoms. They bring a curse on the land. This man was told to leave as soon as he delivered his message, but he hasn't left. I will send some of my men to escort him out of Ringsaker."

Harald said nothing more. He could see that his father was upset, even though he wasn't sure why.

"It is almost time for the Yule feast. We must see to our guests," his father told him with the scowl still on his face.

There were many guests arriving from the neighboring estates. Each year it seemed like there were more people invited to spend Yuletide with Harald's family at Tande Manor. Soon, it was time to go into the great hall where the feast was prepared.

"Halvdan, what has happened to the food and mead?" asked a worried Ragnhild. "The tables were all prepared when I checked them a short while ago."

"Is this a game? Check with the serving women," Halvdan ordered.

The guests had all entered the hall and were surprised to see that there was no food for the feast.

"The serving women said they have put all of the food out on the tables," Ragnhild reported breathlessly.

"Then, where is the food......Guttorm, where is that Finn? Was he escorted away from Tande Manor?" demanded Halvdan.

"I gave the order as you said and sent ten men as an escort," replied Guttorm.

"Go tell the men to find that Finn. It is he who has stolen our food, I'll wager."

"What shall we do without any food?" Ragnhild questioned.

"I will take care of this, my dear," the King whispered to his wife.

"We beg your pardon, friends and neighbors, we have a problem to sort out. The feast will need to be postponed until next eve," spoke Halvdan apologetically.

The surprised guests reluctantly prepared to leave. There was some whispering and speculating among those who were leaving, but Halvdan was too upset to notice.

"I told you the Finns practice evil magic. No one person could walk out of our house with food and drink for forty people. That Finn has removed the food with a magic spell," he told Harald with a frown.

The men soon found Svase and brought him back to the manor house to face the wrath of King Halvdan.

"What did you do with the food and drink from my feast?" he demanded.

"Why, I did nothing, Your Majesty. Would I steal from you?" whined the Finn.

"Yes! You are a Finn, and you use your powers to accomplish your evil designs," roared Halvdan.

"I am not guilty," replied the Finn calmly. "Why would I steal your food?"

"Because I ordered you to leave our home and never return," was his angry reply.

"But, My Lord, how could one man carry out the food and drink of so large a feast?" he questioned with a smile.

"Do not try to fool me," shouted Halvdan, "I know about you Finns. I want the food and drink restored this instant or you will pay dearly."

"I am sure that a fine and noble judge such as you would not harm a poor, innocent man like me," was the Finn's sly response.

"Take him out and tie him to the large tree by the barns...and beat him until he confesses," was Halvdan's loud order to his men.

As the Finn was being dragged from the room, he came close to where Harald was standing. His eyes looked piercingly into those of Harald's.

"My young prince, save me and you shall be rewarded greatly," the Finn whispered as he passed.

"Maybe he is innocent," spoke the boy to his father as the room was emptied.

"Do you think you know more than your father after three summers of sitting beside me on the judgement seat?" glared Halvdan.

"No, I just feel like he is innocent," countered Harald.

"Then go out and watch his beating and you can be the first one to hear his confession!" answered Halvdan as he stormed from the room.

Harald watched as Svase took his beating, but there was no confession. Finally, the men decided to leave off until the morning. After the men had gone, the Finn whispered, "My Young Prince, come to me."

"How did you know I was standing here in the shadow?"

"Because I can feel your good spirit. Your spirit is speaking to my spirit. You believe I am innocent, do you not?"

"I am not sure," Harald answered hesitantly.

"If you will free me from this tree, I will bless you with the reward I promised," coaxed the Finn.

Harald felt strange. He knew his father would be very angry with him if he let the Finn escape, but he really wanted to do it. There was that same tingling feeling on the back of his neck and he was having a hard time resisting.

"Alright, I will set you free, but you must promise to leave Tande Manor and never come back."

"Of course...I will do whatever you say, Young Prince," crooned the Finn.

But when he was freed, Svase had one more favor to ask of Harald. "Please, just help me find my way to the trail...so I can leave as I promised."
"I will help you, but just until we reach the trail," agreed Harald.

However, when they came to the trail there was another request.

"You are such a kind Young Prince, could you follow along with me just a small distance farther. I am afraid I might get turned around in the dark and find myself right back at Tande Manor."

Harald knew that would not be good, and so he agreed. Soon he was walking so far into the woods that it was almost morning. Somewhere in the back of his mind, he knew he should turn around and return home, but each time he suggested it, the Finn had some reason to convince him otherwise.

Ragnhild felt a sense of panic after she awoke. Where was Harald? She could not find him anywhere. She had not seen him since that awful scene last night with the Finn. She had rarely seen her husband that angry and she had chosen retreating to their bedchamber rather than having to listen to the shouting. She ran outside to search for Halvdan.

She saw him standing with a group of his men next to a large tree by the barns. "Halvdan, I can not find Harald. Is he with you?" she shouted.

Halvdan looked down at the rope in his hand as a terrible thought crept into his mind. "Have any of you seen Harald this morning?" he asked the group of men.

None of them had seen him since the night before. "Look in the barn and see if he is with May Day," ordered Halvdan.

"He is not there," came the reply.

"Check to see if Torda is with the other dogs."

When Halvdan realized that Harald was not in the house, not in the barn, and Torda was not missing, his heart began to sink. He did not want to share his suspicions with Ragnhild, but she was running back and forth, calling Harald's name, and he could not bear to watch her panic any longer.

"Come back up to the house with me," Halvdan suggested gently. "Let us look there one more time."

As he walked Ragnhild back up the hill to the house, he turned and gave a signal to Guttorm who was standing with the men near the tree. Guttorm had had the same thoughts about what could have happened to Harald. He did not want to alarm Ragnhild either, but as soon as she and Halvdan were out of sight, he ordered the men to arm themselves and mount up quickly. There was no time to lose.

Despite the fact that Guttorm and the men had Torda and several other dogs with them, they could not seem to find any trace of Harald or Svase.

The Finn was having a difficult time controlling Harald. He needed to have him look directly into his eyes and make suggestions if he wanted Harald to resist his urge to turn around and return home. The Finn knew a cave in the hillside a ways off the path. He needed to get Harald into the cave before Halvdan and his men came searching for them.

"I am such a tired old man and you are such a great help to me, Young Prince. I must rest for a short time and then things will be better. Just follow me through these trees."

Harald hesitated, but then followed obediently. When they were safely in the shelter of the cave, the Finn offered Harald some dry berries that were hanging from dormant branches.

"These will give you strength for your journey home," he coaxed.

Harald ate the berries and fell into a deep sleep. The Finn smiled as he watched him close his eyes. This Young Prince was a fine specimen and surprisingly easy to control. He would show that high and mighty Halvdan the Black who was the most powerful. Taking his only child and heir would be the best punishment the Finn could devise.

Harald slept through the whole day and awoke to see stars shining through an opening in the top of the cave. "Where are we?" he asked the Finn.

"We are making a journey to my master's home in the north. I have spoken to your parents, and they have generously agreed to allow you to escort me safely home."

Somehow, somewhere in Harald's sub-conscious, that statement eased his mind. He would just escort the Finn to his home and then he would return to Tande. He could not be gone too many days because he was training his May Day and hoping the horse would be strong enough to be ridden next summer.

Guttorm and the men spent the entire day searching for Harald. At one point Torda started barking as if he smelled something, but then he turned back, looking bewildered. Guttorm had checked the trees in the area, but could see nothing. He hated to return to Tande without any news, but he knew Halvdan would want to lead the search in the morning.

"How could they have gotten that far on foot?" questioned Halvdan.

Guttorm did not have an answer he wanted to give. Both he and Halvdan knew that a Finn could hide Harald in plain sight if he wanted to. Ragnhild was sick with worry. She was sure it was the old scheme to destroy Harald before he had a chance to fulfill his destiny.

Halvdan armed himself with Frey, his fighting sword, and mounted his great black stallion. He divided his men into three groups. Thirty five men would ride with Guttorm traveling north. He would travel to the top of Lake Mjosa and search where they hadn't searched the day before.

Thirty five men would ride with him traveling south through Hedmark. His wolfdog, Thor, would go with him. He would travel faster with a smaller group. Thirty strong men would be left at home to protect Ragnhild and Tande Manor...in case this was a conspiracy and not just a kidnapping.

Ragnhild was overcome with worry and sorrow. Why had she become so careless as to seek sleep without first checking on her son? The Finn would not have succeeded if she would have been more vigilant. It had been a number of years since Harald had been in trouble, so she had ceased to worry as much.

Would Odin take away the important calling he had assigned to Harald because she and Halvdan had not protected their son against this new danger? Ragnhild had not felt threatened by Svase the Finn, but Halvdan was on guard immediately. He had some experiences with Finns that taught him to be wary.

Ragnhild spent her waking hours praying to Odin for his help. She pleaded for the life of her son. She promised to sacrifice anything he wanted, her favorite horse or even May Day.

At night she prayed for a dream that would tell her where Harald was and if he was unharmed. This continued night after night, but no dream came. She tried to think of what she could offer, what was as precious to her as Harald that she could give to Odin in exchange for his safe return. She promised Odin anything, anything at all. Later, Ragnhild would come to regret that promise.

Halvdan was having those same thoughts as he traveled south through Hedmark and down to Raumarike. What had he done or not done to deserve the taking of his only son? Hadn't he been faithful to offer the blood sacrifices to Odin at the Yule festival, the spring equinox and the harvest season? What more could he have done?

When that question came to the forefront of Halvdan's mind, his conscience condemned him. He should have tried not to anger the Finn. He should have given him an escort away from Tande Manor the very day he arrived. He should have spoken to his son in a more reasonable manner when he saw that Harald was wont to help him. Mostly, he should not have told Harald to go outside and watch the beating.

Watching a person receive a beating, when you felt they were innocent, would be a hard thing. It could be hard for a man to watch, but even harder for a boy...especially a boy who had been raised to have a kind, loving heart...just like his mother.

Halvdan did not pray to Odin that often. He left the praying to Ragnhild. His part was to make the sacrifices and do the outward acts of obedience...the kinds of things a man does. He had received that dream about his descendants, however. Maybe he could ask Thorleif the Wise again for another dream...or he could just count on Ragnhild to get the message for both of them.

Maybe Ragnhild had already had a dream and knew where Harald was hidden. Halvdan decided he and his men would head back for Tande in the morning, searching and asking as they went.

Guttorm was having no success either in his search for Harald. He had asked to take Harald's dog Torda with him, in case the dog would pick up a scent that would lead to the Finn's hiding place. But even the dog's keen sense of smell was no match for the strong magic that was holding Harald captive.

Svase was keeping Harald drugged by day and traveling by night. Whenever the spell would start to wear off, Svase would peer deeply into Harald's eyes and reassure him that his parents had given him their permission for this trip.

When Halvdan returned to Tande Manor, he was hoping to hear some good news. "Have you asked Odin for a dream, my wife," he asked.

"I have prayed and pleaded and begged, Ragnhild responded, but Odin has chosen to keep me suffering! I have offered to sacrifice my horse and even May Day, if that would appease the Gods!"

"Sacrificing May Day might just break one more bond between Harald and home, but I think we should sacrifice your mare tomorrow," was Halvdan's suggestion.

Sacrificing Ragnhild's horse did not bring any visions or dreams. Neither did sacrificing their prize bull, nor their best boar. Halvdan decided he would travel southwest to Ringerike and Guttorm would go farther north through the Uplands. These trips yielded no information on the whereabouts of Harald. Neither man wanted to be away from Tande too long. They were worried about Ragnhild.

There was good cause to be worried about her. She could not eat and she could not sleep. She lay in the bedchamber at night, praying for a vision or dream, but none came. One night she had a new thought. Maybe Odin would want her life as a sacrifice!

Ragnhild wondered how she would suggest this to Halvdan. She knew he felt guilt when he thought about Harald's kidnapping, even more than she did. It would not work to have Halvdan sacrifice his life...he was needed to rule his eight kingdoms until Harald was eighteen. But what if they never got Harald back? Would they just die of worry and guilt...two lonely old people whose future was suddenly taken from them?

"I think Odin wants a greater sacrifice," ventured Ragnhild when Halvdan returned.

"There is my great black stallion Sleipni," he suggested.

"I was thinking of a greater sacrifice than that," she replied.

"What else do we have that Odin might want?" he asked.

"I think Odin might take me as a worthy sacrifice for Harald!"

Halvdan jumped up and grabbed her by the shoulders. He stared into her eyes in unbelief. "You do not mean that! Surely you would not ask me to choose between my love for you and my love for Harald!" he cried.

"Harald is more important than me," Ragnhild whispered. "Do you not remember our dreams about the great good he was to accomplish during his lifetime? I have already done my most important work here on this earth. I gave you a mighty son who will carry on your reign of peace and justice after you are gone. But what of me? Can I bear you another child to replace the one we so carelessly let slip out of our grasp? No! I am now barren and that makes me useless! I would give up my life for Harald's eagerly!" With that last, Ragnhild began to sob.

Halvdan stared at his wife in disbelief. He had not realized the depth of her sorrow and anguish. He took her limp body into his arms and cradled her in his lap.

"Shush, now, my lovely wife. You must not speak so. We will not give your life for that of our son. Even Odin would not wish it so. I have been selfish to leave you here with no one to share your torment and grief. We will not speak of this again."

With that comment, he picked her up and carried her into the bed chamber and lay down beside her. She was exhausted from lack of sleep and worry. Halvdan laid her head on his arm and stroked the still beautiful golden hair. Ragnhild fell asleep listening to the soothing words of reassurance spoken by her husband.

Halvdan did not sleep, however. He was horrified at the thought that he might have come home to see his lovely Ragnhild hanging by a rope from the large beams over their bed. He must not leave her again. She would come with him when he traveled next to Toten and Hadeland. They could stay at the King's estate in each area. It might even help Ragnhild to be out of the house and seeing other people.

Harald was getting restless. It was becoming harder to keep him in the trance-like state that Svase needed to convince him that he should not return home yet. "Soon," is all the Finn would say when the boy questioned him.

As Ragnhild rode in the sleigh across the frozen Lake Mjosa, she could not help but think about the joy and relief she had felt crossing the same lake while being rescued by Halvdan. This trip was not that joyful, but it was probably better than sitting home at Tande and waiting for news of Harald.

The fresh snowflakes caressed her cheeks as she snuggled deeper into the folds of the soft fur robes that Halvdan had wrapped around her. It did feel better to be outside and she had always loved the beauty of a new snowfall.

Halvdan and his men were riding ahead of the sleigh. She could pick out the broad shoulders and commanding presence of her gentle giant of a husband even amidst a large group of horsemen. Her life had been wonderful with a kind and loving husband and a clever and charming son to rear. Had her life been too easy? Is that why she was having to endure this trial? She had promised Halvdan that she would try to think more positive thoughts, but it was difficult.

Jarl Arvid and his wife Aud welcomed them warmly at Greftegrev Manor. The buildings were located on a hill above Lake Rand and the view from their hill was almost as fine as the view at Tande Manor. Aud was careful to try and talk about everything except Harald.

A messenger came to Greftegrev with an invitation to a wedding feast for the son of a neighbor across the lake at Bredsvold Manor. They were particularly pleased that King Halvdan and Ragnhild were visiting in the area. It would be a special honor and a mark of good fortune to have the King bless the wedding couple.

When the day of the wedding feast arrived, Ragnhild was feeling unwell. "I am afraid I won't be able to attend the feast," she told Halvdan.

"Then I shall stay back at Greftegrev with you while Arvid and Aud are gone."

"That would not be fair to the wedding couple. They are counting on a blessing from their King," she responded.

"But, are you sure you will be alright?"

"I just need to lie down and rest this night."

"If you are sure," replied Halvdan, "I will go, but I will return tonight instead of staying until morning."

"Thank you for that," said Ragnhild with a smile. "I always sleep better when you are by my side."

Halvdan gave her a gentle kiss on the forehead, wished her a good rest, and left for the feast. He donned his heavy robe and his sword, Frey. He certainly would not need his sword tonight, but it made him look more like a king to wear it. As he walked out the door, he saw that his men had hitched up the sleigh instead of saddling his stallion. They did not realize Ragnhild would not be coming.

"Would you rather we saddle Sleipni?" asked one of the soldiers.

"No, the sleigh will be fine for tonight," he replied.

A wedding feast was always a happy occasion and this one was particularly grand because the King was in attendance. The food was plentiful and so was the mead. As the hour drew late, Halvdan told the host that he would be leaving.

"Are you sure you want to travel back in the dark?" he asked.

"Ragnhild will be waiting for me," Halvdan answered. "We shall travel by the light of the moon."

There was a moon in the sky, but it was covered by thin clouds. They would count on the horses to find the trail across the ice of Lake Rand. Just ten of Halvdan's men had traveled with him to the wedding feast. The others had stayed behind at Greftegrev Manor.

The King and his men were most of the way across the frozen lake when they heard the first sound of ice cracking. It was too dark to tell just what was happening. There was the clanging of metal as horses fell and swords hit the ice. Men were shouting, horses were neighing, and water was splashing. Before they could stop, the horse team, sleigh and King were all in the ice cold water.

As the heavy sleigh plunged into the icy water, it overturned and trapped Halvdan beneath it. He struggled to reach the surface, but his heavy robe and sword were weighing him down. He could not see anything in the dark depths of the lake. As he kicked and thrashed he called out, "Ragnhild, my Ragnhild!" Those were the last words Halvdan would utter in this life.

At that moment, in the bedchamber at Greftegrev, Ragnhild heard Halvdan calling for her. In her dream he was in water and reaching for her hand. She tried to reach him, but she could not quite make it. She tried and tried, but it was no use. He called to her again and then he was silent.

Ragnhild awoke with a start. Her nightgown was wet with perspiration and she realized she had been struggling in her dream. What was the dream? She finally had the dream she had been praying for, but it was not Harald she saw in the dream, it was Halvdan.

Halvdan! Where was Halvdan? He had he been calling to her, but where was he? She was trying to remember the dream. Halvdan had been in the water and he was calling for her. She was trying to reach him, to grab his hand and pull him out of the water, but she could not. And then he had.............. Suddenly, Ragnhild screamed as she could see Halvdan sinking in the dark, cold depths of Lake Rand.

She jumped from the bed platform and reached for her over gown. She was screaming Halvdan's name as she ran through the long hall. Where would Halvdan's men be? She knew he had left a number of them at Greftegrev with her.

"Help me," she screamed. "Help me!"

A group of men came rushing into the great hall just as Ragnhild reached the door.

"Halvdan is drowning! He is drowning in Lake Rand!" she screamed.

The men rushed for their horses and galloped as fast as they could to the edge of the lake. As they got close, they could hear the shouting of men and the neighing of horses. It was too dark to see what was happening out on the lake, but they could guess. They could hear the splashing of water and they knew the water should be completely covered by a thick layer of ice.

"Where is Halvdan?" shouted one man.

"Where is the King?" shouted another.

"We do not know! We can not find him!" was the answer.

The first two men in the group had managed to get out of the water and up on the ice. The other eight men and King Halvdan the Black died a cold death in the frozen waters of Lake Rand that night.

Ragnhild was in shock. How could this have happened? What would she do now? Her beloved Halvdan was gone and she was alone. She wished she had gone to the wedding feast so she could have died with him. She would never forget her dream and the sound of his voice calling to her. She would never forget that he had reached for her and she could not help him. It made her want to go down to that hole in the ice and drown herself.

Of course, Halvdan's body was no longer in that dark water. When daylight finally came, there was a gruesome sight of dead bodies, of men and horses floating amid the ice chunks. She had to get herself together! People were asking for her direction and she needed to make the right decisions.

Word spread quickly about the death of King Halvdan the Black. He had been such a fair and just ruler and had given his people peace and prosperity. There was fear that things would take a turn for the worse now that he was dead. Not only was King Halvdan dead, but his heir, Prince Harald, was missing. What were they to do they wondered?

Somehow, Ragnhild got through that first day. Halvdan's frozen body lay in an outer building and she was in the bed chamber alone. How could she bear to go on living? Her world was empty. She quietly sobbed until sleep overcame her.

Then came the dream she had prayed and pleaded for. Odin was there, standing before her and relaying his message.

"You were willing to offer yourself as a sacrifice for your son. You are a worthy vessel, but I have taken your husband in your stead. He had accomplished much good in his life and he will now live in Gimli, the hall of righteous men. The blessings come after the trial of your faith. Your son Harald is on his way back to you. He will need your help as well as Guttorm's to become the great man I have planned for him to be. You must continue to support him yet a while...and then you may come to join your Halvdan."

When Ragnhild awoke, she was sad, calm and relieved all at the same time. She was sad that Halvdan had been sacrificed instead of her. She was calm because now she knew that he was in a place where he was being rewarded for his good deeds. She was relieved to hear that Harald was still alive and on his way home. Her life would not be empty with her son Harald in it...and Odin had said she was still needed.

CHAPTER 8

HARALD, THE WARRIOR KING

That morning when Harald awoke, Svase the Finn was standing over him with an evil look in his eye. "Thy father took it much amiss that at Yule, I took the food and drink from his feast. But you helped me to escape and now I will repay thee the reward I promised. Thy father is dead and now thou shalt return home, and take possession of the kingdom which he had...and then thou shalt lay the whole kingdom of Norway under thee."

Harald was stunned and shaken. His mind was confused. What had the Finn just told him? That his father had been right about him and the stealing of the food? That his father was dead? That this was his reward? That he should lay the whole kingdom of Norway under him? It was too much to take in at one time. Harald just knew he needed to get away as quickly as possible.

Svase gave Harald a horse and told him to ride with all speed to Greftegrev Manor in Hadeland. There he would find his mother and the body of his father.

In parting, Svase said, "We shall meet again, Young Prince. But now you are King Harald! Nevertheless, we shall meet again and next time you will reward me!"

Harald rode off without a backward glance. Most of the time he had spent with the Finn, he could not remember. His mind seemed clear for the first time in a long while. His father had been right...you really can not trust a Finn.

Guttorm arrived shortly after Ragnhild awoke. He had ridden to Greftegrev from Ringerike when he heard the news of Halvdan's death. Ragnhild was relieved to see him and they embraced in their sorrow.

"The people of Hadeland want to bury Halvdan in a mound here, but I wanted to take his body to Tande Manor for burial. What do you think, Guttorm?" asked his grief-stricken sister.

"The people of Ringerike also want to bury Halvdan in their area," responded Guttorm. "They are afraid their peace and prosperity will end with the King's death."

Just then Jarl Arvid came into the room. "We have Jarl Eystein from Vestfold, Jarl Seamon from Vingulmark, Jarl Vemund from Raumarike, Jarl Thorn from Toten, and Jarl Atle from Sogn in the great hall. They all want to ask for the body of Halvdan so they may bury it in their kingdom."

Ragnhild looked at Guttorm, "What shall I do?" she pleaded.

"I have an plan," Guttorm replied. "You may not like it, but it may work."

"What is your plan?" she questioned, almost afraid to hear what he had to say.

"You could take Halvdan's head to Ringsaker and make a mound for him near you at Tande Manor. Then, we could divide his body in four parts and cast lots for them. That way, at least four kingdoms will be satisfied."

"I do not want my husband's body cut in pieces and buried in five different mounds!" she answered with a frown.

"I know you do not," said Guttorm with an understanding tone in his voice, "but you must think of Harald. He needs to have the support of the people in these kingdoms if he is going to maintain rule over them. Though he is Halvdan's son, his rule has yet to be proven. I think you need to give them Halvdan's body to help Harald."

That was the one thing Guttorm could say to make Ragnhild agree. She was choosing to let go of the dead to protect the living.

"You are right, Guttorm, I will do it for Harald," she said. "We must wait until Harald arrives before Halvdan is dismembered. He and I will need some time to say our farewell's to Halvdan's body, before his spirit returns to Odin."

"I will tell the jarls of your decision. We will cast the lots after Harald has arrived and we have said words over Halvdan's body," agreed Guttorm.

Harald arrived the next day. He was relieved to be back with his family...at least his mother and Guttorm. He did not like the idea of dividing up his father's body either, but after listening to Guttorm's reasoning, he agreed to the plan.

The lots fell to Ringerike, Raumarike, Vestfold, and Hadeland. His head would go home with Ragnhild and Harald to Ringsaker in Hedmark. Halvdan was to have five mounds raised to him in five kingdoms.

He was forty years old when he died. He had been one of the most respected kings in all the land. Through the Code of Laws he had established and his just rule, his people had enjoyed much peace and prosperity for more than twenty years.

When Harald walked into the building where his father's body had been laid, he felt very humbled. He needed a chance to say goodbye to his father...and tell him he had been right about Svase the Finn. He wanted to ask forgiveness for doubting his father's wisdom and thank him for the good example he had set.

During the two days it had taken Harald to travel to Lake Rand, he had done much thinking. How was he even going to be half as good a king as his father had been? He would surely need the help of his mother and his uncle. He would also need the inspiration of Odin if he was going to complete all the important work he was sent to the earth to accomplish.

Even though Ragnhild had agreed to share Halvdan's body with the four other kingdoms, she refused to allow his weapons to go with his body parts. "I will bury his weapons with his head in Ringsaker," she told the jarls.

A warrior's weapons were usually buried with him so that he could use them in the next life. Ragnhild was willing to bury Halvdan's spear and dagger with his head, but not the sword, Frey. She knew the story of the sword and how Aasa had removed it from beside Gudrod's body so that Halvdan would have it. Ragnhild also knew that Harald would need that powerful sword by his side to help protect his life.

She decided to give the battleaxe to Guttorm as a token of the time they had spent together. Halvdan had trained her brother to become the head of his armies and Guttorm had served faithfully in that calling. She knew that he would also serve Harald in the same way. Yes, he would need a strong battleaxe to help protect his young nephew.

Their father, Sigurd Hjort, had enjoyed the reputation of being the strongest man in the Uplands, and it looked as if Guttorm had also inherited that same strength. Not only was he handsome of face, but he was taller than almost any man, except for Halvdan. They had stood eye to eye when Guttorm attained his full growth. With Halvdan gone, it would now fall to her brother to act as guide and protector to ten year old Harald.

Ragnhild, Guttorm and Harald had just returned to Tande Manor when there was a rider with an urgent message for them. King Gandalf from Aust-

Vingulmark and his son Hake were planning a sneak attack on Vestfold. Hake was marching with an army of three hundred men and Gandalf was preparing to come by ship across the fjord.

His mother was the first to say they must pray to Odin for his help in defending Vestfold and defeating their enemy. Guttorm and Harald readily agreed. Even though they knew that Harald was destined to succeed in battle and rule the many kingdoms of Norway, they also knew Odin to be a jealous God who wanted them to plead for his help in every battle.

It gave Harald even more respect for his father's twenty year peaceful reign when he realized that these kings were right there, waiting to overtake his kingdoms as soon as they heard the news that King Halvdan the Black was dead.

During those summers when he had ridden with his father and Guttorm and the one hundred soldiers from kingdom to kingdom, it had just seemed like an ordinary trip. Only now did he realize how much power Halvdan's presence had wielded.

He also remembered asking his father to sword fight with him and the great sword, Frey. Halvdan's sober comment had been, "Frey is not for sword practice. Frey is for killing."

Now, Harald carried Frey by his side, and it had definitely been used for killing. The rune inscription of Harald's name had been added to those of all the former warriors who had carried Frey into battle. With this sword in his hand, Harald felt invincible.

Harald also rode his father's black stallion, Sleipni, as he traveled to defend his kingdoms. The fact that Halvdan had ridden in a sleigh across Lake Rand had saved Sleipni from certain death. Harald felt Odin had arranged that because he knew the ten year old king would need every advantage he could give him. Both wolf dogs, Thor and Torda, traveled with them and protected the backs of Harald and Guttorm in hand-to-hand combat.

Just the sight of a warrior king riding at the front of hundreds of armed soldiers on the great black stallion, with the sun reflecting off the gold and silver of the sword Frey, along with his gleaming helmet and battle shield, was enough to strike fear in the hearts of the faint hearted. Even though Harald was big and strong for his age, it would be years before he would reach the stature of his revered father, Halvdan the Black.

Hake was the first to die, along with most of his three hundred men. At the point of victory, Harald and Guttorm saw a vision of Odin riding across the battlefield on his eight-legged horse, with the two wolves by his side and his ravens on each shoulder. This was the same victory sign they would see after each battle, and it reassured them that Odin was watching over and helping them...so that his will might come to pass.

As Harald and Guttorm headed north to return to Hedmark, they came upon King Gandalf and his army. He had just crossed the fjord with the intent of attacking Harald's army from the rear. Gandalf had hoped to come to the aid of his son, Hake, but he was too late.

The two armies marched against each other in a great battle, but Odin was with Harald and Guttorm again. When Gandalf saw the piles of bodies and realized that most of his men lay dead at the water's edge, he ran to his dragon ship and retreated back across the fjord.

Harald and Guttorm led their men in a cheer as they watched the now humbled Gandalf fleeing for his life. "To Odin be the victory! To Odin be the victory! To Odin be the victory!" was to be the famous battle cry that would be heard throughout Norway in the years to come.

The successful warriors once again started on their northward journey. If they had expected a time of rest, they were disappointed. Their army now consisted of warriors from Agder, Vestfold and Hedmark, more than one thousand strong, and they were reveling in the feeling of victory over Hake and Gandalf.

The armed forces camped in a field to the north of Vestfold where there was feed for their horses and friendly subjects to help feed the men. The hide of the bear that had attacked Torda so long ago, now traveled with Harald. It covered the rump of Sleipni during battle to protect him from arrow wounds. The thick bear skin also acted as a cushion on the ground as the young king slept with Torda by his side.

Harald drifted off to sleep to the sound of wood crackling in the fire pits and the quiet murmur of men telling of their successes of the day. Harald was also dreaming of their victory when he saw Odin galloping toward him, waving his spear in the air.

"How can you lay there in slumber while your enemies plot to attack Tande Manor?" shouted Odin.

Harald awoke with a start. What was it that Odin had shouted to him? His enemies were plotting to attack Tande Manor! It was guarded by a mere fifty men while he lay here resting with his thousand.

"Wake up, Guttorm, we must march to Tande. Odin has just told me in a dream that our enemies are plotting to attack my home. I should never have left Mother there with so few men for protection!"

Guttorm was up instantly and began shouting orders to the men.

"Let us speak quietly, lest our enemies have spies across the fjord who might hear our panic and guess our movements," whispered Harald.

"You are right," Guttorm agreed. "We will leave our campfires burning as we depart and it may be that our enemies will think we still sleep."

Soon, one thousand men and their leaders were moving north toward Hedmark and Ringsaker. Horses and men were weary after two hard battles, but they responded to the commands of their young King. As the army traveled though Ringerike, Raumarike and Toten, all of Halvdan's nine hundred trained warriors, and the jarls that had supervised them, joined with Harald's thousand.

There were now about two thousand warriors following Harald and Guttorm. Halvdan had prepared men in every kingdom to be ready for just such an attack, but it did not come during his lifetime. Instead, the cowards waited to attack his ten year old son. Fortunately, his uncle Guttorm was by Harald's side...and they had Odin's support!

Frode and Hogne, sons of King Eystein from North Hedemark had been anxious to conquer Ringsaker and its rich farmland and ideal location along Lake Mjosa. They knew they weren't strong enough to attack Harald and Guttorm on their own, so they asked Hogne of Ringerike and Herse from Gudbrandsdal to join them. If they were successful, each man would have his own kingdom to rule and they would no longer have to abide by King Halvdan's strict laws.

Spies had been sent ahead of the troops to find out where the plotting kings were meeting. The four were spending the night at Herse's estate in Gudbrandsdal. Harald's army marched day and night until they arrived outside the longhouse at about midnight.

Guttorm ordered both houses to be burned and Hogne Karuson and Herse Gudbrand died in their sleep. Frode and Hogne Eysteinsson escaped the burning building with some of their men, but died by the sword instead of the fire. Valhalla awaited the two fallen warriors.

Odin was once again seen riding over the flames of the burning building and the warriors shouted three times their chant, "To Odin the victory!" Thanks to Odin's warning, Tande Manor and Ringsaker were saved from attack.

After the fall of these four chiefs, King Harald, with Guttorm's leadership, had subdued North Hedemark, Ringerike, Gudbrandsdal, Hadeland, Toten and Raumarike. These kingdoms could now be added to Vestfold, Sogn and Agder.

Even though their army had been successful in killing Prince Hake, his father, King Gandalf, had raised another army and was determined to avenge the death of his son. When Harald and Guttorm heard that he was trying to attack Hedemark from the south, they marched to meet him. The battle took place in the fertile valley of Osterdalen, where Gandalf also met his death.

The whole of Gandalf's kingdom of Aust Vingulmark was now under Harald's rule as far south as the River Raum. Most of Harald's early success was due to the great leadership of his Uncle Guttorm. Even though Guttorm had not been with Halvdan the Black during his conquering of the seven kingdoms as an eighteen year old, he had ridden by Halvdan's side for the last ten years and had gained wisdom from the mighty King.

There was much rejoicing and celebrating as Harald and Guttorm returned to Tande Manor. Ragnhild had prayed for them daily and she knew that Odin was helping them with each victory. Not only had they finally redeemed all seven of the kingdoms Halvdan had ruled for twenty two years, they had added Gudbrandsdal to the north and Vingulmark to the south, plus the rest of Hedmark. It seemed like they were due for a nice long period of rest.

They were home in time for the celebration of Harald's eleventh birthday in September. This was also the harvest season and a time for jubilation. The fields had produced grain in abundance, which meant food for both animal and human during the cold winter months ahead.

"Odin has blessed us with a plentiful harvest again this year. That should be a sign to everyone that you will be as fine a King as was your father," said Ragnhild.

"I did not really think about what a great man father was until now that he is gone. Perhaps it is hard to appreciate what you have until you have it no longer," replied Harald. "I do know what a blessing it has been to have Guttorm by my side. Without him I would probably be lying dead on the fields of Vestfold."

"You give me too much credit," protested Guttorm. "Remember, it is you that Odin has given the challenge to accomplish a great work. He has just allowed me to help you."

Ragnhild added,"In my vision, Odin told me that he had accepted your father as a sacrifice for your safe return from the evil clutches of the Finn, but that he had left us to aid you in your conquests. Let us be thankful to the Gods that they have protected you through these battles."

"We shall offer a great sacrifice to Odin this time, to celebrate not only an abundant harvest but our success in battle," shouted a grateful Harald.

Suddenly, he had a sobering thought. "We won't have to sacrifice May Day, will we?" The great warrior bravado turned to the tender heart of the boy.

"No," his mother reassured him, "we have many worthy animals to sacrifice without taking your magic horse!"

CHAPTER 9

THE OATH.....THE VOW

It was Yuletide at Tande Manor and Ragnhild was trying not to feel cheerless when she thought about celebrating this season without her kind and compassionate husband. At night, when she lay alone in the large bedchamber they had shared, she tried to imagine what he was doing in Gimli. She always felt that he was looking down at her and wishing he was there beside her.

Harald could not help but think about the traumatic Yuletide of last year and the fateful encounter with Svase the Finn. His guilt hounded him when he thought about his immature behavior and the outcome of his decisions.

When his mother told him that Odin had taken his father as a sacrifice for the safe return of their son, she thought that would help him to understand the special mission he needed to accomplish. Instead, it just made him feel more guilt. Tande Manor just wasn't the same without the presence of King Halvdan the Black.

He fell asleep that night with these thoughts on his mind. This time it wasn't Odin that came to him with a message. Freya, the golden haired Goddess of Love, stood by his bed. She was a wonder to behold, but her words were sobering. "There is a lovely Princess called Gyda, daughter of King Eirik of Hordaland, who is living in the house of the powerful Jarl Sivert in Valdres. You must go there and ask for her hand in marriage."

When he sat up to question her, Freya vanished. Harald was surprised by the message. His parents had married when his mother was twenty and his father was thirty. His father had been twenty when he married the first time. Why was he being told to marry when he had just turned eleven?

Those were the questions he asked his mother and Guttorm the next day. "We must not question the Gods," counseled Ragnhild. "You must do as you have been instructed."

"Send me," suggested Guttorm. "Then perhaps Jarl Sivert will allow Gyda to travel to Tande Manor to meet you."

"That is good counsel," Ragnhild agreed.

And so it was that Guttorm started off for Valdres in Oppland. Harald wasn't sure what he felt. There was some excitement at the thought of being married, but there was also apprehension. What would Princess Gyda be like? His parents had such a deep feeling of love for each other and that was the kind of marriage he wanted also.

Ragnhild could see the worried frown lines on Harald's fair face. "What is troubling you, my son?" she asked.

"I am wondering about getting married to a girl I do not know and may not like," Harald answered.

"Your father and I did not know each other before he rescued me from Hake the Berserker, but we fell in love quickly after we were together. We always felt like the Gods brought us together because they wanted us to be your parents. You must trust the Gods. They know your future, even if you dono t. There is a good reason you have been asked to seek this girl's hand."

That reason became apparent when Guttorm returned without Gyda. "She said no!" was the message Guttorm told to Harald and Ragnhild.

"She is a remarkably handsome young woman, but a very high spirited one. She also thinks very highly of herself! She asks you to come and see her in person. I think she was offended that you sent a messenger, even if it was your uncle," Guttorm said with a smile.

"Well, if the Gods will it, I shall go!" declared Harald.

Gyda had been pleased to hear that there was a King in Ringsaker who wished to marry her, but she just could not agree. From the time she was a young girl, she had dreamed that one day she would be the wife of a great king. This king was not just a ruler of a few kingdoms; he was the ruler of all of Norway.

She did not tell her dreams to anyone. They would think she was a foolish child, she who was the rejected daughter of Eirik Roreksson, King of Hordaland. Gyda's mother had died just after she was born and her father had been so brokenhearted at the loss of his wife that he blamed her death on the infant.

Eirik, who wanted his first child to be a son, did not care for this girl child. He asked a friend, Jarl Sivert, to foster his daughter. From the day he left her in Valdres, Eirik had never once come to visit. Gyda grew up knowing she was a princess and daughter of King Eirik of Hordaland and Alov of Rogaland, but very little else.

However, when she was six she learned that her mother had died giving birth to her and she gave up asking when her father was coming to visit. Jarl Sivert and his wife Ingeborg were kind people who had no children of their own, but Gyda needed much more love than she was given.

In her loneliness, she pretended that a handsome king would come riding up to the manor house and take her away to live with him on his great estate. She would ride off with him and he would love her as she needed to be loved and she would be so happy.

When she got older, she actually had these dreams. She wasn't really sure if she wanted that life so much that she dreamed about it while she was asleep...or if her dreams were a foretelling of her future. One night she dreamed that a young golden haired king would ask for her hand, but that she should refuse to marry him until he had become King of all Norway.

That dream had been so vivid that she knew she would recognize him as soon as she saw him. When the uncle of Harald Halvdansson arrived and told her that his nephew wanted to ask for her hand in marriage, she had to ask that Harald come himself. She needed to know if he was the king in her dream.

Within a fortnight, Harald and Guttorm set off for Valdres. They all agreed that it wasn't safe for Harald to travel without a large retinue of warrior soldiers. There were still plenty of petty kings out there that would like to see Halvdan's son and heir go on to Valhalla.

As they were welcomed into the great hall of Jarl Sivert's manor house, Harald was a bit anxious. Should he tell this proud girl that she wasn't his choice, but he was commanded to have her by the Gods? He decided he would only tell her that if she outright refused him.

He could not believe his eyes as Gyda entered the room. Instantly, he felt his heart begin to pound. She was proud, yes, but so beautiful. She had copper red hair that framed her face and lay in a mass of curls around her shoulders. Her piercing green eyes shone above rosy cheeks and ruby lips. He thought she was the most beautiful maid he had ever seen.

Similar thoughts were going through Gyda's mind. When she saw him standing in the great room, she knew he was the king in her dream. She was tempted to say, "Yes, take me away with you right now!" but she knew she must do as she had been instructed.

Harald did not appear to be an eleven year old boy. He looked strong and straight, with muscular legs and broad shoulders. His face, though beardless, was very handsome to look at and his head was covered with golden curls. She thought he was even more striking than the young man she had seen in her dreams.

"Thank you for traveling to meet me," said Gyda with a smile. She knew her cheeks were red, but she was determined not to show any weakness of her position.

"The pleasure is all mine," replied Harald with a smile. He could actually see himself marrying such a beautiful girl.

There was an awkward silence in the room. Finally, Harald decided to move forward boldly. He walked over to Gyda and looked into her lovely green eyes.

"I have come to ask for your hand in marriage, Princess Gyda," said Harald confidently.

He wanted to reach for her hand, but she hadn't offered it.

"My father was King Halvdan the Black, son of Gudrod the Hunter, King of Vestfold and Aasa, Princess of Agder. My mother is the daughter of King Sigurd Hjort of Ringerike and Thorny, Princess of Jutland. I have a fine estate in Ringsaker on the edge of Lake Mjosa and I am now ruler over twelve kingdoms from Gudbrandsdal to Agder."

His words sounded impressive even to him and he waited for her reply.

"You have a fine start as a warrior king, and your family is very respectable, but I want more. I have dreamed of becoming the wife of a king who rules the whole of Norway as King Eirik rules Sweden and King Gorm rules Denmark. When you have succeeded in conquering all of Norway and can say you are ruler over thirty kingdoms, then will you truly claim the title of Warrior King and I shall be honored to call thee husband!"

Guttorm and Jarl Sivert stood in shocked silence. Harald said nothing for a moment. It was as if he was listening to a message that only he could hear. In truth, he was. As Gyda spoke, it was as if she had turned into the Goddess Freya with a message just for him.

The message was that he should not sit home at Tande Manor and be content to rule his twelve kingdoms. He knew there was a greater work for him to do and he needed to get about doing it. This was not the time for him to marry Gyda, but she was the messenger. She would be there for him when he had fulfilled his mission and conquered all the kingdoms of Norway.

Finally, Harald answered. "Thou hast spoken well, Princess Gyda, and reminded me of something which I have known before. It shall be my quest to conquer all the kingdoms of Norway. Odin has spoken it and thou hast reaffirmed it. I make a solemn oath, and take God to witness, who made me and rules over all things, that never shall I cut nor comb my hair until I have put all the kingdoms of Norway beneath me. Then shall I vow to return for thee!"

Gyda graciously offered Harald her hand. He pressed it to his mouth in a gallant gesture and said, "My vow is sealed with this kiss!"

As she felt the closeness of his presence, Gyda said a silent prayer that his quest might be accomplished with all possible speed.

CHAPTER 10

KING HARALD MARCHES NORTHWARD

Harald and Guttorm traveled from kingdom to kingdom, proclaiming their intent to establish the Code of Laws practiced by Halvdan the Black. They shared the ancient plan of Odin with taxes paid for the safety and protection of all. Through the southern kingdoms they rode and gathered a large force of men from all of the kingdoms that Halvdan and now Harald ruled. When they had succeeded there, they moved northward...through the Uplands, the Gudbrandsdal Valley, over the Dovrefields and then on to Orkadal.

In each place, they sent out an ultimatum declaring that men must decide their own fate. They could take service with King Harald and pledge their allegiance to him and his cause of uniting all of the kingdoms...or they could choose to fight and die. Some chose to leave the country and find new lands to the west.

King Harald attended the Thing in each of the kingdoms. There he proclaimed the cause he would make his life's work...to give the people peace and justice in their lives.

He addressed the crowd at each Thing. "Fellow countrymen, join with me. For my cause is just, yea, it is the cause set upon my father by the Odin himself. Let us all follow the same Code of Laws that allows for fair judgement and punishment that fits the crime."

"Now, if there are no laws, and no punishment given for breaking the laws, many men would not be afraid to continue their cruel and evil ways. Some men desire to do evil. Let them practice their wickedness on their enemies, not on their own countrymen and kinsmen. I will execute the law and the law will inflict the punishment."

"I will follow my father's system of fair laws and taxes. His system required everyone to pay land dues based on their possessions. In exchange, he offered protection and employment. I will equip up to three hundred soldiers in each area. A jarl will be chosen to maintain order and to judge according to the law of the land at the local Thing. He is to treat the people with fairness and see that justice is served. Twelve lawmen will be chosen from among the free men of every district. They will promote a system of justice in our country."

"Now is the time to decide. You must either be with me, or against me.

There is no middle ground. You may come forward right now and take an oath for yourself and your men...or you may leave the Thing and meet us tomorrow on the battlefield!"

The best and strongest men chose to pledge allegiance. Harald and Guttorm did not like fighting their own countrymen, but they knew they were carrying out Odin's plan. Those who did not choose to follow Harald as their king would continue to cause trouble and would thwart his ability to make one united country out of the many kingdoms.

The next area Harald and Guttorm came to as they traveled north was Gaulardal. Jarl Hakon Grjotgardson from Stjordal came to join with him there and brought seven hundred men to enter into Harald's service.

This pleased the King greatly, for he would rather have men offer their allegiance to his cause than to slay them. Harald took a sword and shield and placed them on Hakon as a sign that he pledged his loyalty until death. Then, he made him a jarl and gave the Stjordal district into his hands. This was a great lesson to the other chieftains whose kingdoms lay in the path of Harald's conquest.

The young king and his uncle fought eight hard battles and slew eight kings in the Trondelag area and laid the whole of it under him. He then was ruler over Gaulardal, Strinda, Stjordal, Vaerdal, Skeyna, Sparbyggja, Eyin Idre and Eyna.

After Trondelag, Harald and Guttorm traveled north to Naumadal where two brothers, Herlaug and Hrollaug, were kings. When they heard that King Harald and Duke Guttorm were on their way, Herlaug hid himself in a mound with eleven of his men. Then they covered up the entrance. Hrollaug went out to meet King Harald and offered him the whole of Naumudal and asked to enter his service. He swore an oath of allegiance and was made Jarl of Naumudal.

Despite the icy cold winds that swept over the land from the frigid waters of the Trondelag Fjord, Harald and Guttorm decided to return to Nidaros for the winter. They knew Ragnhild would wish to have them come to Tande Manor for Yuletide, but they needed to keep a large force of men in the Trondelag area to maintain the kingdoms they had just captured.

The year was 865 A.D. and Harald was now fifteen years of age. He had grown much in his quest of conquering Norway. It was great to have Guttorm always by his side. He was thankful that Odin had allowed him to have his uncle as foster-father.

Jarl Hakon Grjotgardson had invited them to spend Yuletide at his estate in Stjordal and they were happy to have a place to camp for the winter. It was much colder this far north and near the Norway Sea. Harald liked the area, but it wasn't as pleasant as his home in Hedmark.

"We are pleased to have you at Lanke Manor," said Jarl Hakon. "You honor our home with your presence."

He was relieved that Harald had accepted him, his sons, and his men into the large army that was moving through Norway. Had he chosen to fight King Harald and Duke Guttorm, he would probably be in Valhalla right now with the other kings they had overpowered.

"My men and I are grateful for your kind hospitality," Harald answered. "Guttorm and I welcome the opportunity to over winter in your home."

The two warriors had changed into clothing suitable for the Yuletide feast. They were anxious to partake of the roast boar they could smell and the other special foods that were prepared for Yule. They were also looking forward to drinking as much mead as they could hold and then sleeping in a warm room.

"You shall sit in the high seat, King Harald, and Guttorm and I will take the seats on each side," said their host.

Harald looked at Guttorm, who nodded acceptance. He knew he was the highest ranking person in the room, but Harald was still young enough to think that the high seat should be filled by the father of the home.

"Thank you, Jarl Hakon," Harald responded. "Your warm welcome will be rewarded."

"It is enough that you have allowed me and my sons, Grjotgard and Herlaug, into your service."

When the men were seated, the rest of the family entered the long hall. "This is my wife, Malfrid, and my two daughters, Asa and Disa."

The three women bowed low to the King and he thanked them for sharing their Yule feast with him. There were many other friends and neighbors who had also come for the feast. They sat at the long tables and looked in awe at the young man they had heard so much about.

As the feast progressed, Harald noticed the oldest daughter staring at him. He wondered if she was looking at the mat of curls that was his hair. He might have been a little hasty in vowing not to cut or comb his hair until he had succeeded in conquering all of Norway, but he would not consider breaking his oath...no matter how he looked.

Actually, Asa was thinking what a handsome man was sitting in their high seat, despite the fact that his golden curls were matted and needed combing or cutting. She had heard so many stories about this young king that she could hardly stop staring at him in fascination.

When the feast was finished, Jarl Hakon asked Harald if he would like to hear his daughters play the lyre and sing.

"That would please us greatly," he answered. "Guttorm and I have enjoyed many Yuletide celebrations listening to my mother and his sister playing and singing."

As the music started, Harald closed his eyes and tried to imagine he was home at Tande Manor listening to his mother's voice. The girls sang sweetly and he was enjoying the beautiful sounds in his ear. The next thing he knew, he saw the Goddess Freya in his mind. She had a smile on her face and bent down to whisper in his ear.

"The oldest daughter, Asa, will be your first wife. She will love you faithfully and will bear you four fine sons."

A startled Harald opened his eyes and Freya was gone. He looked at the two young women that were playing and singing. Asa was staring at him. Had she heard Freya's whisper also? She was lovely in a soft sort of way. She did not have the striking beauty of Gyda, but he thought he could grow to love her.

Several days passed at the manor house in Stjordal. It was pleasant to eat and sleep and rest one's body after the hard battles he and Guttorm had been fighting. Each day as he watched Asa at her loom, at the table or singing sweetly, he felt more attracted to her. She always seemed to be looking at him also, but they had not really spoken to each other.

They met while walking through the hall one day, after Harald had been at Lanke a fortnight.

"I take pleasure in listening to your music each night," said Harald.

Asa blushed and said, "Thank you, My Lord."

She could not think of anything else to say, so she blurted out, "You have two beautiful horses, My Lord."

Asa could not have said much else that would have pleased him more than to recognize his prized horses.

"Do you like to ride?" he asked her.

"Oh, yes, My Lord, but I haven't a horse as fine as yours."

"How would you like to come for a ride with me, on my horse May Day?" he asked.

"That would be very pleasurable," Asa responded.

"Then, we shall do it. You can show me the best places to ride in Stjordal. I will have my two stallions saddled and ready in a short while."

"I shall be ready," she answered with a smile.

There was not much Asa enjoyed more than riding a spirited horse. Harald was astride the big black stallion as he led his May Day to the front door. He jumped down and helped her mount. Her body felt light as a feather as he lifted her into the saddle. Asa tingled at the touch of his hands on her waist. She was trying to contain her excitement at the thrill of riding with King Harald.

Asa lost her shyness as the two galloped side by side. When they stopped by the Stjordal River, he told her the story of his white stallion, May Day. She could hear the emotion in his voice as he told about the miracle of his horse's birth. She was happy to see that this warrior king had a tender side.

He felt at ease in her company. Her eyes looked more blue and her hair seemed more golden out here in the sunshine. They made a nice looking couple as they rode the snowy trail toward Ofsti Manor.

Guttorm usually rode Sleipni, Halvdan's black stallion, now that Harald had May Day trained to ride. They were an amazing pair of horses and Harald loved to be able to ride them just for enjoyment. They were fierce and brave in battle, but gentle and obedient on a pleasure ride.

That same description could be used to describe King Harald Halvdansson. He had been raised by a mother who was gentle and trained to be obedient by a father who held himself and his family accountable to obey the just laws he had established. His uncle Guttorm had shown him how to be fierce and brave in battle.

After that first time, Asa and Harald went riding every day. Much as she loved the thrill of the ride, the part that Asa enjoyed the most was when

Harald helped her mount and dismount.

On the tenth day of riding, she challenged Harald to a race on the way home. Harald loved a challenge, but this one surprised him. He wasn't sure she was a good enough rider to stay on May Day's back through an all out race.

"Are you sure you want to try this?" Harald asked.

"Are you afraid I might beat you?" Asa asked with a grin.

"I think you would like to try," he answered. "But you should know that I am accustomed to winning!"

With that, Asa slapped the reins on May Day and he bolted down the road. Harald was taken by surprise, but he gave a war shout and Sleipni sped off at a full gallop. The two horses were neck and neck as they rounded the last corner and headed toward the barn.

Asa barely stayed in the saddle as May Day came to an abrupt halt near the barns. Harald and Sleipni were right behind, but Asa and May Day won by a few seconds. The hood of her cape had slipped off her head and Asa's hair looked wild and wonderful. Her cheeks were flushed and her laughter showed the thrill she felt in narrowly beating him in their race.

Harald quickly dismounted and reached up to help her down. As she slid down May Day's side into Harald's arms, he held her tight. Her happy smile faded as he wove his fingers into her tousled hair and tipped her lips up to meet his. It was a long, slow kiss and it took her breath away.

Asa's heart was pounding beneath her fur robe. Could this really be happening? She had dreamed of just such a kiss from the moment she first saw him. She wondered if the kiss meant anything.

Harald withdrew his lips, but held her close. "That is the reward I give to lovely women who beat me in a race!"

She was relieved that his light hearted manner had broken the spell of the moment.

"Pray tell, King Harald, how many women have beaten you?"

"You are the first and you will be the last! My reputation will be ruined if word gets around that I was beaten by a mere woman!"

"It can be our secret," Asa whispered.

"I have another secret," Harald whispered back.

"And what is that?" she asked, trying to keep her heart still.

"I want to make you my wife, dear Asa!"

Asa was startled by his declaration. Was this a real proposal? The look in his eyes and the smile on his face told her it was true.

"I would be honored to have you for my husband," she said with all seriousness.

Harald grabbed her and swung her around and kissed her on the cheek, on the forehead, on the nose, and finally found her lips again. This kiss was not long and slow, but hard and passionate. The affection he had felt for her was deepening into desire.

"I shall ask your father for your hand this very night." He was suddenly serious. "May I tell him you have agreed to the marriage?"

"Yes, you may," Asa replied as her disbelief turned to excitement. "I had better go into the house now and change my clothes before dinner."

She reached up to give him a short kiss in parting, but he grabbed her again for another fervent kiss.

"That is all the kissing you get until you have spoken to my father!" Asa said laughingly as she pushed him away. She wanted more, but she did not want to seem too anxious.

With that, she turned and walked quickly into the house. Harald watched her go and decided that he might just like the idea of marrying sweet, lovely Asa.

"Guttorm, I am going to ask Hakon tonight for permission to marry his daughter Asa."

"I thought you were going to marry Gyda," Guttorm questioned with a look of surprise on his bearded face.

"I think I am going to marry her, too," said Harald. "I haven't told you this, but Freya came to me at the feast the first night we were here and told me I was to marry Asa and she would give me four sons. I did not know how I felt about it, so I did not tell you. My affection for her has been growing...and today I knew it was right."

"Well, you remember what your mother said to you when you questioned Freya's message about Gyda." She said, "Listen to the Gods and they will help you make the right choices."

"Thank you, Guttorm, I can always count on you for good advice."

Harald waited until the meal was finished before he told Jarl Hakon that he needed to speak with him. When the others had left the room, he began.

"I would like to ask you for the hand of your daughter Asa," Harald stated. "Do you have any objection to that request?"

"Any objection?" questioned the father. "It would be a great honor to have my family joined to yours. Asa is a good girl and will make you a fine wife. How soon would you like to have the wedding feast?"

"As soon as Asa is ready," Harald answered. "I will want some time with her before the spring equinox. When construction of my dragon ships are completed, I will be ready for another expedition. This time it will be down the coast of the North Sea."

Soon they were talking about the kingdoms Harald would choose to conquer next and talk of the marriage was forgotten. Asa was waiting for either Harald or her father to come and tell her the news, but she was disappointed. They were busy discussing plans for the spring expedition and had more important things on their mind.

His desire to love and his dedication to war were both part of Harald's makeup. Asa wondered if he really loved her. He acted like it, but conquering Norway and fulfilling his oath were never far from his mind. She decided she would take him any way he would have her. There was no question in her mind if she really loved him.

The wedding feast was held within a fortnight. It was begun on a Friday to honor the Goddess Freya. Many preparations had been made, including enough mead to serve all the wedding guests. Harald had agreed on the bride price he would pay for the privilege of claiming Asa as his wife and Jarl Hakon had agreed on the amount he would give for Asa's dowry.

The great hall at Lanke Manor was decorated with numerous candles, plus fragrant pine boughs and small white mistletoe berries. There was an excitement in the air as preparations were made for the joyous occasion.

Guttorm was to stand as witness for Harald and Asa's brothers, Grjotgard and Herlaug were to be witnesses for her.

Asa wore a beautiful gown of soft lavender with snow white fur adorning the neckline and edging the long sleeves. Silver chains, a gift from her mother, covered the bodice of her gown. Her golden hair lay loose on her shoulders for the last time as a maiden. On her head she wore a wedding crown of shining silver, which had been worn by the women of her family for many generations.

Harald wore his best king robes and his hair, though matted and long, had been washed clean. He had no family jewels with him that he could offer to Asa, but he had rings fashioned from one of his gold arm bands. Her ring had Harald inscribed on it and his had Asa's name.

"This ring I give thee carries the name of your husband and I shall wear a ring bearing your name as my wife," declared Harald.

"I shall cherish this ring forever, and as well, the memory of this day," she responded.

With the rings on their fingers, and their hands joined together, the couple then spoke their vows.

The ring he gave her was enough. She was not marrying Harald for his riches, though he had a great deal, nor was she marrying him for his power, though he was already the most powerful man in Norway. Asa was marrying for love, and her love would grow and deepen as the years passed by.

Her wedding night was something she would remember always. Harald was not thinking about the next kingdom he would conquer, nor was he distracted by other thoughts. He was totally conscious of the fact that this lovely woman was chosen by the Gods to be his mate...and he thought about Freya's promise that Asa would bear him four sons.

If having a son was going to be as great as having his own dog, Torda, or his own horse, May Day, then Harald was anxious to get started.

"There is so much love in your eyes when you look at me," said Harald tenderly.

"Is there as much love in your eyes when you look at me?" she asked.

"I do feel love for you, and I think my love will grow stronger as we join our bodies together. You will have a son for me after harvest season and I will spend next winter here with you both."

With that, he began kissing her. They had shared some kisses after the first one that followed the horse race, but Asa had been careful to keep her emotions in check. Now, there was no reason to hold back. Harald was ready to allow his passions free rein and he could feel that her passion matched his own.

Harald woke with a start. He had been dreaming and he had temporarily forgotten that this was his wedding night. He lay in the dark with a smile on his face. He decided he was going to enjoy having a wife to share his bed. He wondered if he should tell Asa about the message he had received from Freya. He thought maybe he would wait for a time to tell her the real reason he had married her.

The next morning the bridal couple was showered with good wishes. Asa had another new dress, this time of pale blue, and her mother had placed on her head the soft, white headdress that indicated her new status as a married woman. Across her forehead, she wore a blue, white, and silver woven head band that brought out the beauty of her blue eyes.

After the morning meal, Harald stood to offer a toast to his new bride.

"A morning-gift I give to thee, my fair Asa, the choice of all the estates I have conquered here in the north. May you make a home for us and our four sons!"

Asa stood beside her new husband and raised her cup. "I accept your generous gift, My Lord, and I shall choose wisely the home where our sons will be reared."

Harald's bodyguard was waiting outside the manor house to show honor to their king and his new bride. Asa and Harald put their new fur robes over their shoulders and stepped out the main door of the house. Standing in a double row with swords crossed in an arch, were Harald's men. The couple walked through the archway, greeting each man amid shouts and cheers.

At the end of the sword arch stood Sleipni and May Day, saddled and ready. This was a surprise that Harald had planned for his lovely bride.

"We shall enjoy our first ride as husband and wife," he said with a smile as he looked at her surprised expression. "This was how our love first began...and may it ever continue."

"Oh, you are truly my tender hearted warrior king," Asa murmured as she wrapped her arms around his waist under his fur robe. With her face turned up to his, she whispered, "Can we share a kiss in front of your men?"

His answer was to lift her up off the ground in a fervent kiss that brought additional cheers from the one hundred watching warriors. As Harald helped Asa mount May Day, he felt a thrill and said a silent prayer of thanksgiving to Freya who had planned this happy experience for him.

While Harald and Asa rode through the snow that day, they talked about the bride-gift he had promised her.

"Will you really want me to move into the manor house of a defeated king?" she asked.

"We will need a manor of our own, now that we are married," he stated.

"I know we will, but I do not want to choose. You are the one with the power and authority gained through your victories. I want you to choose," Asa replied.

"Alright, my little wife, we shall choose together," he said.

Harald actually appreciated the fact that she wanted to leave the decisions to him. It reminded him of the way his mother always gave that respect to his father. He did not think he would care for a demanding wife.

"You know, I shall be very lonely when you leave for the North Sea. I think I should like to stay at Lanke with my mother while you are gone, especially if...."

"If what?" he asked and reined in Sleipni.

"Well, if I shall be with child," Asa said with a slight blush.

"But of course you will be with child! Did I not tell you that you should have a son after the next harvest season?" he said with a confident air.

Asa just smiled at him and slapped the reins on May Day's neck. She loved a good gallop and she intended to enjoy this lovely ride that was the thoughtful gift of her wonderful husband.

A few days later, Harald decided to take Asa with him as he rode into Nidaros. They traveled the road from Stjordal, through Malvik and continued along the fjord. As they came near to the village, he turned their horses to the north. He rode to an area that had a commanding view of the water on three sides.

"This is where we shall build our home, my little wife," he said with enthusiasm.

"Oh, it is a wonderful place!"

"There is plenty of shoreline to keep many ships...and enemies would be easily seen if they tried to make a surprise attack," noted a suddenly serious Harald.

"I hate to think there would be warriors attacking our home when you are far away," she said with a worried look on her sweet face.

"There will always be a troop of men stationed to guard my home and family. I would not think of leaving you unprotected," he said as he reached for her arm. "You are very important to me, you know."

"I am glad to hear you say that."

"Besides, we need a safe place to raise our four sons!" he said with a laugh.

Malfrid, Asa's mother, was watching her daughter carefully for signs that a child had been conceived. It was important that this happen before Harald left with his troops. Neither Jarl Hakon nor his wife wanted Harald to forget about their Asa during his expedition to conquer the kingdoms along the sea coast, and a child would help to tie his allegiance to their family.

Finally, the signs came and Malfrid counseled Asa to share the good news with Harald.

"You will be coming back to Stjordal when you have succeeded in conquering the coastal kingdoms, won't you?" asked Asa as they lay in their bed wrapped in each others arms.

"I plan to, but the future of each expedition is uncertain," he responded staring at the board ceiling above their bed.

"I feel there will be a surprise for you when you return," she said as she tried to interrupt all thoughts of the coming expedition.

"What kind of surprise will you have for me, my little wife?" he asked as he turned to look at her face in the dim candlelight.

"What would be the best surprise you could ask for?" she teased.

"The best surprise would be for me to find you waiting for me with four healthy sons in your arms!" he joked.

"You are a hard task master, My Lord. Four might be hard for me, but would you accept just one?" she asked with a smile.

Harald picked her up and set her down on his wide torso. He put his hands on her middle and said, "Is there a surprise for me in this little belly?"

"If my mother is right, there is," Asa answered, anxious to see his reaction.

He reached for her arms, pulled her down on top of him, and gave her a lingering kiss. "I am so glad you made me marry you!" he said with a laugh.

She opened her mouth to protest, but he just covered her lips with his. Yes, married life was full of wonderful pleasures.

"We will name him Halvdan after my father," Harald said matter of factly.

"What makes you so sure it will be a boy?" she asked.

"I think we will have four sons," he replied with a secretive grin on his face.

"Well, then you had better plan to spend every winter here in Trondelag," Asa stated emphatically.

"I shall make Trondelag my winter home...at least until you have given me my four sons," Harald teased.

With that comment, Asa reached over and bit him on the ear.

"Ouch, you little vixen! Behave yourself or I shall have to find myself a nicer wife," he retorted and began to kiss her with a passion.

Asa wondered how much truth there was in that statement. She did not think Harald loved her as much as she loved him, but she was happy that she was being blessed to give him a child. She just prayed that it would be a son.

CHAPTER 11

MORE AND RAUMSDAL CONQUERED

The winter months passed quickly. The area around Nidaros was rich in abundant forests and Harald had chosen the best trees to be felled for the great dragon ships he was having built. He and his men would all need sturdy vessels for their expedition along the coastal kingdoms to the west of the Trondelag Fjord and out along the wild waters of the North Sea.

Guttorm and Harald had established a pattern for success when planning their strategies for a take over of the kingdoms. They would counsel together, make a plan, and then ask Odin for his confirmation that their plan was according to his will. Sometimes Odin would answer with a vision and sometimes with a dream. Sometimes, he would just give them both a strong feeling that the plan was right.

This time they decided to start at Orkadal. Guttorm had spent time during the winter traveling in the kingdoms west of Nidaros. He rode a plain brown horse and carried a simple sword so no one would suspect that he was part of King Harald's army.

He had learned that there was a petty king named Nokve who was gathering troops in the Opdal forest. He bragged that he would take over Trondelag as soon as Harald and his men left in their ships. When Guttorm reported this to Harald, it was decided that they would start at Orkadal and take care of King Nokve first.

Harald had a deep booming voice and would lead his troops into combat with a great battle cry. The army surprised Nokve by departing Stjordal a day earlier than had been planned. They landed their ships near the Opdal forest and attacked the enemy army in the woods.

Nokve and his men fled to their ships and rowed furiously to get to open water. The victorious warriors just stood on the shore and laughed at their enemy's hasty retreat. The King was confident that Nokve would not be back this season. If they should chance to meet in the North Sea, then Harald would have to send him to Valhalla.

"O'er the broad heath the bowstrings twang,
While high in air the arrows sang.

The iron shower drives to flight
The foeman from the bloody fight.
The warder of great Odin's shrine,
The fair-haired son of Odin's line,
Raises the voice which gives the cheer,
First in the track of wolf or bear.
His master voice drives them along
To Hel -- a destined, trembling throng;
And Nokve's ship, with glancing sides,
Must fly to the wild ocean's tides.
Must fly before the King who leads
Norse axe-men on their ocean steeds."

Heimskringla

Whenever Harald and Guttorm won a battle, they would hear the cry of ravens in the sky and see a likeness of Odin on his horse with the ravens Huginn and Muninn on his shoulders. That was Odin's signal to them that he had accepted their conquest and that they should press on. The King always led his men in the shout, "To Odin be the victory! To Odin be the victory! To Odin be the victory!"

As he continued his quest, Harald let it be known that it was Odin's will that he should subdue all the kingdoms of Norway and set them under his rule. He wanted to rule with justice and fairness as his father Halvdan had done. Some of the petty kings and chieftains were willing to join Harald's cause and become his men...still others chose to fight, and often die.

Guttorm and Harald had gathered around them men that were remarkable for their strength, courage, and fighting abilities. They had the choice of the best men from every kingdom. It was a great honor to be a member of the King's personal bodyguard. Every one of them would die for him, and many did.

There was no shortage of men to replace those that were lost in battle. The most fierce fighters were called berserkers. They were the forward guard and would attack first to clear the way for the troops that followed behind Harald and Guttorm.

Berserkers made up the personal bodyguard for King Harald. They were remarkable for their large stature, plus their strength, courage and fierce bravery. They formed an impregnable line of defense and could hack through an enemy shield with one blow.

These men wore wolf skins for armor and used the cry of wild animals to scare their victims as they ferociously attacked with their battleaxes flying. While the berserkers were advancing, the archers would shoot arrows over their heads and pick off many men before the berserkers even reached them.

Next, the armed men would stab with their spears before using their swords and battleaxes. If all of these weapons failed, each man carried a longblade dagger with which to pierce the heart or slice the throat of the enemy. Harald's warriors were expert in all areas of combat and spent much time during the winter months sparing and training for the battles that would come with the spring thaw.

Their mighty fleet of ships was a fearsome sight to behold. The largest dragon ship carried King Harald and his body guard. It was fitted out in the most splendid way. The forecastle men were hand picked, for they carried the King's banner. It was blood red and carried the image of Odin's two ravens in the center.

There was never a question of whose ships were sailing into the harbor. Only one man could command so many ships and fill them with so great an army of trained warriors. Harald's ship also carried his lucky bear skin and his wolfdog, Torda. It was important to him to keep them both with him and he knew Odin would not mind him using them for a talisman.

When an enemy saw a warrior with a gold helmet trimmed in silver, they knew it was the King himself. His shield was also covered with gold and silver trim and lined with leather. The famous sword, Frey, was always at his side. It shone in the bright sunlight...wiped clean of blood from the last battle.

His golden hair hung in braids around his shoulders and his golden beard matched the splendor of his helmet. The gold was a great contrast to the white stallion he rode while on land. May Day was now a trained battle horse and it was tradition that an important king would ride a white horse.

Guttorm's helmet and shield were just the opposite...silver helmet and shield with gold as the trim. It was planned that way so that the soldiers could always know where their leaders were and follow their lead during a battle.

From their victory in Orkadal, Guttorm and Harald moved with their armada of ships westward to More. As they sailed into the harbor at Soskel, they were met by a large army of soldiers led by Hunthiof, King of More and his son, Solve Klofe, who were both great warriors. Their family had ruled this area of Norway for many generations and they refused to even consider yielding their property rights to a young King Harald.

King Nokve had sailed to More to warn Hunthiof that King Harald had surprised him at Opdal and was now on his way to conquer the coastal kingdoms. Prince Solve, who ruled over the neighboring kingdom of Raumsdal, was the brother of Nokve's mother.

Hornklofe tells of this battle: --

"Thus did the hero known to fame,
The leader of the shields, whose name
Strikes every heart with dire dismay,
Launch forth his war-ships to the fray.
Two kings he fought; but little strife
Was needed to cut short their life.
A clang of arms by the sea-shore, --
And the shields' sound was heard no more."

Heimskringla

Nokve and Hunthiof were slain in battle, but Solve, seeing the battle was lost, escaped hurriedly by sailing off in his longship. Both More and Raumsdal were now subdued by King Harald, who gave the remaining enemy soldiers the choice of allegiance or death. Most chose allegiance.

The victorious warriors determined to remain in More and Raumsdal for the rest of the summer so that they could assure the loyalty of the people. It was important that Halvdan's Code of Law be established in these new kingdoms, and that took some time and effort.

There was also the possibility that Solve Klofe would return and try to rally his former soldiers and take back the kingdom that had been his father's and his grandfather's before him. He was a strong and mighty warrior, and Harald would have made him Jarl of More if he had been willing to pledge allegiance to the cause...but Solve was not.

Instead, Harald chose Ragnvald Eysteinsson to serve as the new Jarl of More. He pledged allegiance very willingly as a close kinsman of Harald and was given charge of both North More and Raumsdal. He owned large estates in More and there was no question he could command the loyalty of the people in both kingdoms.

Jarl Ragnvald was given the command of a large army of battle trained soldiers, together with their many ships. He took an oath to protect the kingdoms with his own life and would see that the Code of Law would be followed. The fact that he was a cousin to Harald's mother, Ragnhild, meant that he could be trusted to protect the area from those who would seek to reclaim their petty kingdoms from the grasp of King Harald Halvdanson.

CHAPTER 12

A SON, A NEPHEW, A GRANDSON

Standing on a large boulder, listening to the sound of the great sea waves pounding on the rocky shore, gave Harald a feeling of power. He loved the thrill of sailing his great dragon ship while cutting through the waves and moving swiftly along the coastline.

The waters of the Trondelag Fjord and Lake Mjosa seemed tame in contrast to the wild movement of the North Sea. He would miss the sight of the sun going down beyond the horizon, shining a shaft of gold on the water. He would miss the sounds of the sea and even the smell of the salt water in his nostrils.

But it was time to return to Trondelag and Asa and enjoy the protection of the calm fjord water for his fleet of ships. Harald had left a few hundred men at Stjordal to watch over his wife and her family while he was gone. Jarl Hakon and his two sons had sailed with him and had all fought bravely. He hoped there had been no trouble in his absence.

Aside from keeping the peace in Trondelag, Harald had assigned his men to build him a new estate on the promontory between Stjordal and Nidaros. He wanted to spend this winter with his wife and child in his own home. He also needed stables for his horses and buildings to house his bodyguard. The rest of his army would be stationed at the estates that had been left vacant by the death of the kings he had conquered last winter in the kingdoms of the Trondelag.

The first snow had fallen by the time Harald, Guttorm and their army sailed up the deep fjord. He was anxious to see his Asa. He hoped everything had gone well with the birth of their child...their son. Freya would not have fooled him by sending a daughter first, would she?

Guttorm and Harald left their ships to the care of their men and walked the distance from the shore to Lanke Manor. They had considered sending some men ahead to the barns to saddle Slepni and May Day, but Harald wanted to surprise Asa by coming to the manor on foot.

Also, they knew that if they once got in the saddle of those mighty steeds, a short ride would not be enough. No, they would do the right thing and stop at the house first.

"Where is my little wife...and where is my son?" bellowed Harald as he entered the great hall.

There was a flurry of activity, spurred on by the realization that the men were home. Malfrid, Asa's mother, came out first to greet the returning warriors. The smile on her face was enough to reveal that there was good news, but Harald had to ask anyway.

"Is Asa alright and do I have a son?" he questioned.

"See for yourself," Malfrid answered as she led the way to the bedchamber.

There lay sweet Asa, suckling his child.

"Who should I kiss first," asked Harald with a wink.

"Well, it had better be me," she responded smiling.

Harald gave her his teasing kiss, starting on her forehead and moving to her cheeks, nose and finally her mouth. It was good to have a wife waiting for you, he thought, and even better...a babe in her arms.

"Well, how long are you going to make us wait to hear if it is a boy?" asked Guttorm.

"I am tempted to tease you and tell you it is a girl, but I am afraid you two might just get back in your ships and sail away!" she laughed.

"Can I hold him?" asked Harald hesitantly.

"Can you wait until he is done eating?"

"No!" was the quick reply.

"Alright, but if he cries, you'll know he loves his mother best!" Asa said as she removed her breast from the infant's mouth and handed him to his father.

Strangely, the baby did not cry. He opened his eyes and stared into the steel blue eyes of his father. It was almost as if he could feel the great spirit that his father possessed and the affection that now passed between father and son.

"We shall pour water on him this night and name him Halvdan, with your father and brothers and Guttorm for witnesses," Harald declared.

"Can I hold him?" was Guttorm's meek request.

He reluctantly handed over the tiny bundle. There was a look on Guttorm's face that Harald had not seen before. Suddenly, he was aware of the fact that Guttorm had never married a wife. Instead he had devoted his life to being his general and helping him fulfill his oath and his destiny.

How selfish I have been, thought Harald, thinking about myself and my happiness only. I have not even considered Guttorm's feelings or appreciated his selflessness.

"I have changed my mind," he announced, "This boy shall be named Guttorm, after the best friend and foster-father a man could ever have."

Guttorm looked at the proud father in surprise.

"Do you mean that?" he asked with tears welling up in his eyes.

"I do," said Harald reassuringly. "This boy will be fortunate to be fostered by his namesake, the great Duke Guttorm Sigurdsson!"

"We will name our next son Halvdan, won't we Asa?"

Asa just murmured her consent. She knew that Harald would have his way no matter what she thought and Guttorm did look so pleased.

The next morning at sunrise, Guttorm and Harald were having another pleasurable experience. They were riding side by side on their two great stallions. It was exciting to sail a great dragon ship across the water, but there was nothing quite so exhilarating as the feel of a powerful horse beneath you.

It was hard to know who was enjoying the galloping ride more, the horses or the riders. Sleipni and May Day had certainly missed getting the personal attention of their masters over the summer months. Others had ridden them for exercise, but the experience was not the same.

Their ride ended at the new manor house that had been built during the spring and summer. It was an impressive structure sitting on the highest point of the hill overlooking the Trondelag Fjord. The workers had been busy and they had done their job well.

"I want to move into the house right away before the snow really begins to fall," Harald told Guttorm. I have planned a large group of rooms on the far side of the great hall, and I want those to be for Mother and you."

"I know she will be anxious to see your new son, and if I leave soon, we can bring her here to spend Yuletide with us. It may not be the same as the happy days when your father was alive, but we won't have to worry about her being alone at Tande Manor."

"We should find a jarl to manage the affairs at Tande so that Mother will feel at ease living here with us for the winter. Then, you can bring her back to Tande if she wants to spend the summer there while we are gone."

"I think I can convince her to agree with our plan. It seems like a long time has passed since those peaceful trips we would make with your father...traveling the route of his kingdoms while he acted as judge for his people," Guttorm replied with a wistful sigh.

Asa hadn't seen the house that Harald had built for them, but she knew it would be wonderful. Any place where her Harald lived would be wonderful in her eyes. She was also excited to meet her husband's mother, Ragnhild. Harald had talked about her with such loving comments...and she was anxious to show off her little Guttorm.

Ragnhild was so thrilled to see Guttorm after such a long absence. He and Harald had sent messengers to keep her informed of their progress, but it wasn't the same as having them in her own house.

She was overjoyed to hear about the birth of Harald's son and eager to see him. When Guttorm told her about the plan to have her come and spend the winter months with them in Trondelag, she was relieved. The Yule season had been the most difficult time to be alone and the time she missed Halvdan the most.

Yuletide was always a festive time, and it was even more merry in the new house at Lade Manor. That was the name Harald had given his new estate. Lade meant lucky, and he felt very lucky and blessed at this time in his life.

Harald sat in the high seat with Asa beside him and baby Guttorm on her lap. His mother was next to Asa and his uncle Guttorm was next to him. There was a boar roasting over a fire and the hall was filled with the fresh scent of pine boughs. This Yule he would hear his mother play and sing the old songs. Yes, he was a contented man.

Odin had been good to him. He had guided and protected both he and Guttorm through many battles. There were more battles yet to come, but he was making good progress in uniting all of Norway and setting up the judicial system that had been used by his father. As long as he relied on Odin for his inspiration and guidance, he knew he could not fail.

Ragnild enjoyed her stay at Lade Manor. It wasn't quite like being in her own home, but Asa was very sweet and baby Guttorm looked like his namesake, with brown hair just like her brother. Of course, his mother, father and grandmother all had golden hair, so it was easy to say who the baby looked like. It made Guttorm happy when she told him the baby looked just like he had at that age, so she insisted it was true.

CHAPTER 13

ON TO FIRDAFLYKE AND HORDALAND

Spring arrived too soon and signaled the end of the peaceful winter. The year was 868 A.D. and Harald was now seventeen winters old. He had accomplished a great deal for one so young, but he still had not fulfilled his oath to conquer all the kingdoms of Norway.

Guttorm and Harald gathered their great army of battle trained warriors and set sail in their dragon ships for the vast North Sea. They were anxious to spend a few days with Jarl Ragnvald in North More and hear his report of the happenings over the winter in the two kingdoms under his rule.

The news, however, was not good. Solve Klofe had spent the winter months plundering, pillaging and burning the property of estates along the coast for revenge against those who had pledged allegiance to King Harald. He had killed many warriors and Ragnvald was waiting for the large army to arrive with new forces before he went on the offensive.

Assuming that Harald's army would choose South More to conquer next, Solve had also spent time talking to King Arnvid of South More and King Audbjorn from Firdafylke. He was able to convince them that if they joined together, they could defeat this King who was trying to subdue all of Norway.

The petty kings of the coastal kingdoms were more aggressive than the inland kings. The two large armies met at Solskel and a great battle ensued. Solve was determined to avenge the killing of his father from the summer before, but he was unsuccessful once again.

King Arnvid's ship was in the lead as they began the attack. King Harald's ship rowed out to meet the leader and there was heavy fighting from both sides. The fierce berserkers attacked with a vengeance, but the enemy was just as violent and determined.

Asa's brothers, Grjotgard and Herlaug, were part of Harald's body guard. They fought behind the berserkers, but in front of their King. In the midst of the battle, Harald heard a loud shout and turned to see both brothers suffer the death wound while protecting his back.

This so angered Harald that he became mad as the berserkers, wildly killing everyone in his path with a vengeful fury until his sword dripped with blood. The angry rage continued until there was no one left alive, including King Arnvid.

Duke Guttorm's dragon headed for the ship of King Audbjorn. After some time of intense fighting, this King also met his death. Solve was the one they wanted to destroy the most, but he fled when he saw he was the only leader left standing. He did not get his revenge against King Harald this time, but he would continue his attacks on the coastal kingdoms for many years to come.

As Harald and Guttorm watched Solve's ship sail away, they thought they saw Odin on his great steed Sleipni, chasing the coward out to sea. The bloody battle was finally over and once more the two leaders came off victorious. When they heard the raven's cry, they led their warriors in a shout of, "To Odin be the victory! To Odin be the Victory! To Odin be the victory!"

So says Hornklofe: --

"Against the hero's shield in vain
The arrow-storm fierce pours its rain.
The King stands on the blood-stained deck,
Trampling on many a stout foe's neck;
And high above the dinning sound
Of helm and axe, and ringing sound
Of blade and shield, and raven's cry,
Is heard his shout of `Victory!'"
Heimskringla

South More was now added to North More and Raumsdal as the coastal kingdoms under Harald's power. Jarl Ragnvald had been such a strong leader with the first two kingdoms that he was rewarded with the rule of South More as well. He was called Ragnvald the Wise and was not only Harald's kin, but his trusted friend and advisor as well.

They thought the death of King Audbjorn would yield them the kingdom of Firdafylke, but they found that his brother, Vemund, had set himself up as king. Harald was ready to launch a new attack on Vemund, but Guttorm counseled him to wait until the next summer.

"It is Odin who shall decide our course, whether to continue on to Firdafylke this season or return to our home in Trondelag," Harald decided.

Guttorm hoped Odin would take pity on him. He felt tired and cheerless. Besides Grjotgard and Herlaug, they had lost Jarls Asbjorn and Olav in the battle for South More. A great number of soldiers would remain with

Ragnvald over the winter to aid help him in protecting their territory. It was enough.

"Yes, it was enough," said Odin in Harald's dream that night. "You have proven yourself a worthy servant, and you may return to Lade for the winter."

As it was, Jarl Ragnvald took care of Vemund for them. While he was traveling through Eid, Berdaluke the Berserker came to him with good news. Their enemy from Firdafylke was visiting a friend in nearby Nausdal.

The jarl traveled to the estate under cover of night, secretly discovered where Vemund was sleeping, and set the building on fire. That night, Vemund burned to death along with ninety of his men.

Ragnvald took all the ships left behind by Vemund and returned to More. Berdaluke had captured a completely armed longship and traveled to Trondelag to give a report of their conquest. The berserker pledged allegiance to King Harald that winter and fought beside him for the rest of his life.

CHAPTER 14

A DOUBLE SURPRISE

The appearance of the great fleet of warships pulling up to the long shoreline at Lade was a surprise to everyone. Guttorm and Harald had not been expected back until after the harvest season.

"My Lady, My Lady, the King is home, the King is home," shouted a maid servant as she ran into the great hall.

Asa was sitting at her loom weaving a decorative braid when she heard the news. There wasn't even time to check her appearance before she heard the familiar voice and saw her handsome Harald enter the room.

"Where is my little wife and where is my little Guttorm?" he shouted.

"Your little wife is here at her loom and your little Guttorm is asleep...at least he was before that booming voice came in here," she said with a smile.

"Aren't you glad to see me?" Harald asked with an expression of disappointment on his face.

He walked over to the loom and knelt down to collect a kiss from his fair Asa.

"What is this, my sweet maiden? Hast thou been keeping secrets from your warrior husband?" he asked in surprise as he felt her rounded belly.

Suddenly, Asa burst out in tears and began to sob.

"Are those tears of joy or sorrow, my little one?" he asked as he lifted her gently off the loom bench.

Harald carried her to the high seat and cradled her in his arms. "What is it that causes such sorrow that you must greet your husband with tears?"

"I carry a child that will not live," sobbed Asa.

"Who told you this child will not live?" he asked with a hint of anger in his voice.

"All the old women know it. If you get a child in the belly when your baby is still suckling, the child always dies!"

"I do not believe it. I do not think Odin would reward me for my good service by giving me a dead child. We must pray to him and ask him for this blessing," he declared.

Even though she did not believe Odin would grant the favor, Asa was glad that her husband had such faith. His confident words made her feel better. She was blessed with one stout little boy and now her husband had come home safely again...and that was enough for her.

Odin did grant the favor, however. Actually, he granted two favors. Asa was delivered of not one, but two little boys. The first head to crown was covered in black hair. The second head was covered in golden hair. It was quite a blessing to get two babies at once...and to have them both live was an even greater blessing.

Harald laughed out loud when he saw them lying in their mother's arms.

"We shall have a little Halvdan the Black and a little Halvdan the White!" And so it was when water was poured over them.

There were times when Harald wondered if Odin had given Asa these two boys to replace her two brothers who had died defending him in battle during the summer. Maybe he should have named his sons Grjotgard and Herlaug in their memory, but he really wanted to honor his father Halvdan.

Guttorm could not wait to get to Tande Manor to tell Ragnhild the news. Not just one, but two Halvdan's had been born. She was just as anxious to get to Lade Manor to see them. This would indeed be a special Yuletide.

Not only did little Halvdan the Black remind her of her dead husband, but Halvdan the White reminded her of her dead father. It seemed Odin was paying her this kindness for having taken her father and then her husband from her.

Little Guttorm received much less attention from his mother now that she was busy with two babies, but he received much more attention from his great-uncle Guttorm. They played together through the long, dark winter days. Guttorm carved little wooden toys while little Guttorm looked on in fascination.

The winter months consumed the men in busy preparation for the battles that would surely come with the next summer. Keeping muscles toned and fighting skills sharp was important to the men of the army. Each soldier was responsible to keep his weapons in good repair. Swords, battleaxes and daggers needed sharpening and leather goods needed mending. The blacksmith's forge was kept busy making or repairing swords, battle axes, spear heads, daggers and chainmail.

Evenings were spent in the warmth of the great room, where a fire burned day and night. One of Harald's favorite games was skak, played on a board divided into squares with playing pieces of various shapes made out of bone. The placing of the pieces was decided by the throwing of dice. He was good at this game as well as many others.

It was expected that high-born people became expert at the game, but he allowed all of his soldiers to improve their skills as well. The game was especially popular during long voyages on a ship. There was a lot of competition, but only his mother or uncle could beat Harald. Ragnhild and Guttorm were fortunate to have their father's valuable skak board, which was made of gold with playing pieces of carved walrus tusk.

There was great moose hunting in the forests and any man who brought home an animal got the first choice of the meat. He would also have a good fur to use for a blanket or a shield cover. In addition, the antlers could be carved into useful as well as decorative items. Many men enjoyed falconry and trained the birds to find squirrels and field mice.

When she saw the ships being taken down from their staves and turned right side up along the shoreline, Asa realized it was almost time for her husband to sail off again. She knew she aught to be grateful for having had him with her through the long winter months, but she would miss his cheerful laugh and happy smile. She had given him three sons and she knew he loved her for that.

The day of departure soon arrived. Guttorm, Harald and their men were in the dragon ships and ready to shove off from the shore. Asa and Ragnhild were standing in front of the house, each holding a baby in their arms with little Guttorm standing between them. Just as the men stood to wave farewell, little Guttorm started running down the hill to the water's edge.

He was crying and running and crying. Harald got out of his ship to pick himup and return him to the house, but the boy ran right past his father and headed for the ship that held his friend and companion, Guttorm. He was calling, "Gaga, Gaga!"

Harald just stood and watched as big Guttorm scooped little Guttorm into his arms for one last hug. He was both pleased and also saddened to realize that his first born son chose his uncle over his father. The two Guttorms seemed to have developed an inner connection that was to continue to mature throughout their lifetime.

CHAPTER 15

MORE COASTAL BATTLES

The spring season was wet and cold, with low clouds and overcast skies, but the great army of the north would not let the weather stop them. As they sailed out to sea and passed by Orkadal, Harald was reminded of the battle they had won on those shores. When they rounded the coastline and came to More and Raumsdal, additional memories assailed him.

Harald was grateful to Odin for the victories he had granted them. Though many good men had fallen in these battles, many good men survived. He was looking forward to meeting with Jarl Ragnvald to get a report on the happenings in the coastal kingdoms over the winter season.

There had been no new attacks from Solve Klofe and the jarl was still feeling proud of his accomplishment in getting rid of Vemund. Ragnvald was indeed an able leader. Harald felt a debt of gratitude for his service and honored him at a great feast.

Most of the warriors that had been left to guard More and Raumsdal through the winter now joined Guttorm and Harald as they sailed down the coast to Firdafylke. With both King Audbjorn and his brother Vemund dead, the task of subduing their kingdom was not difficult.

The two brothers had left a great estate and Harald decided to give the rule of Firdafylke to Asa's father, Jarl Hakon Grjotgardson. Hakon was a great warrior and loyal to Harald and his cause for justice, but the son-in-law did not want to return to Trondelag next winter with the news that the last male of Asa's family had met his death.

Jarl Hakon was pleased to be made ruler over the vast fjord district. The North Sea here stretched for miles into the interior of the country and it was awe-inspiring to look at the deep blue of the water against the steep sides of the cliffs. He only wished his wife, Malfrid, could be present to enjoy the beauty of the area.

The great army of the north, with their fierce looking dragon ships and colorful banners flying, came rowing into the harbor of Bergen in Hordaland.

Here they met no enemy army ready for war and Harald was pleased. However, different sort of foe was discovered.

It was found that King Eirik Eymundson of Sweden had taken over both Hordaland and Rogaland and all the kingdoms in the southwest along the North Sea. Eirik had set Jarl Hrane to rule this area and was collecting taxes from all the landed people.

Harald was furious when he heard of this. It was sometimes difficult for him to cause the death of fellow Kings of Norway in his conquest of the country, but it would not be hard for him to rid these kingdoms of an intruder like King Eirik.

The troops King Eirik had left with Jarl Hrane were no match for the thousands of soldiers that were under Harald's command. The jarl fled for his life and left his army at the mercy of the invaders. No doubt, he hoped to sail to Sweden with a message that King Harald and Duke Guttorm had succeeded in the takeover of both Hordaland and Rogaland.

The conquerors made these south western kingdoms their home for the rest of the season and enjoyed the bounties of life they found in the warm waters of the Stavanger Fjord. Harald succeeded in establishing the Code of Law and set up the Gulathing at Gulen near Bergen. He knew the people would find more peace when there were fair rules judged by their twelve lagman and jarls with enough men to enforce them.

Guttorm and Harald planned to spend some time in Firdafylke on their way back home to Trondelag. As they sailed up the fjord, they were met by Jarls Arne and Trond who told them a sad tale.

It seemed Jarl Hakon had it in his mind that he should rule not just Firdafylke, but also the Sogn district that bordered his kingdom on the east. Harald had set Jarl Atle Mjove as ruler of Sogn just after Halvdan died. Hakon thought he had more authority as the father-in-law of King Harald.

But Atle Mjove refused to abdicate and said he would wait until he was able to speak to Harald face to face. Hakon became so angry at the thought his word was being questioned by a less important jarl that he took the troops under his command and marched to Sogn.

When word reached Atle Mjove that an army was on its way, he marshaled his forces and went out to meet them. The battle took place at Fialar in Sogne Fjord and took the life of both Jarl Hakon and Jarl Atle. The senseless death of two great men was caused by both pride and greed.

"He who stood a rooted oak,
Unshaken by the swordsman's stroke,
Amidst the whiz of arrows slain,
Has fallen upon Fjalar's plain.
There, by the ocean's rocky shore,
The waves are stained with the red gore
Of stout Jarl Hakon Grjotgardson,
And of brave warriors many a one."

Heimskringla

CHAPTER 16

SORROW AT HOME

As Harald and Guttorm listened to the details of this fatal confrontation, they were greatly saddened. The plan to leave Jarl Hakon at Firdafylke so that he might not be killed in a battle had been in vain. Jarls Gudbjorn and Trond, who had served faithfully as troop leaders for their King, were now rewarded to take over the rule of Firdafylke and Sogn.

That night, as Harald slept in the bedchamber that had so recently been occupied by his wife's father, Hakon Grjotgardson, Odin came to him in a dream.

"Thou art doing well, my son, but sorrow is about to enter your life. You must leave for Lade Manor in the morning and not stop off at More on your way. Time is of the essence!"

After delivering his message, Odin was gone. Harald tried to ask him what was happening at Lade, but there was no response.

The men of the army gave no complaint about rushing home to Trondelag when Harald gave the order the next morning. They could see by the look on their King's face that all was not well. Most of the soldiers thought he was just unhappy about having to tell Asa and Malfrid that their father and husband had gone to join his sons in the great hall at Valhalla.

Guttorm knew there was something more to this sudden hurried journey. He had learned to read Harald's thoughts in the years they had traveled and fought together, and there was a look of deep distress on Harald's face this day.

As the two walked to the shore and their separate war ships, Guttorm asked what was wrong. Harald told him about the message from Odin and Gutthorm's face took on the same worried look.

The one person Guttorm worried about the most was his little namesake. He would be turning two years old just after they returned and Guttorm had been carving a small wooden horse to give him. So many accidents could happen to a small child in their growing up years and he selfishly hoped the problem involved someone else.

It was someone else who had the problem. Asa was with child again and she was having the same trauma she had had while carrying her twin boys. The old women continued to say it was bad luck to have a new child in your belly while you were still giving suck to your babies.

Malfrid and Ragnhild had both tried to comfort her and remind her that she had carried the twin boys last year while suckling little Guttorm. The two babies had been born alive...small, but alive.

Asa tried to overcome her feelings of doom, but the long days stretched on and on and there was no word of Harald's return. Little did she know that at that very moment, he was sailing up the Trondelag Fjord ahead of the rest of the army, with just Guttorm and his ship beside him on this dark night.

The two men walked up the hill to the house in silence. This time Harald did not enter the great hall at Lade shouting, "Where is my little wife? Where are my little sons?" He entered quietly and went immediately to the bedchamber that he shared with his wife.

Asa was lying on her back in the soft folds of the eiderdown mattress. A linen sheet covered her body and Harald could see the outline of a full belly in the soft glow of the bedside candle.

"What are you doing with another child in that belly?" he asked in a whisper as he took her hand and sat down on the edge of the bed platform.

"Oh Harald, I am so glad you have returned! I have been praying for your return every night, but I did not think Odin was listening," she sobbed.

"Odin was listening. He came to me in a dream and told me to hurry home to you," he said. No need to tell her that Odin had said there would be sorrow on his return.

Guttorm looked in on the three boys in the adjoining bed chamber. A smile crossed his face as he saw that his little Guttorm was sleeping peacefully. He could hear the murmur of voices in the next room and he hoped all was well with Asa also.

But, all was not well with Asa. By her reckoning, this baby should be ready to come forth. Even though she could feel movement in her belly, she was sure the child would not live. That was a given. Her two boys had been spared last time, but she did not dare ask for so great a favor twice.

Harald dared to ask, however. He was sure Odin loved him and wanted the best for him. He knew the favor would be granted if it was his will. Through his fears, he kept remembering the words of sorrow that Odin had foreseen for him.

He did not have long to wait for the sorrow to arrive. The child began its painful descent in the early morning hours a fortnight after his return. Harald felt the warm liquid fill the bed next to him before he heard Asa's moan. He was up quickly, calling for the women of the house to attend to her.

Men were not invited into the birthing chamber and Harald was glad of it. He and Guttorm sat in the great hall and listened to the screams. Why did Odin make women suffer so with the birthing of a child? They did not know.

Ragnhild was brought back in memory to the time when her beloved Harald was the child that was struggling to enter the world. She had thought many times that all the pain was worth it when you held that new, precious life in your arms.

"Why don't you two go out to check on the horses?" she said.

"Do you think we should?" Guttorm asked.

"I think it will be better for you than waiting in here. We have a long way to go I am afraid."

They left the hall with a mixture of guilt and relief written on their faces. Sleipni and May Day were housed in stalls in the barn at the bottom of the hill and the two men decided to relieve some of their anxiety by brushing down their horses. The barn was within calling range and Ragnhild had promised to call them when the baby was born.

However, there was no baby that night, nor the next. Ragnhild suggested to Malfrid that they take the baby from Asa through an opening in the belly, as they had done with her. Malfrid asked Harald what they should do. He did not know, but he trusted his mother, and she thought it was the only way to save both the child and the mother.

Asa could not have held on for another day. Her body was worn from the struggle and all she wanted to do was sleep. When her mother suggested slicing open her belly, she was too weak to even agree.

A tiny boy child was taken from the opening. He was red from blood and his head was blue from being stuck in the birth canal for so long. He gave out a weak cry when he was lifted from his mother's womb. Harald had come into the room at the sound of that weak cry.

"You have another boy," was all Malfrid could take time to say. She was busy trying to help her daughter cling to life.

He felt like crying when he saw his sweet little Asa lying there covered with blood. Her face was as white as the linen sheet that was tucked under her chin.

"You look beautiful, my little wife," he said to her as he held her weak hand to his lips.

Asa almost managed a smile through her haze. She had loved him from the first day she saw him sitting in the high seat at Lanke Manor four years ago. She loved him even more now. He could always make her smile, but right now she could not even manage a weak grin.

"We have another boy," Harald whispered in her ear.

Asa heard him but she could not respond. Now Harald had his four sons, she thought. At least she had given him his four sons.

She barely heard his next words, "I love you, Asa."

Those were the last words Asa heard while her spirit was in her body. Just then, her spirit slipped its earthly bonds and she was floating above the bed. It was strange. She could see herself lying there, covered in blood, but she could feel no pain.

She was glad to see the look of love in Harald's eyes as he gently kissed her lips.

"She is gone," he said quietly to the women who were trying to stop the bleeding. "She is gone," he said again, to no one in particular.

Suddenly, he knew how much he meant those last words he had whispered into Asa's ear, "I love you." He hoped she had heard him. He wondered if he had told her those three little words enough in their short time together. Wherever she was now, he hoped she would know how much he really did love her.

Asa knew now, because she could see him clearer than she had ever seen him before. She could see not only his body, but also the thoughts in his mind. She began to realize that death was a wonderful release from the pains of life.

Even as she looked down on the small child that had caused her death, she felt no sadness. Her spirit moved through the wall to the next bedchamber where her other three boys lay asleep. Somehow, she knew they would be cared for and loved, though she would not be able to do so herself.

This wonderful spirit body was allowed to watch over her physical body until it was buried in the ground near their home at Lade. Harald had a large stone placed over her that he had taken from a spot on the Stjordal River where they were wont to stop and talk while enjoying a ride together.

On the large stone he carved this rune inscription:

To the mother of my sons
and the wife of my youth.
Odin gave you to me and
he has claimed you again.

Harald wondered what name he should give to this little infant. He was so thin and hungry all the time. Maybe he would yet die. A male child was always named after his grandfather, but he already had two Halvdan's. He wasn't sure if Asa's mother would want the boy named after her dead husband Hakon. It was bad luck to give a great name to a child that had caused the death of its mother.

Just then, Malfrid walked into the long hall carrying the infant in her arms. "What name have you chosen for this son?" she asked.

"I haven't yet chosen," Harald replied.

"I would like him to be named after my father, Sigrod. Then I shall take him and raise him up as my own. My sons are gone, my husband is gone, and now my Asa is gone. I do not blame him for his mother's death as others do. I feel he must have a great purpose in this life for Odin to let him live."

Harald liked her words. She was a good woman and would do her best to help him with his sons.

"Sigrod it shall be then. We will pour water over him this night." And so he did.

It was a sad Yule feast that year at Lade. There were four boys, two women and two men. Only the boys were somewhat oblivious to the somber mood of the adults around them. Guttorm gave his carved wooden horse to little Guttorm and talked to him about the day when he would have his own big horse.

The two of them spent many hours in the stables, caring for Sleipni and May Day. Little Guttorm would sit on the stallion's back while Guttorm brushed and groomed each horse. The man would tell stories of the mighty grandfather who had first ridden the big black stallion and also stories of the mighty father who still rides the big white stallion. The boy would listen intently...he was a serious little boy.

"We really ought to breed some more stallions from Sleipni before he joins Halvdan in Gimli," suggested Guttorm.

"You are right," Harald answered. "We will need a stallion for each of my boys. We need at least one black one for little Halvdan the Black, don't you think?"

"I think little Guttorm would like a black horse also."

"Well, that is probably because he always sees his favorite uncle riding the black," Harald teased.

Guttorm knew Harald was just making fun with his words, but he was always slightly sensitive when it came to little Guttorm. It was generous of Harald to allow him to treat the boy as if he was his own son and sometimes he imagined he really was.

"Alright, two black and two white colts next spring. Be sure you tell that to Sleipni and May Day tomorrow when you are giving them their daily brushing," said Harald with a laugh.

There wasn't much that made Harald laugh these days. Despite the fact that Malfrid had moved over from Lanke to be near little Sigrod and his mother was doing her best to care for the two Halvdans, the house still seemed empty without Asa in it.

The nights were especially bad. How had he ever been happy without a soft woman by his side, Harald wondered. He guessed that was why God had made women, so that they could please and comfort a man. Of course, they were also needed to carry children in their belly and feed them from their breasts.

Harald was glad God had not chosen men to bear children. That would have been too hard. He would rather go off with his army and fight battles than stay at home with crying babies all day. Yes, it was good that God had made women.

Asa had always marked the day to celebrate and remember their wedding feast. Harald felt more lonely than usual that day. When Malfrid reminded him that it had been four years since he and Asa had made their marriage vows, he knew the reason for his sadness.

As he lay in his bedchamber that night, he wondered why it was that he could not fully appreciate those he loved until they were gone. It had been that way with Asa and it had been that way with his father.

He went to sleep longing for sweet Asa to wrap his arms around. Suddenly, there she was in his dream. What was she trying to tell him? He was so happy to look upon her face. It looked soft and pink and not white and pale as he had seen it last.

"I am here, my love," she said as she looked down at the reclining body of her handsome husband. "Odin has allowed me to bring you this message, so that you will see that I am happy. He does not want you to be sad. He still has a great work for you to do and you will need all your strength to accomplish it."

Harald sat up and reached for her. "Can you come and lay beside me?"

"I can, but you will not be able to feel me."

"It is enough that I can look at you and fix your lovely face in my mind."

"There is another face that you will see when you travel south in the spring. Odin has planned to give you Svanhild, daughter of Jarl Eystein from Vestfold."

"I miss you so much, my dear little wife," whispered Harald, all but oblivious to the message Asa was trying to give to him.

"Odin has promised me that we can be together when you have finished your work for this life. That is my reward for giving you your four sons."

"Please tell Odin I am grateful for the wife and sons he gave me."

"I saw the rune inscription you put on my stone, dear husband."

"I touch it each time I enter or leave our home."

"Thank you for that, my love. Now I must depart."

"Oh please...." he pleaded with outstretched arms, but she was gone.

Odin still watches over me, Harald thought to himself. He knew his mother always spoke of being together with his father when it came her time to die, but he hadn't thought about that for himself. It was comforting to know that his Asa was happy in her next life and that they could be together when he died.

"We cannot tell the precise moment when love is formed. As in the filling of a vessel drop by drop, there is at last one which makes it run over." **Author Unknown**

CHAPTER 17

VESTFOLD AND THE SOUTHERN KINGDOMS

That was the last view Harald had of his sweet wife Asa. The next visitor was Odin. He came to him the night before he prepared to leave Lade Manor and travel through the Trondelag Fjord and out to More.

"You must prepare for a long journey this time, my son. You may plan to stop at More and Raumsdal and on to Firdafylke to check on your jarls and gather men, but do not remain too long. King Eirik of Sweden has taken over the lands to the south and has plans to capture your kingdoms of Vestfold, Raumarike, and Vingulmark. Be strong and brave and I will continue to bless you."

Who did that King Eirik think he was, wondered Harald. The kingdoms of Vestfold, Raumarike, and Vingulmark had been ruled by his father before him and he thought he had strong jarls in each area. They probably needed additional troops and a visit from their King to bring things back in order.

Bring things back in order is exactly what Harald did when he arrived in the southern kingdoms. Vestfold was his first stop, just as it had always been with his father Halvdan. He and Guttorm both felt comfortable in the surroundings where they had spent so many years.

Now was not the time to be pleasant, however. They sent out messengers to all the jarls, herses, and bondes of each area. A Thing was to be held at Haugar in Vestfold, and all who had pledged loyalty to King Harald were told to be in attendance.

"Where is my father's half-brother, Olaf?" questioned Harald. "Has he given in to the Swedish King also?"

"Not so. He was severely challenged by King Eirik because of his relationship to your father, but he would not agree to pay the scat. Eirik first challenged him to come with his men and see who held the most power, but when it was told that Olaf was sickly and could not stand against the King, Eirik chose to humiliate him instead."

Jarl Eystein continued, "It was told about that Olaf was a coward, he who shared the blood of the great King Halvdan the Black. Olaf was so shamed by those words that he would not leave his home at Gokstad and died a pitiful death just a fortnight ago."

Those words made Harald even more determined to see that King Eirik paid for his crime of stealing. He had stolen not just the scat that was due to him from his father's kingdoms, but he had also stolen the good name of his father's brother. Revenge would be taken on King Eirik of Sweden...all in good time.

Harald sat in the judgement seat with Guttorm on one side and Jarl Eystein on the other. Eystein had held out against the pressures placed on him to give obedience and taxes to the Swedish King, but many men had not.

"We shall begin with an oath taking," shouted Harald to the assembly. "Every man who has pledged allegiance to me or to my father, King Halvdan the Black, raise your right hand. Now say after me, 'I swear that I will obey the Code of Law that has been set for the people of Vestfold, Raumarike, and Vingulmark and pay taxes and scat to no King but Harald Halvdanson.'"

Guttorm and Eystein marked those who did not take the oath. These men were charged with treason as set up under Halvdan's rule. Some paid fines and some were punished. Some tried to defend themselves by saying that they would not have paid King Eirik if King Harald had been there to defend them.

Harald scoffed at that excuse. "Never did I hear messages from this district that there was a lack of fighting men. If I had, I should have sent many ships with many warriors. You are cowards to accuse such! You will pay your fines and accept your punishments, or you may leave your estates and join King Eirik in Sweden. Then you will see which King takes care of his people!"

He spoke with such power that no man dared question his authority. The jarls who had served under King Halvdan were proud to see the son of that great man take over his rule and earn the respect of his people.

There were some dissenters who fled with their families after the Thing was over, but they did not seek out King Eirik of Sweden. Mostly, they traveled west by ship and settled in the islands of the sea.

That night, Guttorm and Harald were invited to a feast held in their honor at Sem Manor, the estate of Jarl Eystein in Vestfold. It wasn't until he was seated in the high seat next to Guttorm and Eystein that he saw her. Eystein had not thought to introduce his family to them, because the two had stayed in his home many times as they traveled the route with Halvdan.

So...this was Svanhild, he thought...the little girl with the big eyes who used to watch while he and her brothers practiced sword fighting. He must have been just ten years old the last time he saw her. She had turned into a beautiful girl, or woman. Harald wasn't sure how old a girl had to be before she could be called a woman.

Svanhild was small in size, like Asa had been, but her hair was golden brown and she had eyes to match. Harald thought she must be only fifteen or sixteen. Was that too young to become a married woman? Asa had been eighteen when they married and his mother had been twenty. He would just have to trust that Odin knew what was right.

The next day, Harald, Guttorm and Eystein rode to Gokstad to check on Olaf Gudrodsson's estate. It was the nephew's intent to raise a great mound in memory of his uncle. He also wanted to show the people of Vestfold that Olaf was to be rewarded for his loyalty. As they rode through the countryside, Eystein surprised him by offering sympathy for the death of his wife.

"How is it that you know about that when you are way down here and Trondelag is far to the north?" Harald asked.

"All the people under your rule want to know about you and your affairs," the jarl answered.

"Yes, we spent a sorrowful winter at our home in Lade last year. Asa gave me four sons in four years and then she passed to that heaven where lovely queens go to rest."

"I have a matter to speak to you about," said Eystein with hesitation. "I fear if I do not speak this to you, one of my sons will say it in jest."

"And what is the matter that I need to hear?"

"From the time you came here as a boy, traveling the route with your father and Gutthorm, my daughter Svanhild has always said she would have Harald Halvdansson for her husband. Her mother and I thought it amusing when she was just five years old and you were eight. But now that she is sixteen, she continues to refuse any suitors."

"I think she has even told her mother that she had a dream about being Married to you. Her brothers think she is just being foolish and like to tease her about it. When it was told that you were traveling here to Vestfold after all these years, and that your wife had just died...well, I am afraid Svanhild has really imagined her dream coming true."

He listened with interest to the tale that Jarl Eystein told him about his daughter Svanhild. Was it possible that Odin was planning his future even then? I guess he was, because he had given both his mother and his father dreams about his future.

Harald's response to Eystein's story shocked both of his listeners. "I would like to ask for the hand of your daughter, Svanhild, in marriage!"

The jarl turned so quickly in the saddle that he almost came off his horse. "What did you say? Do you jest?"

"I do not jest, Jarl Eystein, nor do I ask for Svanhild's hand to fulfill a girl's childish wish. Odin sent my Asa to me in a dream when I was sorrowing from her loss. She gave me the message that I was to marry Svanhild Eysteinsdatter from Vestfold. I wasn't sure which girl that was until I saw her last night at the feast."

"This is remarkable," exclaimed Guttorm, "Odin really does have your future in his hands!"

Eystein had agreed to let Harald ask Svanhild in his own time and in his own way. He had even promised not to tell her mother of their conversation.

"Guttorm and I will be spending the summer months here in Vestfold, as well as in Vingulmark and Raumarike until we feel like affairs are back in order. There will be some time for Svanhild and me to get better acquainted," Harald assured him.

Harald wasn't quite sure how to go about telling Svanhild that he would marry her. He certainly could not say he loved her for he hardly knew her. Of course, he had felt that same way when Freya had told him he was going to marry Asa and, without question, he had grown to love her with an intensity he had not known was possible.

His dilemma was solved for him one night as the family was eating their evening meal. Svanhild's brother, Halvor, was whispering in her ear and trying to get her to say something. Their father noticed the situation and told Halvor to quit teasing his sister. He stopped for a time, but then started up again.

Svanhild was obviously uncomfortable with what he was asking her to do. Harald could see that her face was flushed...and it wasn't just the light from the fire causing it.

Halvor just could not contain his joke any longer and he burst out with, "King Harald, Svanhild wants to ask you to marry her!"

He was laughing so hard from the trick he played on his sister that he almost missed the response.

"I accept," Harald said, loudly enough that even Halvor heard the words.

With that, he got up from the high seat and walked over to where Svanhild was sitting. Harald reached for her hand and pulled her to her feet. Right there, with her astonished family looking on, he dropped down on one knee and said, "Svanhild, would you do me the honor of becoming my wife?"

The only sound in the room was the crackling of the wood in the fire pit and the gasp that came from Svanhild's mother. Finally, Svanhild found her voice and answered, "I will."

Halvor was speechless as her mother and father got up from their seats and walked over to congratulate the couple. Guttorm just sat in his seat and smiled. There was no doubt in his mind that Odin watched over Harald.

The wedding feast was set for the day of the summer solstice, which would bring the couple good fortune.

"Summer is the best season for weddings," said Svanhild's mother Dagny, "Then your baby is born in the spring, and they have a chance to get a good start before the cold of winter."

If anyone but Harald noticed the blush on Svanhild's cheeks at the mention of a baby, they did not let it be known. It was a little bit awkward that Harald and Guttorm were living in the same house as his future bride and watching all of the preparations for the wedding.

Of course, the situation had been the same with Asa, but at least the couple had had their rides in the country together to be alone and get better acquainted. He wished he had Sleipni and May Day here to help him.

He finally asked Svanhild if she would like to go for a ride across the fjord with him. He was making a trip to Varna in Vingulmark and was using Jarl Eystein's small boat.

Svanhild agreed to go and they were finally alone. The sun was bright on the water and the easterly wind blew their boat quickly across the fjord. Dagny had packed them some food to share and Harald was already hungry by the time he got the boat secured.

"Can we sit right here by the water's edge?" he asked.

"How about under that willow tree?" she answered.

He carried the food and she carried the cloth they would sit on. It was hard to imagine they were planning to marry in a few weeks.

Harald could not think of anything else to say, so he blurted out, "Is it really true that you told your mother you were going to marry me when I was only eight and you were only five?"

It seemed like the worst thing he could have said, but it turned out to be the best. Now the story was out in the open and Svanhild did not have to hide behind it any more.

"Did Halvor tell you that story?" she asked.

"Actually, your father told it to me the second day I was here because he was fearful that Halvor might do just what he did. At first the story surprised me, because I could not remember much about you from that time, except for your big, golden brown eyes."

"I have wondered why you asked a silly girl like me to marry you."

"I do not think you are a silly girl, I think you are a lovely young woman who knows her own mind and will not let others dissuade her."

"But you still have not told me why you asked me to marry you."

"Do you want to know the real reason?" he asked.

"I do," she answered solemnly.

Harald hesitated. He had never told Asa that he married her because Freya told him to. What would Svanhild think if she knew the real truth? The look on her face told Harald she wanted the truth and not a story.

"Some months after my wife Asa died, I was feeling so sad and lonely. I must have been praying to Odin for help, because he sent my Asa's spirit down from the heavens to comfort me. She had been in such a bad state when she died that he wanted me to see that her spirit was just as perfect as she had been when we first married."

Harald continued, "After she lay with me on our bed, she told me the message Odin had sent her to deliver. The message was that I needed to continue with my conquest of all the kingdoms of Norway as I had sworn to do. And then she told me that I would marry Svanhild, daughter of Jarl Eystein of Vestfold."

He watched her face closely for some indication that telling her the truth was the right thing.

"I see that you are an honest man, King Harald. If you had told me you had also decided to marry me when I was five and you were eight, I should have know that you were not telling the truth. I believe that you saw your wife's spirit, because she came to me also in a dream. She told me her name and said that she loved you very much, but that she was now in the world of spirits and she wanted you to have a wife of flesh and blood. She also said that she had not chosen me, but Odin had chosen me to be your wife when we were just children."

It was like a huge weight was lifted from Harald's shoulders as he listened to Svanhild tell him about her dream. He now knew that she was truly destined to be his wife...even from their childhood.

Harald rose to his feet and, for the second time, took her hand and pulled her up to him. This time he did not kneel before her as he had done in front of her family. He drew her close, lifted her arms up around his neck, put his arms around her waist and gazed into her beautiful brown eyes.

"May your future husband show Odin he agrees with his choice by sealing our agreement with a kiss?"

Svanhild raised her lips to meet his and replied, "Your future wife answers yes!"

It wasn't a passionate kiss...it was a tender kiss between two friends who were destined to become lovers. Harald knew the passion would come later.

The ride back across the fjord was comfortable. The earlier ride had been uncomfortable. Both Harald and Svanhild had been uncertain what to do with the information they had been given by Asa's spirit. Now they were comrades, sharing the same adventure, and they knew their union had been the will of their God.

The day of the wedding feast came quickly. The friends and family of Eystein and Dagny were too numerous to hold the ceremony in the great hall at

Sem, so Svanhild had suggested they speak their vows under the branches of the huge willow tree down by the water's edge. Harald said he thought that would be perfect. Dagny looked at the two of them with concern in her eyes, but she agreed.

It seemed that Harald never was in possession of family jewelry to bestow on his bride. Maybe it was just as well, for his mother had said she wanted her wedding ring to be given to another Ragnhild. Was there going to be a Ragnhild in his life? He did not know and for today, he did not care.

Once again, he had two wedding bands created out of one of his gold arm bands. Once again, he had his name inscribed on Svanhild's ring and her name inscribed on his. He did not really want to take off the ring that bore Asa's name, but he knew he must.

Svanhild looked radiant as she came walking from the house, down the hill to where Harald stood under the willow tree. Her hair wasn't bright gold like Asa's had been, but in size they were almost the same. For a moment, he wanted to imagine that the woman walking toward him was his Asa in the flesh, but his conscience would not let him. This was his new wife and she deserved to have all of him, body and soul.

He would never forget watching her walk down that hill. Her dress was fashioned of gold silk that had come from some distant land. Around her neck, she wore long stands of amber beads and more beads were entwined into her golden brown hair. They glistened in the sunshine as Svanhild came to greet him. Afterward, he came to calling her his golden girl and she liked having that special name.

They spent their wedding night in Svanhild's bedchamber at Sem. It was small in comparison to the great bedchambers at both Tande and Lade, but Harald told himself it wasn't the size that mattered. It was the person you were sharing it with.

Dagny had provided a new eiderdown mattress for her daughter's bed and newly woven linens to cover it. The candles on the bedposts had been lit before the couple entered the room. Harald hadn't seen Svanhild's bedchamber before tonight, but he had the thought that it was small like her.

Harald wasn't nervous...but he could see that his bride was. A pale gold nightgown lay on the bed and Svanhild knew she needed to take off her wedding gown and put on her nightgown, but she did not really want to do that in front of Harald.

They had not been alone together since that day they sailed across the fjord. She did feel comfortable around him after they had had a chance to share their secret, but no man had seen her body since she was just a child. Her mother had told her she must put on her nightgown and climb into the bed with her new husband, however, she had not thought about undressing in front of him.

"Would you feel more at ease if I blew out the candles?" he asked softly.

She just nodded.

Harald undressed and climbed into the bed. The new linens felt soft against his skin. Soon he felt Svanhild's legs crawling across his feet at the end of the bed. She lay down next to him without touching any part of his body. When he tried to put his arm around her, he could feel her body tremble.

"Are you afraid of me, my golden girl?"

It was the first time he called her that pet name.

"No," she replied hesitantly...lying there stiff and still.

"What do you think husbands and wives do on their wedding night?"

"I am not sure," was her reply.

"Should I tell you?" he asked gently.

"Alright," she answered.

"Well, first they take off their wedding clothes and put on their bed clothes. Then, they climb into their bed. They cover themselves up with their new linen sheets and......and then they talk!"

That made Svanhild laugh. He was talking to her like he used to when she was a little girl. Maybe she felt like a little girl tonight, a little girl who had just captured the man of her dreams and now did not know what to do with him.

"I think the next thing they do is lay real close and put their arms around each other," he continued.

Now he was not just telling her, but showing her at the same time.

"Then they search around until they find each others lips, because they have blown out all the candles!"

Svanhild was starting to relax while listening to her patient husband describing his actions. He did finally find her lips in that dark room and she answered his seeking lips. It was not like the kiss they had exchanged under the willow tree. It was the kiss of an experienced husband with an inexperienced wife. It made her feel like a woman...and then the little girl was gone.

Harald wasn't quite sure what to do with Svanhild now that he had her. He had only planned to stay in Vestfold until the end of the summer. Then he was planning to go in search of King Eirik of Sweden. He thought about his empty manor house at Tande, but Ringsaker was several days travel from Vestfold and he did not think she would like to be there alone.

If Ragnhild was still living there he would take his new wife to stay with his mother, but she had moved up to Lade when the twins were born and now had full charge of his little Halvdan the White and Halvdan the Black.

Jarl Eystein's home was too small to be their permanent home. Harald was telling Guttorm about his problem as they headed down the road on borrowed horses.

"I heard that Jarl Eyolf took his family and left their estate in the dark of night to avoid paying you the fine he owed. Let us ride over and see what all he left behind."

"You see why I always ask for your advice," Harald replied, "because you always know how to solve my problems!"

Guttorm just smiled and rode on ahead. It was good to see his friend feeling happy again. He did not think Svanhild would ever make Harald forget Asa, but he was doing a good job of acting like a newly married man.

It was obvious Jarl Eyolf had tried to leave without discovery for he had left behind most of his possessions at Viken. His servants were still living in their quarters and they did not seem to know where the family had gone.

"It is too bad that Eyolf had to sneak off like that," said Harald.

"He did not have to leave, he chose to leave! The fine you assigned him was well within his means, but his pride would not allow him to admit he was wrong to support King Eirik when he had sworn an oath to your father."

"You are right, Gutthorm. I guess I will just take Viken Manor to pay the debt."

"He is the loser, he and his sons. May be they will find a place in the western islands where they will have to pay scat to no one. Let's go to the barn and see if he has left any good horseflesh to help with that debt."

"That is a good idea!" they both agreed.

"Guttorm and I have decided to take over Viken Manor, Jarl Eyolf's estate down the road. He has gathered his family and sailed off to find a new home. His ships are gone, but his animals, his furnishings and his servants are left. It seems like a ready made home for a newly married couple," Harald announced at the evening meal.

Svanhild was excited to think of having her own home. A newly married woman was supposed to get the keys to all the locks to hang from her belt. It was a sign that she was in charge of the household. Right now, her mother kept all the keys and she still felt like the young daughter she had been before her marriage.

Harald took her to look at the Viken estate the very next day. She had been at a feast in the home sometime ago, but she hadn't remembered much about it. The rooms were actually bigger than the ones at Sem, her parent's home. As she walked through the great hall, she could imagine sitting with her husband in the high seats and serving food to her guests from her own pantry. Yes, she was going to enjoy being the woman of the house with the ring of keys hanging from her belt.

She looked like an excited little girl to Harald, as she walked from room to room and imagined her life within these walls. He was glad that he could make her so happy. She hadn't complained about living with her parents, so he thought it was only he who needed more space and privacy.

They walked to the end of a long hallway and opened the door to the master bedchamber. It was a very large room with rich woven tapestries covering the walls.

"I feel sorry for the woman who had to leave these wonderful wall hangings behind," said Svanhild. "I think this is the most beautiful room in the house."

Harald turned to look at his new wife when he heard the quiet wistful sound in her voice. He put his arms around her waist and pulled her to him.

"It is too bad they did not leave their eiderdown on the bed, or I would show you why this is the most beautiful room in the house!"

He lifted her up off the floor and kissed her lips. She blushed in his arms.

"You had better put me down. What if Guttorm should come to the door and see us?"

"That is alright. I am sure he knows what happens in a master bedchamber!" he teased, but he let her go. "There will be plenty of time to enjoy my golden girl in that large bed before I leave for Sweden."

He and Guttorm divided the rest of the summer season between Raumarike and Vingulmark. They needed to set things in order again and make sure the people were following the Code of Law. New lagmen were chosen to speak the laws at the local Things.

By the time of harvest, they found two strong chieftains that had pledged their loyalty and taken the oath to follow the system of judgements and to collect the fair amount of taxes for themselves and for King Harald. Jarl Einar would govern Vingulmark and Jarl Finbo would rule in Raumarike.

This freed the two warriors to begin their journey eastward in search of King Eirik of Sweden. They were sure he must have received messages telling him of King Harald's re-capture of the three kingdoms that had started paying him scat. He had probably also heard that they were coming to find him.

"Must you go seeking after King Eirik," asked Svanhild as they lay in their bedchamber. "I fear you may be killed and leave me a widow when I have only just become a wife!"

Harald rolled unto his side and looked into the lovely eyes of his young wife. The candle light flickered over the sweet face that now wore a frown.

"Do you not have any faith in your husband?" he asked. "Do you think an old man like King Eirik can give the death blow to a body as strong as this?" he said with a smile as he pounded his fist on his chest.

She ran her hand over the hard muscles of his chest and down the rippled muscles of his arm. When she came to the gold ring on his left hand she lifted it to her lips. "I hope you will think about me when you look at my name on this ring and know that I need you to come back to me."

"Have no fear, my golden girl, I will think of you each night when I lay with empty arms. I think it is time to blow out the candles and let you show your departing warrior how much you are going to miss him!"

Svanhild just smiled, climbed over his muscular body, and reached to extinguish the candles. As she felt for the bed in the darkened room, she found his hands reaching for her. He lifted her light body and laid her on top of him. She felt like the most fortunate woman in all of Norway and wondered what she had done to deserve the blessing of becoming the wife of handsome King Harald.

CHAPTER 18

KING EIRIK OF SWEDEN

The great army of the north sailed into the large harbor at Vermaland. Here lived a great bondeman named Ake who had formerly served under King Halvdan the Black. When he received word that King Harald and Duke Guttorm had arrived, he traveled to meet them.

"Please do me the honor of attending a feast I shall make in your honor within a fortnight," pleaded Ake.

"You have honored my father and now I shall be pleased to accept your offer," answered Harald.

With that promise secured, Ake also sent word to King Eirik of Sweden to join him at a feast on the same day. King Eirik accepted as well.

Now, it was the plan of Ake that he might reconcile the two Kings so that bloodshed might be avoided. He knew King Halvdan had always preferred to live in peace and he hoped young Harald might feel the same.

Ake was the wealthiest man in all of Vermaland and he did not want to see his district turned into a bloody battlefield. Neither King Eirik nor King Harald knew the other was also invited to a feast on the same day.

In order to accommodate both Kings as well as their personal bodyguards, Ake had a second feasting hall built and furnished it with all new tables and wall hangings, plus vessels and horns adorned with gold. When the day appointed for the feast arrived, Harald and Guttorm and all their men were ushered into the new hall and served the best of food and drink.

Next came King Eirik and his men. They were ushered into the old hall, which was very splendid, though old-fashioned. Good food and drink was also given these guests and they ate and drank their fill.

When the hour was late and both Kings were made merry from drink, Ake bade them have some words together. Eirik was apprehensive as he approached the new hall and his enemy. He sat down opposite Harald, with Ake acting as a barrier between them.

"If Eirik agrees to keep to his own lands and not go again into your lands, will you cease following after him?" asked Ake of Harald.

Harald looked at the scowl on the face of the King across from him. He still felt anger that Eirik had tried to take over his kingdoms, but he wanted to honor Ake for his efforts to maintain peace. He thought about what his father would do in the same circumstance and gave his answer.

"If King Eirik will swear an oath to keep to his own lands and never again come into my lands, I will leave here in peace and no blood shall be spilt."

Ake looked to King Eirik. "Can you so swear in the presence of King Harald?"

King Eirik's face kept the same frown, but he had decided he must agree or there would be a battle and Harald would likely win the victory. "I so swear," he growled.

With that, Eirik stood up and walked from the hall. Ake nodded to Harald and followed King Eirik back to his feast hall. Harald did not think this would be the end of his conflict with the Swedish King, but he had chosen to take the peaceful route for now.

The next morning, as Harald prepared to leave, Ake came to him and praised his actions of the night before. "You remind me of your father and that is the highest praise I could give any man."

It meant a great deal to Harald to be compared to his father. "I shall carry those good words with me. Guttorm and I thank you for the splendid feast."

The bondeman went next to the feast hall of King Eirik, but found him in ill humor. The King mounted his horse and took the road to the east. Ake followed after him and asked to know the source of his displeasure.

"How is it that you gave King Harald a new feast house and the best of everything and gave me of everything old?"

"I think that your feast failed in nothing, My Lord. You received the same food and drink and entertainment as King Harald. However, King Harald was given everything new because he is a young man in the bloom of youth. You were given that which was old because you are now an old man such as I am."

"You had no right to treat King Harald in a better way while you are bondeman to me!" shouted Eirik.

"I was bondeman to just one King, and that was King Halvdan the Black, King Harald's father. I have never been your bondeman," Ake replied emphatically.

This speech so angered King Eirik that he drew his sword and pierced the heart of Ake and left him bleeding to death on the road. Eirik rode off quickly, hoping that no one would look for his host until a great distance had been put between them.

Now Harald and Guttorm were mounted and ready to take the road to the west. "I will speak one more time to Ake," said Harald.

When the servants went to find him, all they found was his body lying in the dirt of the road with hoof marks all around him.

"Ake is dead! Ake is dead! He lies in the dust of the road which King Eirik took to the east!" shouted the servant as he ran toward Guttorm and Harald.

They took one look at each other, spurred their horses, and headed down the east road. They stopped at Ake's body long enough to see that blood poured from the wound in his chest. Guttorm gently lifted the lifeless body. There was just enough breath left for Ake to speak one word, "Eirik."

They handed his body off to a servant. Then an angry King and his Duke raced down the road in search of the murderer.

King Eirik rode as fast as he could, but Harald and Guttorm with their men caught up to him by the wood which divides Gautland and Vermaland. There they did battle and many were the soldiers of Sweden who went to Valhalla that day. Eirik hastily fled the battle scene when he saw most of his men were dead or dying.

As they heard the call of the ravens in the sky, Harald and Guttorm realized the victory was theirs and Odin was satisfied that they had avenged Ake the bonde. Much as Harald wanted to continue after Eirik, he realized that a better punishment would be to take over the country of Vermaland and lay it under his rule...and so he did.

After setting Ake's affairs in order, they traveled throughout the land, setting up Halvdan's Code of Law. Jarl Haavard was chosen to rule over the people and collect taxes for himself as well as King Harald.

Yuletide would soon be upon them and they wanted to return to Viken Manor in Vestfold. Harald was relieved that he did not have to spend Yule in Trondelag this year. He would like to see his sons, but he knew they were being well cared for by his mother and Asa's mother.

It would be too painful to sleep in his bedchamber at Lade and dream that Asa was lying in his arms. Besides, he had Svanhild to think about. He was thankful that Odin had given her to him to help ease his sorrow.

As they passed through Tunsberg, Harald decided to visit the markets there and choose a gift for Svanhild. There was much silver to be had, but he wanted gold to give to his golden girl. He found a very beautiful neck band of gold strands that were twisted together. He could see in his mind how the gold of the neck band would bring out the golden brown color of his new wife's eyes.

There was excitement in the air as the two men with their body guards rode into the yard at Viken. Svanhild had heard the jangle of metal and the sound of horses' hooves and hurried out the door. The sun was shining, though there was snow on the ground, but she did not even take time to grab her cape from its hook. Harald had dismounted and removed his helmet just as she reached him.

"Are you so glad to see your returning warrior that you will brave the snow and cold?" he asked as he lifted her up for a quick kiss.

"I was hoping you would be back to spend Yuletide with me in our new home," she answered with a smile.

"Well, let me just wrap you up in my cloak and carry you back inside before you take sick," he said as he hugged her to his chest.

"Guttorm, will you take my horse with you to the stable while I take care of my Golden Girl?"

Guttorm just smiled and nodded. He grabbed the reins and led the king's horse to the large barn. Harald was a fortunate man, he thought, a blessed man.

When they got inside the house, Harald set Svanhild down and noted the radiant expression on her upturned face. "Have you missed me then?"

She reached up for another kiss, but he took her hands and brought them to his lips.

"I think My Lady will be more pleased to kiss her King when he has had a chance to wash the soil of a long trip from his body and put on some clean clothing."

Svanhild took his hand and led him down the hallway to their bedchamber.

"Come with me and I will help you get out of those soiled clothes," she said with a mischievous grin.

"Is this really the same girl who would not take off her wedding gown in front of her new husband?"

"Shhh," she whispered, "Do you want the serving women to hear?"

She pulled him into the master bedchamber and closed the door behind him.

"Now, my warrior husband, let us just see what is under all that chainmail and soiled clothing," she said as she unpinned the cloak from his shoulders.

This was a different Svanhild from the shy girl he had left behind four months ago. After his mail and clothing lay in a pile on the floor, she once again took his hand and led him to the large bed platform and bade him lie down.

"Now, you just lay here and I will fetch some warm water and cloths," she said as she kissed him lightly on the cheek.

She was gone just a short while, but Harald had closed his eyes and was almost asleep when she returned.

"Shall I start at your head or at your feet?" Svanhild said with a laugh.

"You had better get this face clean before you do any more kissing!" he laughed back.

She poured the warm water into a basin and wet the soft linen cloth. She started at his forehead and gently washed all the creases of his face and neck, staring into his eyes as she did so. She was enjoying seeing the look of pleasure on his face.

When she moved down to his chest, he closed his eyes. He wanted her to hurry, but he wanted her to go slowly also. Soon, she was washing his left arm and hand, then his right arm and hand. Suddenly, she stopped, dropped his hand, and went rushing out of the room.

What? Harald sat up in surprise. What had happened? Where did she go? He lay back down and put his bare arm on his forehead. As he did that, he caught the gleam of a gold ring on his finger. So...that was it. He had forgotten about the fact that he had put the gold ring with Asa's name on his right hand when he left for Sweden.

He got up from the bed and found some clothing in the large chest next to the bed. He went to the door of the bedchamber and called for Svanhild. There was no response. He walked out to the great hall, but she was not there. He finally found her in the small bedchamber next to theirs. She was sitting on the bed crying.

He walked over to her, lifted her up and set her on his lap.

"I am sorry that I hurt your feelings. I should have remembered to take Asa's ring off before I got here."

"Why are you wearing her ring? Aren't you my husband now?" she sobbed.

"Of course I am," he said softly, "Of course I am."

"Then why are you wearing her ring?"

Harald did not know what to say. Should he tell the truth, or would it be better to lie? He thought about the day they had told each other about their messages from Odin that Asa had delivered. Svanhild had said she wanted to hear the truth. He decided he would choose the truth again.

"I really did not want to take Asa's ring off my finger when we married, but I did it out of respect for your feelings. I did not think it would hurt to wear it while I was traveling, but I had intended to remove it before I got back to you."

She sat quietly on his lap at the edge of the bed. Her head was bowed and her eyes were looking down at his hands.

"You see, I have your ring on my left hand so it is closest to my heart. I want you closest to my heart and I want to love you as much as I loved Asa. But, I do not want to forget about her either. She is gone and you are here. She is not going to come back alive and take your place in our bed, but I spent four long years growing to love her deeply and I can not just forget about her. I will take off her ring so that you will not see it and feel sad."

She lifted her head and looked into his eyes. He took the corner of her apron and wiped away her tears.

"Thank you for being honest with me. I will feel better if you do not wear her ring while you are here. Maybe some day I will feel alright about sharing you, but not now."

Harald took the ring off his finger and set it on the bed.

"Are you ready to give your warrior that nice welcome home gift now?" he asked.

"Yes, I think so," she answered hesitantly.

Harald stood up, her small body cradled in his arms, and walked back to the master bedchamber. This time it was he who shut the door behind them. He carried her to the large bed and laid her down.

"This time I will be the one taking the clothes off," he said as he dropped his clothing on the floor. "Are you ready to let your husband see what is under your gown in the bright light of day?"

"I think so," came her quiet response.

Harald slowly removed her head dress, then her apron, next her overgown, and finally, her undergown. Her lovely white skin was the color of the linen cloth upon which she lay. She wasn't anxious anymore, but she was willing, and he loved her gently.

As they sat at the evening meal that night, Guttorm said, "You forgot this pouch in your saddle bag this afternoon."

"Ah yes, my Golden Girl caused me to forget the gift I had chosen for her at the market in Tunsberg," Harald said as he picked up the leather pouch.

"You brought me a gift?" Svanhild asked in pleased surprise.

"A golden necklace to match your golden eyes," he said as he held it out for her.

She took the chain and held it to her breast. With tear filled eyes, she looked lovingly at her husband. "Thank you," she whispered.

"Let me place it around your neck." Harald rose and bent to fix the clasp on the heavy chain.

"Now you truly look like the wife of King Harald Halvdansson," Guttorm said with a smile.

Svanhild smiled too. She was pleased that Harald had thought of her as he traveled back to Viken. It made the thought of him wearing both her and Asa's rings seem less important. She knew it wasn't fair of her to expect him to forget about Asa so soon, but it was hard to think about sharing his affections with another woman, even if that woman was now dead.

The Yule celebration at Viken Manor was almost as nice as the ones at Tande Manor and Lade Manor. It was good to sit by a warm fire with the smell of delicious food and the company of good friends.

Svanhild invited her family to share the Yule feast with them and it was nice to see her joy at fulfilling the role of a wife in front of her mother and father. She had a full set of keys hanging from the belt on her dress and there was no question she was taking on the responsibilities of being a married woman.

Dagny watched her daughter for signs that there would be a baby in the spring, but she did not see any. She hoped her daughter would not have any trouble producing children for this young King. Even though he already had four sons from his first wife, Svanhild's parents knew it was important that she give him children as well.

Svanhild was worried too. She had been sharing the bed with her husband for almost seven months now and still she had no baby in her belly. Her mother kept asking if there was something wrong. She did not know if there was anything wrong, but she worried.

Her mother had told her she needed to do her part to see that a baby was conceived, but Svanhild wasn't sure just what she meant by that. Her mother also said that there had better be a baby in her belly before Harald left in the spring, or else. Or else what, she wondered.

They were lying in their large bed, wrapped in each others arms, keeping warm under the soft furs that covered their bodies.

"Do you want to have a baby with me?" Svanhild asked in a quiet voice.

"Yes, I want to have a baby with you...of course I do," Harald replied.

"Then why do I not have a baby in my belly?"

"I do not know," he answered. "It was always so easy with Asa."

Svanhild rolled over and put her back to him.

"I guess that was the wrong thing to say. I am sorry."

"Will I always be compared to Asa?" she asked.

"No. I just meant that I do not know everything about babies either, except that I just make love with you and pretty soon there is a baby in your belly," he said as he tried to explain the words that had hurt her again.

"Do we make love as much as you and Asa did?" she asked.

"Do not ask me that. You are not Asa and I do not want you to feel like you are trying to be her."

"Do you love me Harald, even a little?"

"Of course I love you...more than a little!"

"How much?"

"Well, you just turn around here and I will show you how much!" he said as he turned her small body toward him. He started to kiss her lips, softly at first and then more passionately. He was glad she wanted to have a baby, but he wished she had more of Asa's passion.

CHAPTER 19

HOME TO LADE

Spring had turned to summer and the willow trees along the shore were full and green. Returning from a successful battle in Gautland, the two warriors beached their ships and walked the path to the manor house at Viken.

"I have been thinking about our plan for me to travel to Lade. I think you need to go in my stead. I am very anxious to see my sister and little Guttorm, but I feel the people in the Uplands and Trondelag need to see their King and know that he is still interested in their welfare. I can stay here and see to the defense of these southern kingdoms," counseled Guttorm.

"You are wise, my friend, and I will take your counsel. I think I am ready to see Lade again...and my family there," Harald answered.

This time, Svanhild was not at her loom in the great hall. Harald walked down the hallway to the master bedchamber and quietly opened the door. He saw his wife sleeping peacefully on their bed and walked silently into the room. As he knelt down to kiss her lips, she awoke with a start and threw her arms around his neck.

"I have a baby in my belly!" she cried excitedly.

"Well, I had better give him a kiss, too," he said as he pulled back the sheet and kissed her abdomen.

"Do you think it will be a boy?" she asked.

"I hope so. A man can not have too many sons!"

Svanhild was in such high spirits. She had finally managed to conceive a child and she knew Harald would love her more now. Her happiness was diminished slightly when he told her about his plans for the summer.

"I will be traveling up to Lade in a fortnight. I will visit my kingdoms around Lake Mjosa, then through the Uplands and on to Trondelag. My mother and three of my sons will return with me and live at Tande Manor in Ringsaker.

That way, they will be closer and Guttorm and I can see them more often," he told her.

"Do you have to leave so soon?"

"You do not need me here, now that you have gotten a baby in your belly, do you?" he teased her.

She blushed and said, "I will miss having you near me."

"Guttorm will be traveling throughout the southern kingdoms this summer, but he will be close enough if you have need of him."

"That will be good," she said quietly.

Harald seemed happy to be leaving her and anxious to begin his journey to Trondelag. Even though she knew it was wrong, Svanhild could not help but feel jealous of the fact that he would be sleeping again in the bed he had shared with Asa.

She thought he would probably dream he was holding his first wife in his arms and not even give a thought to his second wife. Well, at least she was going to have his baby and that gave her comfort. Hopefully, he would return in time to be there when their child was ready to come into the world.

A large majority of the army was left under the command of Duke Guttorm. Harald followed the example of his father and traveled with a retinue of seasoned warriors. In addition, he took his faithful bodyguard of berserkers, twenty-five fierce fighters.

His trusty wolfdog, Torda, stayed behind at Viken. He was getting too old for a long travel and Harald knew he would soon need to breed a pup to take the place of his dependable companion. He would be glad to see his two great stallions again and he planned to bring them back with him.

He and Guttorm had taken the horses from his new estate for their own but they did not compare to Sleipni or May Day. The colts that were bred for his sons would come with them to Tande Manor as well as their dogs. He wanted each of his children to have the experience of having a special horse and a special dog...just as he had.

Tande Manor looked so good to him as he came riding up the road next to Lake Mjosa. He would always think of this as home, no matter where else he might live. Jarl Knudt, who had been placed in charge of the estate when his mother moved to Lade, welcomed him and his men.

"You will be able to return to your Solberg estate in Loten when my mother arrives," Harald told him. "We shall probably be here just after harvest. You have been a loyal subject and I would reward you by allowing you to keep my portion of the taxes you collect this fall."

"You are very generous, My Lord. My wife, Dorthea, will be happy to return to her own home and close family, but I shall continue to be of service to your mother if she needs me."

"That will be deeply appreciated," responded Harald.

He slept in his old bed that night and dreamed of the many experiences he had had growing up on this estate. He saw his father killing the bear that was attacking Torda, he watched again as his father cut the cord that was wrapped around May Day's neck...and he saw Svase the Finn tied to the large tree by the barn, smiling through his beating.

That brought him awake with a start. The dream had begun with pleasant memories, but had ended with that eerie feeling that the Finn evoked in his senses. Harald hadn't felt the sense of guilt for his father's death in a long while, but it was still there, hidden in the far recesses of his mind.

From Ringsaker, he traveled northward, through the Uplands, over the Dovrefjeld, and on to Trondelag. At each place, he stopped at the estate of the jarl who was administering the affairs in that kingdom. Word had gone ahead of him, telling his subjects that their King was traveling the route. He held a Thing in each area and was pleased to see Halvdan's justice system working successfully.

When he finally reached Lade, he was welcomed joyously. His mother looked like she had aged in the time since he had left her in charge of his three oldest sons. Little Guttorm remembered him and came running into his arms, but the twins clung to Ragnhild's skirt, peeking out to see who this big stranger was.

"Have they forgotten me?" Harald questioned.

"I am sure you look like an unfamiliar person right now, but they will warm up to you soon...especially if Guttorm is in your arms. They are trying to do everything they see him do these days!" exclaimed Ragnhild.

"What about Sigrod, is he here?"

"Malfrid is visiting at Lanke Manor. She will come with the boy as soon as she receives word of your arrival."

That night, when the four boys were finally asleep, Harald told his mother and Malfrid his plan.

"It will be so nice to be back at Tande Manor again. I have enjoyed being here, but Tande is my home and it will be good for the boys to be close enough to see you and Guttorm frequently." responded Ragnhild with enthusiasm.

"What about Sigrod?" asked Malfrid apprehensively.

"I gave him to you to raise when Asa died and I do not intend to take him away," he responded.

Malfrid heaved a sigh of relief. "He will stay here with me, then, and I shall raise him at Lade."

"You are a good woman and I am glad that I am able to give you a boy child to take the place of the sons and the husband who gave their lives in my service," Harald told her sincerely.

Malfrid just nodded. She had lost much, too much. Seeing King Harald again brought those thoughts back to her mind.

"I hear you have taken a new wife," she said suddenly.

Harald looked at her in surprise, uncertain as to her meaning.

"I do have a new wife. Her name is Svanhild Eysteinsdatter and she reminds me much of the lovely daughter you gave to me!"

That seemed to satisfy Malfrid and she excused herself to retire for the night. Ragnhild was happy to have her son all to herself. She had wanted to ask Harald about his new wife, also, but she wasn't sure how Malfrid would feel about that conversation. Now, mother and son were free to share their feelings in private.

"Before I left Lade, Asa came to me in a dream and told me it was Odin's will that I choose Svanhild as my new wife. I did not say anything about the dream before I left here, because I wasn't really ready to talk about it. I still miss Asa, but the wound in my heart is beginning to heal."

"I am pleased that Odin is still taking care of you. When I hear word of another battle you and Guttorm have won, I thank Odin for his protecting hand. I see you still have your father's sword by your side."

He fondled the handle of his prized sword.

"Frey has helped me win many battles, and for that I am grateful. Odin continues to lead and guide me. He shows himself to Guttorm and me at the end of every battle and we ask him for direction in our plans. Now that King Eirik of Sweden has been vanquished, perhaps our fighting days will be over."

"I would hope that could be true, but I will continue to pray for you," she said with a sigh.

Mother and son embraced as they said good night. They were both happy to be back in each other's company. It was nice to be at Lade Manor, despite the sad memories that came to him. He would try to focus on the happy times.

Harald and his men spent a fortnight traveling around Trondelag, holding a Thing at Frosta. Once again, he found the jarls that were in charge had been following the laws and exacting just penalties for crimes. They had been fair in the collection of taxes and had maintained the hundreds of soldier warriors who were ready to defend his kingdom if needed.

"I shall be sailing for More in a few days," he told his mother. "It is pretty peaceful here, but I have had word that Jarl Ragnvald has been having some trouble."

"Will men never desire peace more than war," Ragnild asked.

"We are an independent people," he said, "and there are many outlaws among us. Most of the men who meet at a Thing are willing to live under a just law, but there are always those who would choose the old ways."

"Odin has said there will be rewards for those who choose good and punishment for those who choose evil while they live on the earth. Perhaps those who refuse to obey the laws hope that Odin will be looking the other way and will not see their guilt," was her reply.

"Father was so wise in setting up the Code of Law and the system of justice for his kingdoms. The people who are also wise can see the good that comes from everyone following the same laws and receiving the same penalties. Those who can not see are better off if they leave Norway, but they probably will not find a fairer system, no matter where they travel."

With that, mother and son sat in silence...each thinking about the husband and father who had so influenced their lives. Ragnhild knew Harald still needed her, but she would be happy when she had finished her life on earth and could join her husband in Gimli.

CHAPTER 20

TROUBLE IN LOFOTEN

Harald, along with Jarls Trond from Vaeradal, Gudbjorn from Hegre, Gudmond from Steinkjer and Hrollaug from Naumadal traveled to More with a full complement of men and ships. Ragnvald had not said just what the trouble was in his kingdoms, but Harald planned to bring enough power to deal with whatever was needed.

Jarl Ragnvald was very glad to see his King sailing into the harbor with so many men and ships. He had been trying to defend More and Raumsdal from vikings who would attack and pillage and then sail off to return another time. The law strictly forbade attacks on a man's own countrymen. Many of Harald's men had been killed or wounded in these attacks.

Word had come that there was a chieftain to the north on the island of Lofoten who was bragging about the fact that he had not been conquered by the great King Harald Halvdanson. His name was Olaf Tvennumbrunni of Borg and he had as sons, Helgi the Steady, Tore the Vigorous and Vade the Young. He was a proud man who commanded many men and dragon ships.

Each summer Olaf sent his three sons south to raid on Raumsdal and More. They would sail in quickly, burn and pillage the villages along the coast and retreat back north to their home in Lofoten. The three brothers had bragged about taking the lives of soldiers who were charged with the protection of these coastal kingdoms.

In the summer of 876, King Harald determined to put an end to these raids. He gathered troops and ships and sailed north, past the islands of Hitra and Froya and on to Lofoten. The ships entered the harbor at Borg in the early morning hours. Harald's men lashed their vessels together, stern to stern, creating a barricade so none of Olaf's ships could escape.

Harald's warriors, led by his berserkers, began a shrill battle cry...beating their shields in a thunderous roar. Olaf, together with his sons, Helgi, Tore and Vade, came rushing out of the longhouse in full battle attire. They were leading the warriors who had also been asleep in the great hall when the battle cry was heard.

The rising sun reflected as a blinding ray from the swords, shields and battleaxes of Harald's men as they leaped from their ships to meet the oncoming foe. Olaf and his sons fought bravely, but they were greatly outnumbered.

The berserkers had been instructed to surround Olaf and his sons and disarm them, but not kill them. When that feat was accomplished, the cry of victory was shouted and Harald came forward to demand their surrender. Olaf, realizing he had a choice between yielding and dying, shouted to his men to lay down their weapons.

"I will meet with you and your sons in the house, while your men are being held captive outside," shouted Harald to Olaf over the din of weapons being laid on the ground.

Olaf agreed with reluctance, "As you wish, My Lord."

Olaf, Helgi, Tore and Vade marched resolutely up the hill to the imposing longhouse that dominated the settlement at Borg. Harald and his bodyguard followed them. Jarls Gudbjorn, Gudmund and Trond were put in charge of the warriors left behind on the beach.

Once inside the great hall, Harald wasted no time getting to the point. "You know why I am here, don't you!" he demanded.

"You have attacked us without reason!" asserted Olaf.

"Do not think you can play games with me, Olaf of Borg! Your sons have been burning, pillaging, and killing in Raumsdal and More for two summers, and I am here to say, this is the end!" shouted Harald.

"You are mistaken, My Lord, my sons....."

Harald interrupted the apologetic Olaf, "Stop this talk! Lying does not become a great chieftain such as you. I am here to offer you your life and also the life of your sons in exchange for an oath of allegiance. I need a strong jarl to rule in Lofoten, and as you are already established here, I am offering you the chance to be that man. You may have charge of all the lands from Vager down to Haleygja, but there will be no more raiding by you or your sons. What say you?"

Olaf was silent for a time as he thought of the offer made to him by the Warrior King. Did he really have a choice? Harald's men were outside holding his warriors captive and the King's bodyguard was here in his hall, ready to run him and his family through if he did not agree.

Finally Olaf replied, "You do my sons and I great honor by offering to allow us to pledge our allegiance to so great a King as yourself. We shall be happy to accept your conditions."

"No," shouted Tore, "We shall not be made vassals at the point of a sword!" as he lunged at Harald.

Berdaluke, the berserk, and three other men of Harald's guard had their swords drawn and pressed to Tore's chest before he could get close to his target.

"Forgive my reckless son, My Lord," Olaf said with haste. He is called Tore the Vigorous for this very reason. Please allow his brothers, Helgi and Vade, to hold him in check. He will follow his father's orders, I assure you."

Harald told his men to lower their weapons. "Will you take an oath on your son's lives, that you will rule this land northward to Lofoten in my stead and keep law and justice as I have established it in the kingdoms to the south, Olaf of Borg?"

"I take an oath that I will rule in the name of King Harald Halvdansson, all the lands of Haleygja and as far north as Vager, as long as I shall live here at Borg in Lofoten," swore Olaf with a raised right hand.

"Then let it be done!" declared Harald, though there was an uneasiness in his mind. "Because you are charged with protecting this area against enemies of mine, I want you to keep your weapons. But because you may need some time to persuade some of your men that you have sworn allegiance to me, we will take all the weapons with us and leave them at the end of Lofoten Island. It may be that your men will find acceptance in their souls as they march to retrieve their weapons!"

With that, Harald turned and walked through the doorway of the longhouse. His bodyguard followed behind him. He gave the order to collect all the weapons that had been laid down by Olaf's men and to return to the ships.

Olaf, Helgi, Tore, Vade and all of Olaf's men watched as the dragon ships turned and headed out to sea. It was a sad day at Borg. The ships were barely out of sight when Tore turned on his father with an angry shout.

"How could you do this to us, Father? We do not want to be King Harald's men! We want to be free to do as we please...as we have always done."

"Would you have chosen death versus allegiance, my son?" asked Olaf with a sigh.

"Yes, I would have chosen death!" replied Tore. "Death in battle brings a warrior certain glory in Valhalla!"

"And what of your mother and your sisters?" asked his father.

Tore was about to answer boldly, when he looked up to see his mother, Hilde, standing in the door of the longhouse. She was wiping tears from her eyes with the corner of her apron. Suddenly, Tore knew that his father had chosen the better part.

Harald was relieved to have the matter of northern Norway settled. But was it really settled? Olaf of Borg was a good man, a worthy chieftain, but his sons were a different matter. They were like many others who wanted to spend their summers raiding and pillaging. He did not mind them partaking of those activities, he just could not allow them to attack the areas he was responsible for. He hoped Olaf could control his errant sons.

Olaf was indeed having a hard time controlling his sons. One day a group of ships came into the harbor at Borg. It was led by Hilde's brother, Bjorn. He was leaving Norway to settle in Iceland and had come to tell his sister farewell.

That night around the fire, Bjorn told Olaf's family the things he had heard about Iceland. He said there was land for the taking, with long grass for grazing and wild animals for hunting. The fishing was good and a man could set up his own kingdom and live as he would like.

This was just the news that Helgi, Vade, and especially Tore wanted to hear. They pleaded with their father and mother to leave their farm on Lofoten and go to Iceland along with Uncle Bjorn.

"You forget, my sons, I have given an oath to King Harald and I cannot go against my word," said Olaf with a sad note in his voice.

"But the oath you swore said that you would be faithful to King Harald as long as you lived at Borg in Lofoten," whispered Hilde.

Olaf turned to look at his wife. She was right, that is what he had said. He meant that he would be jarl at Lofoten until he died, but that is not what he said.

"Are you saying that you want to leave our home at Borg and follow Bjorn to Iceland, my wife?" he asked.

"Yes, my husband. I think it will be better for our family, especially for our sons, who have claimed they would rather be dead than to be ruled by another."

Olaf looked at the faces, in the glow of firelight, which were staring at him and waiting for his answer.

"We shall cast lots so that everyone will know they had a choice in this decision."

The same choice was shared by all the family of Olaf and Hilde. They would leave their home at Borg and start a new life on the island of Iceland. They would pack up and go quickly. They would sail off with Bjorn and his family. They would not look back. They would tell no one of their plan...in hopes that King Harald would not come to find them and challenge Olaf's oath.

The family of Olaf Tvennumberunni, who had lived on Lofoten for many generations, took their most valued possessions and sailed for Iceland. There they settled all of Skeid between Tjorsa and Kvita and Sandlok. They called their new home Olaf Fields and lived there until they died.

Harald never bothered them. They were just one of many families who chose to settle on the island of Iceland, rather than be subject to the strict laws of King Harald Halvdansson.

When it was discovered that Olaf and his family had left Borg, Harald decided it was a good thing. Even though he could have had them killed for the breaking of an oath, it was better that they had moved from Lofoten. Olaf had been a man of honor, but it was doubtful he could have kept his sons from their summer raids. Now they would be too far away to bother attacking Norway. Raumsdal and More would be free of their terrorizing.

The situation reminded Harald of his yearly travels to administer justice with his father, Halvdan the Black. When a man was branded an outlaw, it was better for him if he left the country. In that way, the number of trouble makers became less and less and that brought more peace for his people. Harald wondered if he would ever be as good a ruler as his father had been.

CHAPTER 21

YULETIDE AT TANDE MANOR

The trip from Trondelag back to Tande Manor was exhilarating. What a thrill it was to be riding on the back of his magnificent stallion May Day once again. They had missed each other and it was hard to tell who was enjoying the experience more. Halvdan's stallion Sleipni traveled along, but without a rider. The great warrior horse had fought his last battle, but was still able to sire colts for Harald's sons.

There was rejoicing among the servants and workers at Tande that fall. The harvest had been bountiful and there would be plenty of food for both man and beast through the long winter months. They were excited to have Ragnhild back home to stay.

Harald stayed with his mother and enjoyed playing with his three sons and helping them get settled in their new home. Halvdan the White and Halvdan the Black were full of mischief. What one did not think of, the other one did. Little Guttorm was a good helper, but the twins did not want to be restrained very much.

Their grandmother told them stories of the exploits of their father as she put them to sleep at night. They never seemed to tire of hearing the same stories over and over. Harald enjoyed hearing them also. She always made him out to be a hero...whether that was true or not.

Soon the weather began to get cold and he decided it was time for him to return to Viken. He knew there were two people waiting anxiously for him to return. Guttorm was planning to spend the winter months with his sister and the boys at Tande and could hardly wait for his turn to travel to see them.

Svanhild wanted so much for her husband to be present when their baby was born. Harald wasn't sure when the time would come, but his conscience told him he ought to try and be there. Thoughts of the terrible birth of his last son and visions of Asa lying in a pool of blood assailed his memory and he could not seem to rid himself of them.

Fortunately for him, he walked into the manor house at Viken just as the sound of an infant's cry came from the birthing chamber. Guttorm had been doing his duty by waiting in the long hall while substituting for the absent husband.

"Am I glad you are here," was all he had a chance to say before Dagny came to the door to announce the birth of a baby boy. She was also relieved to see Harald at the end of the hall.

"Is Svanhild alright?" he asked.

"She will be just fine, now that you are here!" was the answer.

"Oh, Harald, it's a boy!" cried Svanhild as she saw him enter the room.

"Just what I expected," he said as he bent down to kiss her wet forehead. "I guess he waited until his father arrived."

"I would have liked you here sooner," she told him with a tone of disapproval in her voice.

"I think it was just right," he said as Dagny placed the red-faced bundle in his arms.

The thrill of seeing their baby for the first time made Svanhild forget the irritation she had felt at her husband's absence.

"What will we name him?" she asked.

"As I was riding here, I passed Olaf's mound at Gokstad and thought we should give the child his name if it was a boy."

Svanhild was so excited that she had given Harald a boy child that she did not really care what name was chosen.

"I think Olaf will be fine," she said.

So Harald poured water over his fifth son and called him Olaf after his father's half brother.

Guttorm left for Tande Manor the very next day. He was anxious to spend Yuletide with his sister, but mostly, he wanted to be reunited with Little Guttorm. He did not care that Harald had five sons, as long as he got to claim one of them. It was going to be wonderful to spend the winter months in Ringsaker, playing with the boys and visiting with Ragnhild. There would also be time to check on Stein Manor, his family estate in Ringerike.

Guttorm remembered fondly his time spent in the barns at Lade Manor, brushing Sleipni and telling Little Guttorm that he would have his own horse someday. Now that the old war horse and his colts had been brought down to Tande Manor, the foster father would have his chance to make good on that promise.

"Ah, sister, it is so good to see you," said Guttorm as he embraced Ragnhild. "Where are the boys?"

"They are asleep for the afternoon, but will soon be awake. Let us sit and visit while it is quiet. Sleep time is about the only peace you get with three active boys in the house," she said.

"It is sad that Halvdan is not here to enjoy them."

"Yes, he wanted many sons...but I was able to give him but one."

"Well, I rode beside Halvdan for ten years and I have now fought beside Harald for nine years, and two finer men could not have come into our lives. We are truly indebted to Odin for giving us this blessing when our father was taken."

"You are right, my brother, and now I am blessed with the chance to raise three of Harald's sons. I am happy to be back at Tande and I'm grateful to you for coming to help me during this winter season."

"I think I will get as much pleasure as I will give. I have missed the days of having Little Guttorm follow me everywhere I went. We shall all enjoy this time together. Let us toast to Harald and his sons," said Guttorm as he raised his drinking horn to Ragnhild's.

Suddenly, the quiet of the afternoon was changed to one of excitement. Little Guttorm had awakened and crept down the hall. When he saw who his grandmother was talking to, he ran into the arms of his namesake.

"You have grown into a big boy! Can you say our name yet?"

"You are Guttorm, I am Gutt!"

Both Ragnhild and Guttorm laughed at his words.

"His brothers could not say his whole name, so they came up with Gutt. I guess it is one way to know which Guttorm we are talking to, now that you are both here together," said Ragnhild.

"Do you like being called Gutt?" Guttorm asked the boy.

"I like having your name, but I will be Gutt until my brothers are old enough to say my whole name," was the serious reply.

"That is very grown up of you," said Guttorm. "I think you will make a great king one day. Every great king needs a great horse. I think we should choose one of Sleipni's colts to be your special horse and then we can train him to obey only you."

"You are the best uncle a boy could have!" said Gutt as he gave Guttorm a big hug.

Ragnhild was happy for them both. They had developed a special bond of friendship while they were at Lade Manor and she was glad to see that their feelings for each other had not changed.

"Why don't you two go out to the barn now before the twins awake...otherwise, they will beg to go along."

They were more than happy to take her suggestion. Soon, she could see them walking down the hill toward the barns, Little Guttorm's hand holding tightly to the hand of his great uncle.

Harald wasn't sure how to tell Svanhild that he wanted to spend this Yule season at Tande Manor in Hedmark. She had so enjoyed being the hustru in her own home last year and inviting all her family to celebrate with them. She had told Harald, as they lay together in their bed at the end of the day, that she hoped to spend every Yule in the same way.

"Svanhild, I want to take little Olaf on a trip to Tande. I think it is time both of you met my mother," he said one morning as they sat together at the morning meal.

"Perhaps we can go there in the spring," she replied.

"I was thinking about Yuletide," he ventured.

"But I want to spend Yuletide with my family here at Viken."

"We spent last Yuletide with your family," he countered.

"And you spent the Yuletide before that with your mother in Lade!"

Harald looked at her with an expression of sadness in his eyes.

"We will not speak of this again," was all he said as he left the room.

Svanhild felt bad. She really did not want to go to Tande Manor for Yule. She did not want to have to share Harald with his mother and especially, she did not want him to spend time with his three sons that were there. He had a new son now and she wanted Harald to think of his new life with her and not his old life with Asa. Would she always have to feel this jealousy for Asa, she wondered?

As the Yule season drew closer, Svanhild could see that her husband was not his usual cheerful self. She knew he was missing Guttorm, but she expected him to feel more joy in spending time with her and their young son.

"I think you ought to travel to Tande Manor for Yuletide this year," Dagny told her daughter as they sat together in the great hall.

"Why do you say that?" Svanhild asked.

"I asked Harald why he looked so sad, and he told me you had refused his request to spend Yule with his mother and his three sons," she answered.

"Well, I want to stay here and have my own family close."

"I think you are acting like a selfish wife who is jealous of her husband's family!"

Svanhild opened her mouth to protest, but the look on her mother's face told her the protest would be futile.

"But.....he will be so busy enjoying his mother and his other children that he will forget about our son."

"Olaf won't know the difference and you need to do what makes your husband happy. Then he will feel like making you happy," was Dagny's advice.

She knew her mother was right. She would just have to try hard to act like she was enjoying herself...no matter what.

Harald gave out a loud shout and swung his wife in the air when she told him she had decided she wanted to travel to Tande Manor for Yuletide.

"I hope we do not get caught in a snow storm," Svanhild said, still looking for an excuse to stay at Viken.

"Of course we won't get caught in a snow storm!" answered Harald. He was too overjoyed to let anything dampen his enthusiasm.

The next day they said goodbye to Dagny and Eystein as they set off for their journey. The snow was dazzling white against the black of the sleigh and the jangling metal of the horse's harness sounded like bells ringing. Svanhild was warm in her white hooded fur cape, so she could not complain about that. It would not have done her any good to complain to Harald anyway, because he was in such high spirits.

There was much excitement in the great hall when Svanhild, Olaf and Harald arrived.

"I thought you weren't coming," said Ragnhild as she helped them off with their cloaks.

"We just could not stay away," Harald said with a laugh. "You know I have not spent a Yule at Tande since I was a boy!"

"It will be just like old times," replied Guttorm, "except we will miss your father."

That comment caused a temporary pause in the conversation as Ragnhild, Harald and Guttorm thought about Halvdan, but the sound of six pairs of small feet running to greet them changed the mood.

"Hey there, my boys, come and see your new brother!" Harald shouted as three pairs of hands reached up for him.

Harald took Olaf from Svanhild's arms and knelt down to give his sons a look at the red faced infant. Gutt tried to give him a hug and Olaf began to cry.

"Let's let him go back to his mother now," he said as he rescued Olaf from more fierce hugs. "He needs to get a little bigger before he is ready to play with you big, strong boys!"

Ragnhild showed Svanhild and Olaf to the bedchamber where they would be sleeping.

"It is so nice of you to venture out in the cold with your young child," she said as she tried to make her daughter-in-law feel wanted and appreciated.

Svanhild was about to say that she hadn't really wanted to come, but she remembered the words of her mother and instead said, "I was anxious to meet you and Harald's other sons."

"They surely love their father, and he is so good with them. Halvdan did not play with Harald much until he got older, but Harald enjoys wrestling around on the floor with all three boys. They have some great pretend sword fights with their little sticks and Harald dies over and over again."

It really was enjoyable to watch her husband playing with his sons. It made Svanhild realize that she did not actually have to be jealous of these little boys, because Harald would probably give little Olaf just as much attention when he was older as well.

Everyone was having such a great time celebrating the Yule season. Harald could not remember when he had had so much fun. Ragnhild treated Svanhild like an honored guest and paid a lot of attention to baby Olaf. When her husband pleaded with her to agree to stay at Tande until spring, she surprised him by saying yes.

He and Guttorm played with the boys in the snow and let them help to brush the horses. The boys were excited to think they could each choose a colt to be their very own. It was interesting that little Halvdan the Black chose a black horse and Halvdan the White chose a white horse. Gutt chose a black one also, because he wanted to be just like his uncle Guttorm who had ridden big black Sleipni.

CHAPTER 22

THE FINAL BATTLE

Life was good. The year was 870 and there was peace in Norway. The two mighty warriors had conquered all of Norway from the kingdoms northwest at Lofoten down to Vermaland and Gautland in the southeast. They were sure Harald had finally accomplished the mission he had been given by Odin and thus it was his right to settle down and begin ruling his kingdoms as his father had done.

He had been saying as much to his mother and uncle as they sat in quiet conversation around the fire at Tande Manor. They all agreed it had been a long and hard fought battle, but Odin had been watching over them and had given them victory in each conflict.

Only the Gods know the future...and Odin must have been smiling as he listened to these three obedient servants speaking of peace. At the very time their thoughts were contemplating an end to war, a messenger was traveling to Ringsaker with news of a new threat being planned along the sea coast at Rogaland.

This new rebellion was being led by Sulke, a King of Rogaland, and his brother Jarl Sote; Eirik, a King of Hordaland; Kjotve the Rich of Agder and his son Thor Hakland; and Hroald Hryg and his brother, Had the Hard from Telemark. Not only had these seven men gathered warriors from each of their districts, they had a foreign host of English, Scotch and French soldiers who were willing to fight the great Harald Halvdansson...who had proclaimed himself King of all Norway.

When Harald and Guttorm got word of this, they began immediately to gather forces, ships and weapons from all the kingdoms that had pledged allegiance to the young King. Riders were sent north through the Uplands and on to Trondelag. Riders were sent to More and Romesdal, Firdafylke and Sogn. Other swift riders were sent to Hadeland, Toten and Ringerike.

Men with mail, shields and weapons joined them at every stop as they traveled south to Vestfold with the army from Hedmark. Jarl Eystein, who had first gotten news of the rebellion from a trader at Larvik, had already sent messages to Agder, Vingulmark, Raumarike, Vermaland and Gautland. By the time Harald and Guttorm reached Viken, the harbor between Larvik and

Tunsberg was filled with ships.

When the two leaders asked Odin for help in planning to thwart this new attack, they were told to gather at Hafrsfjord. That was the message that was sent with the riders who had traveled north and west. All the jarls were to bring as many men and ships as they could and travel along the coast to Rogaland as swiftly as possible. They were not to engage the enemy if they should encounter them, but to sail to meet King Harald and Duke Guttorm with the rest of the forces assembling in the depths of the fjord.

As each of the jarls gave the count of men and ships they had brought, Harald and Guttorm realized they were commanding a force of twenty thousand seasoned warriors in more than two hundred war ships.

King Harald and Duke Guttorm ordered the men ashore. When all were assembled, Harald told them the battle plan. He said that Odin would be watching the battle and cheering for them. Then he asked each soldier to kneel with one knee touching the soil of their mother country. Every man laid down his weapons and removed his helmet.

When they were all ready, Harald knelt to pray. He asked Odin for his guidance and his blessing. He asked that the arms of his warriors would be filled with strength and that their very lives would be protected as they carried out the oath they had taken to preserve all their kingdoms as one united nation of Norway.

As the prayer ended, Harald stood up and his men did the same. Then he led his men in a war shout so thunderous that it echoed off the very walls of the fjord.

"To Odin be the victory! To Odin be the victory! To Odin be the victory!"

Odin had told him this would be his biggest and most important battle. As he and Guttorm listened to twenty thousand warriors banging swords on their shields, they knew their army was fully prepared to fight.

King Eirik, King Sulke, and King Kjotve sailed south by Jadar to meet the foreign forces they had hired to fight along side them. The large body of men and ships headed for Rogaland and planned to gather in Hafersfjord. To their great surprise, Harald and Guttorm were already there...waiting and ready for battle.

Three great warships moved swiftly forward and led the attack. They had decided that Harald would take King Eirik, Guttorm would get King Sulke and Jarl Ragnvald would take King Kjotve. The clang of metal was deafening as sword and shield were wielded in offense and defense. Soon the shout of victory could be heard as King Eirik and King Sulke were slain.

As Thor Hakland, a mighty berserk, heard the victory shout, he laid his ship against Harald's and was determined to give the death wound to the mighty King. Berdaluke, Harald's berserk, tried to step in, but the King shouted, "He is mine! The traitor is mine!" Though Harald's_arm felt as if it would break as he wielded his sword Frey in blow after blow, Thor soon fell along with all the men of his ship.

Duke Guttorm exchanged brutal blows with Jarl Sote and gave the victory shout just after Harald. When King Kjotve heard the shouts and realized his companions were all dead, he turned his ship and ordered his men to row out of the fjord. He fled to a little island out from Rogaland and hid from the men he had sought to destroy.

When the enemy army realized all their leaders were gone, they fled also. Some rowed out to sea and others abandoned their ships and hid on the land. The vast army assembled by King Harald shouted with laughter at the sight of the cowards fleeing for their lives.

Odin was also laughing as he rode his eight-legged horse through the sky...in pursuit of the enemy who had tried to thwart his plan for Norway. Guttorm, Harald and Ragnvald looked at each other across the water as they stood in their large war ships. Miraculously, none had a blood wound, but all three had much enemy blood on their swords, shields and chain mail.

That night they gathered their forces in a grand celebration for the victory that was won that day. Harald asked for a count of soldiers they had lost. When the count came in they were amazed to find that twenty thousand warriors still lived. There were countless serious wounds among the men, but not one death.

Many sacrifices were made to the great God Odin who had blessed them in their conflict. The jarls and their men pledged allegiance anew to King Harald and Duke Guttorm. There was no question in their minds that they fought with the men who were blessed by the Gods.

So says Hornklofe,

"Has the news reached you? -- have you heard
Of the great fight at Hafersfjord,
Between our noble King brave Harald
And King Kjotve, rich in gold?
The foeman came from out the East,
Keen for the fray as for a feast.

A gallant sight it was to see
Their fleet sweep o'er the dark-blue sea;
Each war-ship, with its threatening throat
Of dragon fierce or ravenous brute
Grim gaping from the prow; its wales
Glittering with burnished shields, like scales
Its crew of udal men of war,
Whose snow-white targets shone from far
And many a mailed spearman stout
From the West countries round about,
English and Scotch, a foreign host,
And swordsmen from the far French coast.
And as the foemen's ships drew near,
The dreadful din you well might hear
Savage berserks roaring mad,
And champions fierce in wolf-skins clad,
Howling like wolves; and clanking jar
Of many a mail-clad man of war.
Thus the foe came; but our brave King
Taught them to fly as fast again.
For when he saw their force come o'er,
He launched his war-ships from the shore.
On the deep sea he launched his fleet
And boldly rowed the foe to meet.
Fierce was the shock, and loud the clang
  Of shields, until the fierce Haklang,
The foeman's famous berserk, fell.
Then from our men burst forth the yell
Of victory, and the King of Gold
Could not withstand our Harald bold,
But fled before his flaky locks
For shelter to the island rocks.
All in the bottom of the ships
The wounded lay, in ghastly heaps;
Backs up and faces down they lay
Under the row-seats stowed away;
And many a warrior's shield, I ween
Might on the warrior's back be seen,
To shield him as he fled amain
From the fierce stone-storm's pelting rain.
The mountain-folk, as I've heard say,
Ne'er stopped as they ran from the fray,
Till they had crossed the Jadar Sea,
And reached their homes – so keen each soul
To drown his fright in the mead bowl."

Heimskringla

Harald was young in age but large in stature when he became King in Halvdan's stead. After he conquered all of Norway, he was no longer a boy, but a powerful man, a seasoned warrior, and expert in the use of all weapons. The sword, Frey, that had helped Halvdan subdue seven kingdoms, had helped Harald subdue thirty one kingdoms.

After their enormous success in Hafrsfjord, Harald chose to accompany the great army of the north back through More and Raumsdal and on to Trondelag. Guttorm was to accompany the great army of the south back to their homes in Agder, Vestfold, Raumarike, Vingulmark, Vermaland and Gautland.

When they reached More, Jarl Ragnvald planned a great feast for Harald and his men. They were all in high spirits because of their tremendous victory over the jarls who had chosen to become traitors.

"This should be the last challenge to your ruling all of Norway," Ragnvald said.

"Yes, I will wish that to be so," nodded Harald.

"Do you remember now the oath that you took ten long years ago," asked Ragnvald.

"You mean the oath not to cut nor comb my hair until I had subdued all of Norway?"

"Yes, that oath! I think it is time to cut that hair of yours. Will you allow me to have the honor of cutting the hair of the mighty King Harald?"

"Yes, you may have the honor, my friend."

Jarl Ragnvald took a scissor and began to cut. The matted hair fell to the floor in large chunks. Soon there was more hair on the floor than on Harald's head. He went into the bath chamber and came out looking like a different man.

"Yours must be the most thick and fine golden hair I have ever seen," said the jarl. "Your new name should be Harald Fairhair!"

Ragnvald told the new name to all of Harald's men gathered at the feast. The warriors drank a toast to their new, more handsome leader. Soon, the word went around the country that King Harald was not to be known just as just King Harald Halvdansson anymore. From this time forward, he should be known as King Harald Fairhair Halvdansson.

That night, as he was about to lay his sword down on the bedside table, Harald thought of all the battles Frey had defended him through. He knelt to thank Odin, once again, for protecting his life and helping him to fulfill his destiny. He was grateful for the long line of warriors whose names were recorded on his special sword and whose blood he shared.

The ancestral warriors who were named on the great sword blade of Frey were:

Halvdan Whiteleg
720 AD
Fret Eystein
740 AD
Halvdan the Mild
765 AD
Gudrod the Hunter
790 AD
Halvdan the Black
830 AD
Harald Halvdanson
860 AD

CHAPTER 23

THE VOW

"Hail to thee, our Warrior King. Great is the victory thou hast won at Hafrsfjord! May we have peace in our county now and forever more!"

Enthusiastic shouts of joy and admiration overwhelmed Harald as he sailed past the loyal kingdoms along the Trondelag Fjord. Knowing they could enjoy the protection of the victorious army their King had assembled gave his people a feeling of security. He was grateful to the powerful jarls of the Tronder who had joined with him to defeat their enemies. He knew the plan to establish the Code of Law would be the means of providing justice to the upright and punishment to the outlaw.

Harald spent some days visiting his son Sigrod and Asa's mother Malfrid. It was nice to see this little boy growing up strong and true. There had been no serious problems in the Trondelag area since the last Thing was held and he was thankful to the strong jarls who ruled in his absence.

After leaving his Lade estate, he continued his journey toward Hedmark. He always enjoyed traveling down through Oppdal, then across the Dovrefjell and into the Gulbrandsdal Valley. Everywhere he stopped, word of Hafrsfjord had preceded him and the people gathered to hail him as their victorious Warrior King.

Svanhild and baby Olaf had stayed at Tande Manor when Harald and Guttorm left to do battle once more. His wife and mother were both relieved to see him back from yet another battle with no wounds. He was happy to have a few pleasant days to spend with Ragnhild and his sons, but he knew Svanhild was anxious to get back to her home.

The next morning, just as they were planning to depart for Viken, an unexpected visitor arrived. Harald opened the outer door to see a stunningly beautiful woman standing there, a woman with a mass of long, curly red hair and lovely green eyes. This visitor was destined to change the life of Harald and Svanhild forever.

"Is this King Harald who has just won a great victory at the battle in Hafrsfjord and is now the undisputed King of all Norway?" she asked.

Harald just stood in the door way, unable to think of what to say.

"I am Princess Gyda. Have you forgotten your proposal of marriage and the vow you made to me ten years ago? I am here to honor my word and become your bride."

As these last words were spoken, Svanhild stepped boldly forward from behind Harald, her eyes flashing with anger.

"I do not care if you are Princess Gyda. Harald is already married to me and I refuse to allow you to have any claim on him!"

Both women looked to Harald for reassurance that their rights would be honored, but he was still struggling for words.

"You have carried out your quest to conquer all the kingdoms of Norway...and who was it that challenged you to truly claim the title of Warrior King? You said Odin spoke it and I reaffirmed it. You made me a vow, and asked the Gods to be your witness...and took an oath that you would neither cut nor comb your hair until you had put all the many kingdoms of Norway beneath you. Then you promised to return for me. Well, I am here and I demand that you honor the vow you spoke so long ago."

The King finally found his voice. "I did truly make that vow. Now I must ask Odin for guidance," he replied, trying to avoid looking at the glaring expression on his wife's face.

Svanhild stared at her husband in disbelief. "I cannot believe you would so dishonor me by agreeing to take another wife!" she shouted.

"Odin will certainly guide Harald's actions as he has always done," assured Ragnhild, trying to mediate the situation in an effort to keep things as calm as possible

But Svanhild would have none of it. She turned and stormed down the hall to the room she had been sharing with her husband and refused to come out for the evening meal. Harald tried to talk to her and explain that he must follow Odin's instructions if he wanted to continue to be guided, but she wasn't willing to listen to his words.

After his prayer to Odin that night, the answer came in the form of a dream. He was told he must honor the vow he made to Gyda just as she had honored him by waiting for him to fulfill his oath to become King of all Norway.

This confirmation of his obligation to Gyda was lost on Svanhild. No matter what he said, she rejected his plea for understanding. She alternately cried and screamed and begged him to take her home to Viken and stay there with her and baby Olaf.

Ragnhild tried in vain to appeal to Svanhild and tell her of the dreams she and Halvdan had about Harald before he was born. She told her about Svase the Finn and the sacrifice that she had asked for and that Halvdan had paid for. She told her about Harald's dream that he should ask Gyda to marry him even though he was just eleven years old. She explained that Odin had planned the situation so that Harald would begin his quest to fulfill his destiny.

Svanhild was inconsolable. She just could not stand the thought of sharing Harald with another woman, no matter what Odin wanted. She was beside herself and demanded to be taken back to Viken. Harald agreed it might be easier to talk to her without Gyda around. They left the next day.

Through the long journey back to Vestfold, he tried to help his wife recognize his obligation, but she refused to listen. They found Guttorm at Viken and he tried speaking with Svanhild also, but she was too heartbroken to hear his words of comfort.

"You must pray to Odin and he will confirm the message he gave to me," Harald pleaded when they were alone in their bed that night.

"No! I refuse to even ask, because if he says you are right, I still can not accept it."

Harald explained the unhappy situation to her parents, Dagny and Eystein. Her mother told him to go ahead and leave for Tande and she would try to help Svanhild understand. He felt bad leaving her when she was so upset, but he hoped that she would come to understand and eventually forgive him.

Guttorm traveled back to Ringsaker with Harald. It gave them a chance to talk about this new situation.

"I was not really thinking about Gyda during the time we were fighting our battles. Even when Ragnvald cut my hair, I thought of my oath, but not my vow to marry Gyda. Maybe I thought she would have found someone else by now."

"It seems she is just as proud and determined a woman as she was when she was fifteen," Guttorm answered.

"Well I know one thing for sure...she is even more beautiful than I ever remembered her to be. It might have been easier for Svanhild if she had been ugly!"

Ragnhild had asked Gyda to stay with her at Tande Manor until the situation could be worked out. She was glad for an opportunity to get acquainted while they waited for Harald's return. She told her about the situation that had brought about her own marriage and that she had also known her husband a very short time before her wedding in this very manor house, twenty two years earlier.

"I can not imagine a happier life than I had with Halvdan. I feel Odin had a hand in my circumstances also."

Gyda confided her story of being fostered out as a baby when her mother died. Her father, Eirik, had lived far away in Hordaland. He was so displeased that she was a daughter and not a son that he never visited her...not even once. She only knew she was his daughter when her foster mother told her it was so. Her foster parents were kind, but they thought her too proud and assertive and were relieved when she told them she was leaving.

When the two men arrived at Tande Manor, Harald sought out Gyda."I am prepared to honor my vow," he reported to her with all seriousness.

She was relieved to hear him say the words, but was disappointed that he showed none of the interest in her he had expressed during his first proposal of marriage ten years earlier.

The wedding was planned to be held in a fortnight. Ragnhild and Gyda spent their days in preparation for the solemn occasion. Guttorm and Harald spent their days outside working with the horses and the men and trying to make a plan for the future.

"It is too bad she did not come here to marry you, Guttorm. That would surely have made my life easier!"

"It was not me that gave the vow, and it was not me that she has waited for these last ten years."

"That is true. As strange as it will seem to have two wives at the same time, I do not want to question Odin."

"Of course, if you had died at Harfrsfjord, then you could have avoided this situation!" Guttorm said with a smile.

"When you put it that way, I guess things could be worse!"

In the evenings, Ragnhild and Guttorm lingered at the table for a while and then excused themselves so Gyda and Harald would have some time to get better acquainted.

"Have you any feelings of anger against me for the death of your father?" he asked.

"I hold no feelings of anger because my father was a stranger to me. He sent me away when I was a baby and gave me nothing but his name. I think Odin has punished him by keeping him childless throughout the rest of his life."

"Being childless would indeed be a great curse," Harald agreed.

"I think there is no danger of that curse in your life!" she countered.

"You are right. I have already been blessed with five fine sons."

"I pray that the curse of childlessness will not follow me," she exclaimed.

"I pray the same," he said as he moved closer and put his arm around her waist.

She looked up into the face of the man she had agreed to marry so many years ago. If anything, he had become even more handsome than she had remembered. She could feel the hard muscles of his arm as it touched her back and the hard muscles of his leg where it touched hers. He was younger than her, but wore an air of confidence honed on the battlefield...as well as in the bedchamber.

In her mind, Gyda said she was marrying Harald for his power and position as King of all Norway. It was true that she was proud...pride was about all she had. She had grown up without the love of a mother or father, and she wasn't sure she really knew how to feel love, but she thought she just might be able to learn to love this brave, heroic conquering warrior.

Before long, the day of the wedding ceremony arrived. When Harald saw Gyda come walking down the hallway toward him, it almost took his breath away. He was sure now that she was the most beautiful maiden he had ever seen. She wore an emerald green gown that exactly matched her eyes and set off the thick red curls that rested on her shoulders. She wore earrings of gold that fell to the skin of her neck and two large brooches with many colored stones.

Guttorm stood next to Harald and watched her come walking toward them. His mind went back to the first time he had seen her when he went to seek her hand for the eleven year old King. She had been fifteen years old at the time, and yet she had known what she wanted out of life...and now she was here to claim it.

Neighbors and friends, who had known Harald during his youth, were happy to be included in seeing him marry at Tande Manor. They knew he had been married twice before, but now they were able to partake of the large wedding feast and wish the newly wed couple Odin's blessing.

Soon enough, the day came to an end. The guests had left the great hall and Ragnhild was supervising the serving maids in their work of cleaning up after the large crowd.

"Do you need any help, Mother?" Harald asked.

"No. Do not worry about me. You two just go ahead. Most of this will be done tomorrow," she answered.

It seemed an awkward moment as they stood together in that large room. Amid all of the well-wishers, there hadn't really been time to think of the end of the day and the expectations that came with the marriage night. He was surprised at himself. After all, he was the one with experience. It was up to him to guide his new wife through this night of consummation.

"We will sleep in the bedchamber that has been mine since I was a boy," he said as he took her by the hand and led her down the hallway.

She had been using a guest bedchamber near to his in the few weeks since she had arrived.

"I will just change out of my wedding gown in my room," she said, and then corrected herself, "I mean, my former room."

"That will be fine," he said. "I will be waiting for you when you are ready."

She was more nervous than she thought she would be. Even though she did not have a mother to prepare her for this first night of lying with a man, she thought she knew enough to get by. The new white linen gown that Ragnild had given her was laid out on the bed. She had visited the bathing house in the morning, so she was sure her body would smell fresh and clean.

The floor boards in the hallway made a squeaking sound as she tiptoed to Harald's room. When she reached the door, she felt like she should knock, but then thought better of it. She opened the door slowly and looked in to see her new husband relaxing on top of the quilts, also wearing a new linen nightshirt. There was just one large candle burning on the bed stand, but she could see the smile on his face even in the dim light.

"Welcome to my bedchamber," he said as he rose to meet her.

He took her hand and shut the door behind her, then put her hand to his lips and gave it a sweet kiss.

"Your hair looks as lovely against the white of your night gown as it did against the green of your wedding gown," he said as he touched it where it lay on her shoulders.

She was still standing just inside the door, waiting for him to lead the way. They had only exchanged one kiss, and that had been this afternoon after they had spoken the marriage vows. He looked into her green eyes and tried to read the emotions that he saw there. Certainly, this proud woman was not feeling fear.

"Come over to the bed and lie down with me," he coaxed.

She followed him without saying a word. She lay on her back in the middle of the bed and he lay on his side facing her. His left hand held his head as his right hand played with the red curls that lay spread out on the eiderdown pillow.

"It must seem strange to you to lie with a man you hardly know," he said.

"Does it seem strange to you to lie with a woman you hardly know?" she countered.

"Are you asking if I have had this experience before?" he questioned.

She was a little embarrassed by his question. "It seems to be the way of a man......"

"The way of a man can be hard or it can be soft. It can be filled with love or it can be filled with coarseness. I prefer it to be filled with love."

"I have not known love in my life, not even the love of parents, so I am not sure I am capable of love."

"Are you planning to be my wife, but never love me?"
"I cannot say, for I do not know. You certainly cannot say you love me this day."

"Though I have not had time to learn to love you in my heart, I do intend to love you," he assured her.

"When I determined to come here and insist that you honor your vow by marrying me, I expected you to do what you have done today, but I did not expect love."

"Are you saying that you do not want my love?"

"I am saying that I have never felt love from another, and I have never felt love for another, so I am content to live without it."

"But what if I am not content to live without it?"

"I am sure you must get plenty of love from Svanhild!"

"Yes, I get plenty of love from Svanhild, but that doesn't mean I do not want some from you, also."

"I am prepared to give you my fidelity and my body. Is not that enough?"

"A body devoid of love is just a body. I could get that anywhere. I want your body to want my body. That is when there is true meaning. Maybe we can not expect that tonight, but I hope that desire will grow within you."

"Yes, I could hope for that also," she admitted with a low whisper.

"Do you like kissing?" he asked enthusiastically.

"Yours are the first lips that have ever touched mine."

"Well, I like kissing before everything else," he said with a smile.

"You lead the way and I will try to follow," she smiled back.

This was going to be an interesting wedding night, he thought to himself, certainly different from Asa and even different from his first_night with Svanhild. He knew there must be a flame in there somewhere. It would be an enjoyable challenge to try to light it.

She was the first to awaken in the morning and she lay quite comfortably covered by the eiderdown quilts. Her husband was still fast asleep and she enjoyed just looking at his handsome face. Was it really possible to feel love for this great man? She hadn't expected to be treated with such gentleness, but then, she hadn't really known what to expect. She would like to know what love really felt like. She was glad that he expected to love her and wanted her love in return.

Just then, the sleeping giant rolled over and she found herself trapped under a muscular arm and a heavy leg. She stood it as long as she could and then began to tickle his nose with a stray curl. One eye opened and then another, and then a smile crept across his face.

"You are just as beautiful in the morning as you are at night," he exclaimed and tightened his grip on her body.

"You are about to crush me," she said laughingly.

"Oh, if you want me to crush you, how about this?" he asked as he rolled his whole body over on top of hers.

"I can not even breathe!" she panted.

"Let me look! Is there any love in there yet?" he asked as he opened the front of her night gown and peeked inside.

"If there is, it is probably going to get squeezed out of me!" she protested.

"How about letting me see what is under that nightgown?" he teased.

"Did you see it last night?"

"No. I had my eyes closed!"

"That is too bad," she teased back.

"I will show you what is under my night shirt!" he offered.

"But you do not even have your night shirt on!"

"I know, but I will show you what is under this quilt. Did no one ever tell you that is one of the best things about sharing a marriage bed?"

"No one ever told me anything."

"Well, I am telling you now. I will even go first," he said as he threw the quilt aside.

It was something of a shock to see a man's full body without any clothes on it, but his smile was so engaging that it made her laugh.

"Alright, now it is your turn," he encouraged as he began to pull up the bottom of her gown.

She lay staring up at the boards above her head. She could guess what he was doing, but she did not protest. He slowly lifted her gown off her bare legs, and continued on until she was totally uncovered. Suddenly, a shiver went through her body.....not from cold, but from excitement.

"I think that shiver was just a little bit of love trying to escape!" he said as he began to kiss her bare skin.

She wasn't sure what it was, but it felt more wonderful than anything she had ever felt before.

They stayed at Tande Manor for a fortnight after the marriage feast and then traveled back to Tune with Guttorm. Gyda enjoyed the feeling of importance she experienced while traveling with these two important and impressive men. Everywhere they stopped, she could see the admiration and respect that people paid to her husband and his uncle. She thought she also saw admiration and respect in their eyes when they looked at her...and she liked the feeling.

When she shared those thoughts with Harald in their bed that night, he just laughed at her.

"A woman as beautiful as you are would see admiration in any one's eyes, even if you rode next to a thrall! People are probably lying in their beds this night wondering where I found my red haired beauty!"

She did not really believe him, but it gave her a thrill to hear him say it. All those years she had sat at Dalin Manor in Valdres waiting for Harald to come and claim her seemed now but a moment. He had definitely been worth waiting for. She hadn't been sure what to expect when she left her foster parent's home to travel to Tande Manor, but things had turned out even better than she could have imagined.

After a few days in Tune, they were ready to board the ships for the long voyage around the southern tip of Norway. Gyda felt like she was seeing her country for the first time...and she was. She hadn't traveled anywhere, and now she had seen Eidsvold, Raumarike and also Vingulmark all on their journey southward.

They had barely set sail, when Harald mentioned that Vestfold was just across the fjord. She wondered where Svanhild lived, but she did not ask. Soon they passed the large kingdom of Agder, then on to Jadar and Rogaland and up to Hordaland.

When Harald told her he was going to give her Eidsvag, her ancestral home, for a bride gift, she was overwhelmed. She hadn't really thought about where she would live, but to go back to her birthplace seemed like a dream come true. In her heart, she hoped her father was looking down from his place in Valhalla. Maybe living there would free her of some of the hatred she harbored for him...and maybe she could even feel her mother's spirit lingering there.

"Well, there it is," said Harald as he pointed to a huge manor house rising above the surrounding hills.

"Is that really my home?" she asked with a catch in her throat.

"That is Eidsvag Manor, former home of King Eirik. I think you will like it here," he said, turning to her with a smile.

"Thank you, Harald. You have made me so happy!" she exclaimed.

"They say a happy woman makes a happy man!" he teased.

"Then we must both be happy," she replied, ignoring his inference.

The home really was lovely. One could stand at the front door and turn to look at the rolling sea and smell the salt in the breeze. The rooms were large and the walls were covered by wonderful tapestries. Gyda wondered if the scenes portrayed on them depicted her father's successful battles. Beautiful green hangings draped the large bed in the master bedchamber.

"Green must have been your mother's favorite color also."

"Yes, they look as if they must have been here when she was still living. I wonder if she was buried here in the yard."

"Why don't we look outside and see?" he said, as she turned and walked toward the door.

They found the large stone on the side of the house, just outside the master bedchamber.

"I think your father must have loved your mother very much."

"Yes, it does seem as if that must be so."

"Because he died at sea, there is not a burial mound for him. May be you would like to add a stone for him next to your mother's."

She turned to look up at him. "Are you that generous a man that you would pay to have a stone made for a man who tried to kill you?"

"I think I will forget that part of his life and just honor him for bringing me my lovely wife."

"You really do know how to make a woman happy, don't you?"

"I am working on kindling that little flame of love that I lit down in there," he answered as he wrapped his arm around her waist and pointed to her heart.

She reached up and gave him a warm kiss and responded, "You just keep working on that little flame and it just might turn into a fire!"

"I'm counting on it!" he smiled and returned her warm kiss.

Harald stayed with Gyda for two months and then decided he had better return to Viken before the winter storms set in. He knew how Svanhild felt about having him with her at Yuletide, and he did not want to make her any more upset than she already was. He hoped her parents had helped her to understand the importance of keeping his vow...even though it meant marriage to another woman.

"I have always spent Yuletide with Svanhild since we have been married, and I feel I must continue to do that. Are you going to be alright with my leaving you after such a short time?"

Gyda looked at her husband as he sought her understanding. She wanted to say that Svanhild was a spoiled child, but she did not want to fall into the trap of showing the same immature behavior as she had seen in her rival.

"You must choose for yourself how you will manage to keep two wives happy."

"Ah yes, a happy woman makes a happy man!" he said with a smile.

"I suppose two happy women make for a really happy man!" she countered.

"You are so right!" he chuckled and kissed her enthusiastically. "I just hope my little flame doesn't go out while I am away!"

"Well, you had better not stay away too long or you will have to start all over again," she laughed.

It was lighthearted fun, but she really did think she would miss him. It was hard to remember the time when he was not a part of her life, and even harder to imagine what life would be like if he was never to be a part of it again. Fortunately, she did not have to imagine that, because he assured her that he would be back to her as soon as the spring thaw started.

Eidsvag Manor sat right along the coast with the same marvelous sunsets that he had enjoyed while staying in More. How exciting it was to walk along the cliff edge in the afternoon sun and hear the crashing of waves on the rocky shore. Gyda was enjoying life in Hordaland. It made her feel like she was home to be back on her ancestral estate...the one her father had deprived her of while she was growing to womanhood.

From the moment she awoke in the morning, Gyda smiled at the thought of the many blessings now in her life. She had married the great Warrior King and he actually seemed to like her. It was possible he would even grow to love her as she worked at returning some of the affection he showed her. The large estate where she was born was now hers to command in her husband's absence. She could not imagine a better bride gift. She loved walking the same floors that her mother had walked so many years before.

Aside from those blessings, she could feel new life beginning to grow within her, and she felt so fulfilled as a woman. She could not wait for the chance to hold this new life in her arms and shower it with all the love she had been denied in her own childhood. Yes, life was much better than anything she had imagined.

Svanhild had realized she was with child just after Harald left Viken. At first she wanted to tell him because she thought he might leave Gyda at Tande and come back home. Her mother refused to send the message, saying Gyda had a right to have several months with Harald after their wedding just as she had...to enjoy getting to know each other.

But she did not want him to spend time with his new wife, stating that, after all, he does not even love her...he just married her because of Odin's command. Her mother reminded her, gently, that Harald was in that same situation two years ago when Odin told him he was to marry her when he was still in love with Asa. Svanhild did not want to hear that, but she realized her mother was right.

"We will send a message to Harald when you are about to deliver this baby and I am sure he will come then," Dagny said soothingly.

She wasn't actually sure if Harald would come, but she knew she had to say something to pacify her daughter. How grateful she was that her husband Eystein had never taken a second wife. It would truly be hard to share the man you loved with another...especially a woman as beautiful as Gyda.

A message reached Harald that Svanhild was about to have her baby and wanted him to come and be with her. He traveled to Viken in time to see that he had another son. Harald poured water over him and gave him the name of Bjorn. Svanhild was so thrilled to have Harald back with her. She had to force herself to avoid any mention of Gyda.

Yuletide approached and with it came the celebration of peace and prosperity. Dagny and Eystein plus Svanhild's brothers and their families gathered at Viken. No one mentioned Harald's new wife and Svanhild was content to play the happy hustru and show off her new baby.

Most of the winter months were spent at Viken with a few journeys to Tande Manor. Harald went by himself. He knew better than to suggest that his wife travel there with him. He realized that a visit to Tande would always bring the traumatic events of Gyda's arrival into Svanhild's memory.

A pleasant surprise was waiting for him when he traveled to Eidsvag in the spring.

"If you had sent me a message I would have returned to be here when you were giving birth," Harald told Gyda.

"I am not such a child as Svanhild that I can not have a baby without a husband waiting outside the birthing chamber!" she retorted.

"I did not mean to infer that you needed me...but I would have come."

His kind words softened her sharpness.

"I did not mean to say that I did not want you here. I guess I am so used to having only myself to depend on, that I did not think to ask you to return," Gyda said quietly. "Are you disappointed that I did not give you a son?"

"I already have six sons! You have given me what I have not had, a lovely daughter."

Gyda was relieved to hear Harald say that. She knew every man wanted many sons, but she was happy to have a daughter.

"What shall we name this little one?" he asked as he lifted the child up to his face.

"I would like to name her after my mother. Even though I never knew her, I always wanted to feel her presence. Each time I call my daughter's name, I will be calling her name also."

Harald turned to look at his wife.

"Did I hear you say that this is only your daughter?"

"Well, I did say that, but I guess I have to recognize that she is also a part of you."

"We shall see how she acts when she grows up. If she is naughty, I will say she is your daughter. When she is nice, then I will say she is mine!"

Gyda just smiled at that comment. It was nice to have a husband who actually cared about his children. She had seen that in Harald as she watched him with his sons while she was at Tande Manor. Because she hadn't known her own father, she did not really know what to expect of her husband.

He poured water over the girl child and pronounced her name as Alov Arbot. She cried loudly as the cold water ran down her neck.

"Let me take her," said Gyda.

"I will give her over to you now when she is crying, but remember, when she is nice, she is mine!"

Gyda smiled as she soothed the crying infant. She was happy to be a mother at last. Harald, who had never had a brother or a sister, was starting to enjoy having such a large family.

Harald stayed in Hordaland until after the Spring Equinox. He held the Gulathing for Rogaland, Hordaland, and Firdafylke along the coast, then sailed north to More and Romsdal to confer with Jarl Ragnvald. He presided over a Thing there and then traveled up to Lofoten. He was pleased to find there wasn't even one murder to deal with at the northern Thing.

Next, he spent a fortnight at Lade, taking time with his son Sigrod. It felt great to be back in the Trondelag area and meeting with the jarls who were overseeing the eight kingdoms that surrounded the Trondelag Fjord. He presided over the large Frostathing, listening to the many serious crimes that came before him and meting out the proper punishments.

Hundorp was the location for the Thing held in Gulbrandsdal. Harald liked to pay a visit to Thjoldolf at Hvin when he traveled through this area. Thjoldolf was a great skald and an expert in creating verses that told of the life of his friend, King Harald.

He chose to visit Hedmark next and planned to stop at Tande Manor before and after holding the Thing at Vang. He spent the last months of summer traveling through Toten and Hadeland before presiding over the Eidsvolthing in Romerike.

Svanhild was so glad to see him when he arrived at Viken. She knew he always visited the market in Tunsberg to buy her a gift. This time it was some beautiful brown silk fabric with gold embroidery on the edge.

"Oh Harald, this will make a lovely new dress for me to wear during Yuletide," she laughed as she twirled around with the fabric draped over her shoulders. "You will be here for Yuletide, won't you?"

"Do I not always spend Yule with you here at Viken?" he asked with a raise of his eyebrow.

She went quickly to where he was seated and put her arms around his neck. She wanted to mention the Yule spent at Tande, but she did not want to displease him.

"This home is always full of laughter and good cheer when you are here. That is all I meant."

He looked at her bright smile and answered back with a smile of his own. He did love Svanhild, but she could be a trial at times. Olaf and Bjorn were growing to be fine little boys and he was pleased to see that they were healthy and strong.

While Harald was enjoying the Yule season in Viken with Svanhild, Guttorm spent Yuletide with Ragnhild and the boys at Tande. The weather was much more mild along the fjord than in Hedmark, and Harald's bodyguard enjoyed many of the outdoor games, such as pole throwing, bat and ball and wrestling. It was always important for warriors to keep their body strong and healthy...and ready for combat at all times.

In the spring, as Harald set out for Rogaland and Hordaland, Guttorm traveled up through the center of the country, checking on Ringerike, Toten, Hadeland, and Hedmark. He stopped at Tande Manor, where Ragnhild and Gutt, Halvdan the Black and Halvdan the White were waiting to travel with him to Lade in Trondelag. They enjoyed spending the summer months with their younger brother Sigrod.

When Harald arrived in Trondelag, after traveling through the coastal kingdoms, the men and boys enjoyed a long month together swimming and fishing, sailing and riding their horses. Soon it was time for the three oldest boys to travel back to Ringsaker for harvest season and then Yuletide.

Life began to take on a routine...and for the most part, everyone was happy. Svanhild was the least happy, because she had never really reconciled herself to the fact that Harald had another wife. Harald was now twenty four winters and Svanhild was twenty two. Their third son, Ragnar, was born in the year 874. They celebrated the fact that they had been married for six years and had three healthy sons.

Harald spent the first few years trying to convince Svanhild that he still loved her, despite the fact that he had another wife...but talking about it just caused hurt feelings. So eventually, he gave up saying anything about Gyda. He tried to make both Svanhild and Gyda feel that they were loved, and they were...in a manner of speaking...but neither one of them had his whole heart in the same way that Asa had.

He had married Gyda in the year 870, when he was twenty one winters and she was twenty five. She gave him his first daughter and he loved spoiling her with presents every time he traveled to Eidsvag Manor. Gyda told him she wanted to give him as many sons as his first wife...and she succeeded.

Rorek was born in 873, Sigtrygg was born in 875, Frode was born in 877 and Torgils was born in 879. She was proud of the fact that she had three sons after Svanhild had her last son. Gyda felt that meant she had more claim to Harald's time and affection than his other wife.

She really did not want to act childish and jealous like Svanhild, but secretly, she liked the competition and felt she was winning. All of her children were born with red hair and she proudly believed that was a gift from the Gods!

CHAPTER 24

THE SPELL

Peace had come to Norway and all was going well...until the summer of 880 AD when Harald took his yearly trip to the Lofoten Islands. While there, he always stayed at the Borg estate with Jarl Jens who ruled in his absence. After the meeting of the Thing, there was a large feast prepared for him and his men.

Just as the feast was over, a servant came in to say there was a visitor to see King Harald. When the visitor came to stand in front of the high seat, Harald could see that the man looked familiar. Was it just the light of the fire that caused the gleam in the man's eye, he wondered.

Then the man spoke, "Certainly you remember me, My Lord."

"I have met many men in my travels, but there is a look about you that seems to recall a person I might know."

"We spent time together after Yuletide some years back and you made me a promise that you would give me aid if ever I was in need."

"Well, if I gave that promise, then you may be assured I am as good as my word. But, tell me, sir, what is your name?"

"My name is one you will know the moment I speak it. I am Svase the Finn."

Harald rose to his feet and shouted, "Remove this man from my presence!"

"But you have just told me you are as good as your word! Is the word of the mighty King Harald now of no worth?" spoke the Finn as Berdaluke was about to drag him from the room.

All eyes were on Harald. He had just spent the day with these men at the Thing talking about fairness and justice. Now the Finn was challenging his word and accusing him of being a liar. Those who were sitting along the tables in the great hall at Borg could not know of the evil this man had caused in the life of Harald and his father Halvdan.

"What is the aid you are requesting of me?" he asked in a calmer voice.

"My daughter has a great fever. She has said that if she could only touch the hand of the great King Harald, then she would be made whole."

Harald decided he would have to go with the Finn as he had requested. He had nothing to fear. He was not a boy, this time, and he would bring along ten of his most able men.

Though the hour was late, Svase pressed him to leave immediately. The King and his men followed the Finn over the ridge and into the deep forest. They came to the small hut just as the sun was rising.

"Ask your men to retreat down the hill a ways," said Svase, "that they may not frighten my maiden."

Harald gave the order that Svase had requested. The hut was in a clearing but sat in front of a large outcropping of rock. He led Harald to the door and opened it carefully. When the two men stepped inside the dark space, they saw a woman standing behind the fire pit. The golden glow of the flames and the red embers cast an eerie glow on her long white hair and flowing white robe.

"This is my lovely daughter Snofrid."

Harald stared at the young woman whose dark eyes seemed to penetrate his very soul.

"I have come, at your father's request, to offer you my aid," he said as he walked toward her.

"Thou art indeed the generous man my father has told me about," she answered. "Wilt thou share a cup of mead with me?"

"I will," he answered.

Those were the last words Harald uttered under his own power. As he reached to take the cup of mead, his hands encircled those of Snofrid, and a burning raced up his arms and consumed his whole body. He stared into the face of the woman with the black eyes and wild white hair and he was transfixed.

"Please drink your mead, My Lord."

He wanted to drink, but he did not want to let go of her hands. She gently lifted the cup to his lips and let him drink. The hot mead added to the burning sensation that filled his body and he felt weak and helpless.

"Come and lie with me on my bed," she whispered in his ear.

Harald still held her hands and followed her to the bed in the deep recesses of the hut. He had never felt so helpless. He wanted to do whatever she said. Snofrid climbed up onto the bed and Harald climbed up after her. She laid her sinewy body on top of his and wrapped his arms around her.

He was absolutely on fire. He felt like he was lying in the middle of the fire pit as the light from the flames made her face glow red and golden. She ran her hands over his body and he was completely in her power. Just when he was about to succumb to the desires she had awakened within him, he was brought back to reality by the sound of the Finn's voice whispering in his ear.

"A man of your stature would surely not steal that which is most precious from my daughter without first making her your wife!"

Harald looked into the matching eyes of both father and daughter. He could not think for himself. All he knew was that he wanted this woman, wanted her more than he had ever wanted another woman in his life.

"We can call your men to come up and be witnesses for your marriage vows and Snofrid can be in your bridal bed this very day," the Finn urged.

"Yes, that would be simple, that was what he must do," thought Harald.

"Call for my men immediately!" he ordered.

Snofrid never let go of his hands. When they could hear the voices of the men outside the hut, she led Harald to the doorway. There, with her father and his men looking on, Harald repeated the marriage vow that Snofrid coaxed him to say. Immediately, she led him back inside the hut and closed the door.

Harald was in a daze. Snofrid had held his hands and kept his face looking directly into her gaze during the whole time they said the vows. He had a brief impression of his ten men standing outside the hut with a puzzled look on their faces, but now he was back in the dark of the windowless hut. Snofrid was in charge, and he was willing to do whatever she asked of him.

The enticing witch led him back to the bed and made him sit down on the edge. She stood in front of him with the glow of the fire outlining the edges of the gown she was wearing. She reached down, grabbed the hem of her dress, lifted it off her head and dropped it to the floor. There she stood in stark nakedness in front of him. Her body looked as red as the fire behind her and his body felt as hot as if he was filled with fire.

He quickly pulled his clothes off and lifted her on top of him. This

ad ever had before. He wasn't really
felt like an animal, like a bear or a
s.

t really know. The room was dark and
hen he was exhausted, he slept. When
on with more mead. Days went by and
d not even remember his life before the
Finn and his daughter, Snofrid.

eturn to Borg without him. When they
he mountains, he told them he did not
e waited one fortnight and then two.
the hut and ask Harald if he was ready
ned.

nse forest of the mountains before they
looked like the one where they had left
Harald. Unfortunately, there was one inside. The fire pit was there, but there was no fire burning. They found the bed in the corner of the hut, but there was no bedding and no sign that anyone had been there recently.

What Harald's men had not taken into account was the fact that they were dealing with Svase the Finn. He was a warlock and could see the men coming to look for their King before they even reached the forest. In searching the dark hut, they could not see the narrow opening in the fold of the rock outcropping.

Behind this narrow space there was a large cave where Svase and Snofrid had taken Harald. The dark of the cave seemed not that much different than the dark of the hut to him. There was a wide space, deep within the cave, where they could build a fire and keep some bedding on which to sleep. An opening on the far side of the cave allowed Svase to come and go unseen.

After he was sure Harald's men had given up and returned to Lofoten, Svase and Snofrid brought Harald back to the hut. This time Harald was easier to control than the last time Svase had taken him from his home. Then Harald wanted to return to his parents and his dog and horse. Those were the strong yearnings of a boy.

But they were nothing in comparison to the strength of a man's drive for sexual pleasures. With Snofrid's help, Svase was sure he could keep Harald captive for a long time, at least long enough for him to have sired a grandson or two. These grandsons would be legitimate Princes of Norway and would give Svase the power and prestige he had never known as a poor Finnish man.

When they gave up the search for Harald, Berdaluke decided to take charge of the men and sail for Trondelag. After hearing the berserker's report, Ragnhild and Guttorm knew they had good reason to worry. They had not heard the name of Svase the Finn for many years, but it brought back all the old concerns to hear his name spoken again.

"I tried to keep him from going with the Finn," said Berdaluke, "but King Harald's honor was at stake. Svase claimed the King had given his word, so he was bound to keep it. When he came to the door of that hut and said wedding vows to the Finn's daughter, he looked like a man in a trance. I wanted to run up and grab him and take him out of there, but the Finn had put a spell on the ten of us who were waiting for Harald and we were helpless to do anything but witness the sham of a marriage."

"What shall we do?" Ragnhild asked Guttorm.

"I shall travel to Lofoten immediately. Svase the Finn will not stop me from rescuing Harald!" he insisted.

But Guttorm had no more success at finding Harald than Berdaluke had. Though he brought with him a force of five hundred men from Trondelag and More, there was no trace of Harald or the Finn and his daughter. When they finally found the hut, it was empty as before.

As the weather grew colder and the days grew shorter, Guttorm left one hundred of his men with Jarl Jens at Borg and returned to Trondelag. He hated to think of telling Ragnhild that her son was still missing at the hands of the warlock.

"I guess we had begun to take our good fortune for granted," she told her brother. "We thought Harald's battles were behind him and we could live out our lives in peace and comfort. Why could not Odin have protected him from the Finn as he protected his life while he was conquering the kingdoms of Norway?"

"I do not know the answer to that question," he said, "but I know Harald would never have agreed to marry a daughter of Svase the Finn if he was not under some spell."

"How can we get him out from under that spell if we can not even find him?" his mother asked with a note of frustration in her voice.

"About all we can do is pray that Odin will watch over him and help us find him when spring comes to the north."

And that is what they did...pray every day throughout that long winter.

Guttorm sent a message to Svanhild that they would be spending Yuletide at Lade Manor. He knew she would be unhappy about that, but she would be even more unhappy if she knew the real reason Harald was not going to spend Yule at Viken this year.

But spring turned to summer and there was no good news about Harald. Guttorm had traveled to Eidsvag in Hordaland to tell Gyda that her husband would not be visiting her at this time. It was harder to avoid questions when he looked into her piercing green eyes.

"Where is Harald? His children want to see him and so do I!"

"Harald went into the mountain forests outside of Lofoten and he is lost. I am going there with one thousand men in a few days and we will search until we find him!" Guttorm said with an assurance that he did not feel.

Gyda stared at him in amazement.

"Are you telling me he has spent the winter in the forests of the north and you are just now going to look for him?"

Guttorm began to squirm. "I brought five hundred men up there last year after harvest time, but we could not find him."

"I thought you were the great Duke Guttorm, the one who was by Harald's side through every battle...and you left him to fend for himself in a frozen forest?"

She felt a little guilty when she saw the pain come unto Guttorm's face as she asked that last question, but she could not help it. She wanted her husband back. He had given her five children, but that was not enough. She had grown to love him dearly over the last eleven years and she did not want to lose him to death in a snowstorm.

"If I did not have my five children that need me, I would go and look for him myself!" she said in exasperation.

"I assure you, Gyda, I am just as anxious to find him as you are. You have known him only eleven years, whereas I have known him since the day he was born!"

They were both hurt by the other's words, but Gyda was the first to act. She rose from her chair and walked over to where Guttorm was standing. She put her arms around him and began to cry. He patted her on the back and tried to comfort her, but he felt like crying himself.

When Guttorm stopped at More, Ragnvald insisted on traveling with him to Lofoten and bringing an additional five hundred men. Surely, one thousand and five hundred men would be able to find one man, even though the forests were extremely thick in that part of Norway.

Guttorm hadn't told Gyda about Svase the Finn and his daughter. The fewer people who knew that information the better...especially Harald's two wives. The last time the Finn held Harald captive, he had used a magic birch wand, medicinal berries and the power of his gaze to keep him from breaking free. This time, he used all of those things plus his secret weapon...Snofrid.

A boy child had been born to Snofrid in the spring and Svase was overjoyed. He chose to name the boy Halvdan, after Harald's arrogant father who had ordered the Finn off his land. He wondered if old Halvdan could look down and see that he now had a Finnish grandson, he who had insisted, "You can never trust a Finn!"

Svase was about ready to let Harald go after they had gotten a child from his loins, but Snofrid said, "No!" She was enjoying having Harald's attentions. It was much more enjoyable than life had been here on the mountain with just her father for company.

"He will give me at least one more son," she said, "and then we shall see!"

Svase did not argue with her. He could control almost everyone else, but Snofrid knew all of his tricks and she had some of her own.

They spent almost the whole summer in the cave. There were so many of Harald's men combing the forest looking for him, that Svase barely had a chance to collect the herbs and berries he needed to make the potions. And the potions were needed to keep Harald in the trance that made him powerless.

Guttorm and Ragnvald and their men spent the whole summer in the forest outside of Lofoten searching for Harald. Many times they searched the empty hut where he had last been seen, but they never discovered the space in the rock that led to the cave where Harald was being held captive.

After harvest time, they left for the southern waters...before the snow and ice made sailing too difficult. Guttorm asked Ragnvald to travel to Hordaland and try to explain to Gyda why they had not been able to find Harald.

He would sail into Trondelag and try to console Ragnhild and the boys. He knew he should also go in person down to Vestfold to comfort Svanhild, but he just did not have the heart to do it. He sent a messenger instead.

Svanhild took the news better than Gyda. Though she still loved Harald and sorely missed him, she would rather have him missing in the woods than knowing he was in Hordaland...sleeping with Gyda.

The anxious mother had prayed to Odin every day since she first heard her son was missing, pleading with the God to send her Harald back home. Next, she started praying that he would just keep him alive. She was back to praying for a dream that would tell her where he was...but no dream came.

By the time the next summer came and Guttorm was ready to travel back to Lofoten, Ragnhild had begun to wonder if Odin had taken Harald to Valhalla. Maybe her son's work was finished, now that he had fulfilled his mission of uniting all the kingdoms of Norway under one rule and establishing Halvdan's code of law in each area. However, when she asked Odin if Harald was in heaven with him, she felt the answer was, "No."

The summer of 882 was a repeat of 881 for almost everyone. Snofrid had another son who Svase named Gudrod after Harald's grandfather. He enjoyed choosing royal names for these grandsons. He was sure that they would not get treated like he had been. Harald had been so long in the cave that he hardly even remembered he had a former life.

This year, Guttorm and Ragnvald brought two thousand men up to Lofoten to search for Harald. They had no more success than the previous years. There did not seem to be anything else to do but just keep searching. One thing they knew...no one wanted to give up on trying to find their King.

In the year 883, a third son was born who Svase named Sigurd for Harald's other grandfather. Twelve months later Snofrid bore her fourth son to Harald and mysteriously died. Svase, who helped her deliver the infant, was in a panic. Certainly he must know a spell that would awaken her from death. He tried every potion he could think of and spread her body with medicinal herbs, but she would not regainconsciousness.

When Harald came to see her, she would not open her eyes. This confused him. He had become accustomed to asking her what she wanted him to do, but now she would not wake up. Svase tried to talk to Harald and get him to look in his eyes, but he would not move his gaze off of Snofrid.

Day after day, Harald sat by her side. He talked to her, he kissed her, he held her hands, but she would not speak to him. He was lost and did not know what to do. He would not drink the mead or eat the berries that Svase offered him. The Finn was trying to care for the four boys and could hardly be bothered with Harald.

Snofrid had still been feeding her three older boys with the milk from her breasts and now they were crying and trying to climb on her dead body. Harald kept pushing them away. He did not even associate the fact that these were the offspring of his body. Snofrid had been his whole world for the last four years. She had controlled his thoughts and his actions and now he did not know what to do.

Svase was afraid Harald would injure or even kill the boys as he aggressively shoved them away from their mother. He decided to take the boys and the new baby back into the hut and keep them there while he tried to tend to them. He began to wish he had gotten rid of Harald when Snofrid had just one or two boys. Four children were going to be hard for him to manage.

Back in the cave, Harald still sat by his wife's dead body. He was sure she would awaken at any moment and then she would tell him what she wanted him to do. Finally, the fire burned itself out for lack of tending, and he laid his head on her breast and fell into a deep sleep.

Ragnhild finally had the dream she had been praying for. She saw Harald, sitting in a dark place next to a dead body. Odin came into her dream and told her she must ask Thorleif the Wise to travel with Guttorm to Lofoten. "Thorleif has divining powers that will overcome the Finn," he told her.

When the dream ended, she immediately got up and ran into the bedchamber where Guttorm slept.

"Wake up, brother, wake up! I have seen Harald in a dream. He is still alive...in a dark place. Odin told me to have you take Thorleif the Wise with you to Lofoten and you will find Harald!"

No sooner were the ships pulled ashore at the harbor next to Lofoten Island, then two thousand soldiers were ready to ascend the mountain in search of Harald. Thorleif asked that they first kneel in the sand, remove their helmets, and join him in a prayer to Odin. In the prayer the wise man reminded Odin of the important work that Harald had accomplished in his life up to this time...and he asked the God for the guidance he needed to discern where to find the dark place that hid their King.

When the prayer was ended, Thorleif kept his head bowed for many minutes. The men waited in silence. When he finally raised his head, he told them he had seen the place. Harald was in a cave behind the hut of Svase the Finn.

The ten men, including Berdaluke, who had first traveled with Harald and the Finn to the hut four years ago, led the way. It was the first place they had sought to look for the last four years, so by now, they knew the trail well.

When they got close, Guttorm ordered the men to stop. Just he, Ragnvald, Thorleif, and the first ten would go on from here. They did not want the Finn to hear them coming and move Harald to another location.

The sun was just about to set when they came to the clearing. The sound of children crying was coming from within the hut. All but Thorleif drew their weapons, preparing to attack Svase if he should try to harm Harald. Of course, Svase the Finn did not use swords as his weapons. He had weapons more powerful than swords that he had used to bind Harald with for four long years.

As luck would have it, the Finn was out in the woods collecting plants and berries to feed the hungry boys who were loudly crying inside the hut. When the men quickly opened the door, the children were so startled they quit crying. Thorleif walked right to the back of the hut and found the open fold in the rock. Guttorm and Ragnvald followed him. Four of the men tried to comfort the boys by offering them dried meat from their sacks. The other five, led by Berdaluke, went into the woods to look for Svase.

What a pitiful sight the friends saw when their eyes adjusted to the dark of the cave. The only light was the flickering flame of a small fire. There sat their Harald, a mere shadow of his former robust body. His beautiful hair hung in dirty mats around his shoulders and his clothing was in rags.

Before him lay the dead body of a white haired woman. She was dressed in a white gown, with a white silk sheet covering her legs and feet. The stench in the cave was almost overpowering...but Harald did not seem to notice.

Thorleif waved the other two back while he approached the King.

"Harald, my son, this is Thorleif, your father Halvdan's friend from Toten."

At the mention of Halvdan, Harald raised his head and turned to look at the man. The light of the fire was just enough to show the kindly face of the old man. Harald nodded his head and turned back to bend over Snofrid's body.

"Is this your wife, Harald?" Torleif asked in a low whisper.

Again, Harald nodded.

"She is very beautiful. What is her name?"

Harald's mouth opened but only a croak came out. On the second try, he whispered the name of Snofrid.

"What a lovely name," was Thorleif's soft reply.

"You have kept your vigil for quite some time, I see. Some dirt has settled on your beautiful wife's gown."

Harald looked up to see the sympathetic smile that covered the face of his old friend.

"Perhaps we should shake the dirt from her silk sheet and gently brush the dirt from her gown."

The bereft husband had not noticed the dirt that was covering his wife's gown until now. Actually, it was the mixture of herbs and moss that Svase had covered her with, but it looked like dirt in the dim light.

"Shall I help you make her more beautiful?" Thorleif asked with a voice just above a whisper.

Harald nodded once again.

Thorleif removed the silk sheet from Snofrid's legs and Harald instinctively picked up her body and pressed it to his chest. Suddenly, he could see all kinds of ugly reptiles slithering out from the place where she had lain. As he bent to kiss her lips, her mouth fell open and worms began to crawl out. Maggots were coming from her nose and her white hair was turning black.

Her arms and hands began turning to ashes and soon Harald was holding nothing but an empty gown. He threw it down on the bed and looked at Thorleif...really looked at him for the first time.

"My wife is dead!" he said. "My wife is dead."

Guttorm could restrain himself no longer and he rushed forward into the light.

"Harald, my Harald!" he cried.

Harald reached out and clutched Guttorm to his breast. Ragnvald came forward next.

"My friend Ragnvald!" Harald sobbed.

Suddenly, he looked around him.

"Where am I?" he asked.

Guttorm and Ragnvald looked at Thorleif. They were afraid to say anything that might cause Harald to revert back to the trance he had been in when they first saw him.

"You are in the cave of Svase the Finn. He has been holding you here against your will. We have come to rescue you," said Thorleif.

"Where is that rotten scoundrel?" Harald shouted.

"Your men are searching for him as we speak."

"My men? My men are here?" Harald asked excitedly. "How do we get out of this cave?"

Thorleif led the way through the cave to the fold in the rock. Harald walked with one arm around his uncle Guttorm and the other arm around his great uncle Ragnvald.

When they came into the hut, Harald was surprised to see little children in the arms of four of his men.

"What are these children doing here?" he asked.

"We do not know," the men answered.

"They are your children," Thorleif answered, "yours and your wife Snofrid's."

Just then, there was a high pitched squeal heard coming from outside the hut. The door opened and Berdaluke ducked his head and walked through the low door carrying a screeching Svase by his feet.

"Put me down! Put me down!" shrieked the Finn.

"What am I doing here in your cave?" demanded Harald.

"You are the husband of my daughter, Snofrid, and these boys are your sons! I now have four Princes of Norway for my grandsons!" cried Svase.

Harald lunged at the Finn with all the fury of an angry bear. He grabbed the scrawny neck with his large hands and gave a jerk. Just then, Berdaluke dropped the filthy feet and Svase the Finn fell lifeless to the floor of his own dirty hut.

"Leave him to rot as he left me to rot!" shouted Harald as he walked out into the sunshine for the first time in four years.

"What about the children?" asked Guttorm as he followed quickly behind his friend.

"Let them rot as well! They are no kin of mine!" he called back as he walked into the cheering arms of the men who had for years relentlessly searched for their King.

Guttorm looked at Ragnvald and Thorleif. There was a mixture of joy and sorrow in the look on his face. There was great joy in finally finding Harald, but did their father really think he could leave those little children behind to die with the bodies of their grandfather and their mother?

"Bring the children down last," Guttorm said quietly to the men who were holding them. "The King will change his mind later."

Harald and his rescuers spent the night at Borg Manor. A feast was hastily prepared to celebrate the return of the King who had left the same feasting hall four years earlier. Even though he had enjoyed a hot bath and some clean clothes, Harald looked like a skeleton of the man who had sailed to Lofoten in the year 880.

Guttorm arranged to have Harald's children, all boys they discovered, stay for a time with Jarl Jens and his family at Borg. He was sure Harald would want to provide for them once he got back to his normal self again.

As the ships set sail, heading south for Trondelag, Harald stood in the prow and watched the waves of the sea dash against the sides of his warship. He felt a little dizzy from the motion and quickly looked away. Somewhere, in the recesses of his mind, he could feel the twinge of a hypnotic trance coming on. He shifted his gaze to the backs of his warriors, who were manning the oars to aid the wind in bringing them home quickly.

He glanced at the rocky shoreline as they passed. Last night, while he slept in a clean bedchamber at Borg Manor, he had strange dreams. He woke several times in the dark, wondering where he was. Finally, he got up to light a candle so that he would be assured of his surroundings when the next dream woke him.

Had he really been in that cave for four years? It was almost impossible to think about. Was his mind so weak that he could have let Svase the Finn gain control over him once again? Well, at least he did not have to worry about that rotten thief again. What he needed was a return to his former life so he could feel normal again.

All of a sudden, he realized he had two lovely wives to go home to. He wondered for a moment which one he wanted to see first. Well, his mother would come first. She had probably worried about him the most. Guttorm told him that it was her fervent prayers that caused Odin to suggest Thorleif the Wise. Yes, he was glad he was going to Lade first...then he would decide which wife he would visit next.

"Now the King came to his understanding again
    threw the madness out of his mind,
and after that day, ruled his kingdom as before.
    He was strengthened and made joyful by his subjects,
and his subjects by him and the country by both."

Heimskringla

CHAPTER 25

FREE AT LAST

Harald lay in his bedchamber at Lade and stared at the wooden beams over his head. Despite the fact that he was deeply relieved to be back with his family in Trondelag, he could not quite put aside the traumatic events of the past four years. Not that he remembered much of the details, but he knew from what Guttorm had told him that he was lucky to have escaped with his life.

What he really could not understand was why Odin had let this happen to him. Hadn't he done what he was asked to do? Hadn't he fought long and hard and conquered all of Norway as Odin had planned? Hadn't he married three different women as Odin had requested? What more did the God want?

He drifted off to sleep with these questions in his thoughts. No sooner had his mind and body begun to relax than Odin came to him in his dream.

"Awake, my son. I have come in answer to your questioning. You want to know what more I want from you. I will tell you. I want you to always seek to do my will. I want you to ask for my guidance in every decision. I want you to call on me in good times as well as bad. You had come to feel you did not need my help anymore. I let you be overcome by Svase the Finn and his daughter, Snofrid, to teach you a lesson. You still need my guidance and you will until the day you die. Do you understand?"

"Yes, O Great One, I understand. I will never again forget the God who protected me through all my battles and leads and guides my life. Please forgive me," pleaded Harald.

"I forgive you, but you must also forgive. Svase the Finn and Snofrid were evil and I have taken their lives, but the sons who carry your seed must not be punished. They must be fostered in good homes that they might grow to manhood. Only if they begin to practice the evil of their mother can they be destroyed. And now I leave you to your rest."

Harald did not rest, however, but spent the hours of the night thinking about the counsel of his God. He was grateful that Odin had spared his life so many times in the past and that he still guided and watched over him. He prayed that he would never again be so careless as to forget who the real ruler of all Norway was.

In the morning, Harald asked Guttorm to take a ride with him on the stallions that were kept at Lade. Everyone thought that Harald was just anxious to have the feel of a good horse beneath him, but he really wanted to have a private conversation with his uncle and best friend.

As they came to the spot on the Stjordal River where he and Asa used to stop, Harald reined in his horse and motioned for Guttorm to do the same.

"I have a favor to ask of you," Harald said.

"Ask me anything," responded Guttorm.

"I need you to return to Lofoten and get my four sons."

"I knew you would not want to let them die!" Guttorm replied with a sense of relief.

"I would have let them die, but Odin has corrected my thinking. He has said they should not be punished for the evil of their mother. I have been instructed to have them fostered in good homes. I am relieved that he did not ask me to have them raised by Svanhild or Gyda. I do not really want to have them around me and I can imagine how my wives will feel when they find out about them."

"Leave it to me. I will take care of it for you."

"Ah...my great friend Guttorm. What would I have done without you?" Harald asked.

"I might ask the same of you, Harald. You have made my life rich indeed!"

With that, the two friends sat their horses, looking out across the beautiful river...and thought about the experiences they had both enjoyed and endured together.

In the end, it was to Svanhild that Harald traveled to first. It wasn't really that he loved her best, but that she needed him more. She had never really gotten over the anger and jealousy she felt when he married Gyda. If Svanhild found out that he had chosen to visit Gyda before her, it would be like throwing salt on an open wound.

He had developed a love for Gyda and she for him, but Gyda was more independent. Having five children by Harald had given her the confidence and love she previously lacked. Aside from that, the story of a third wife would not bother her like it was going to bother Svanhild.

Harald tried to decide if he should send a messenger ahead to tell Svanhild that he was on his way or if he should just ride up and surprise her. He had sent a message to Gyda saying he would see her in a fortnight, but he decided that surprise would be better for Svanhild.

He arrived at Viken after dark and the gates were already closed. The barking of the dogs awakened the men in the stable and he was quick to tell them who he was before they unsheathed their swords. The dogs ceased their barking when they heard his voice and caught his scent.

"Master," they cried in surprise. "We thought you to be dead long since."

In truth, he looked as gaunt as a man coming back from the dead. Had it not been for the sound of his voice and the gleam of the firelight on his golden hair, they might have deemed him an enemy.

"Care for my horse, Arild, and you come with me to the manor house Egil. I want to surprise Svanhild and not awaken everyone by pounding and shouting at the door."

It felt good to enter into the familiar great room and walk down the long hall to the master bedchamber. He opened the door quietly and looked in to see a candle burning and Svanhild asleep in the large bed. He walked over and knelt down on the bed platform. Then he bent forward and gently kissed the lips of his sleeping wife. Svanhild awoke with a start.

"Harald, is that really you?"

"It is really me, my love."

"Oh, Harald, where have you been? Are you alright? Oh, Harald!" she said, but did not wait for him to answer. Instead, she reached up for him and brought him into the bed with her and kissed him over and over.

When she opened her eyes to look at him and he tried to talk, she just silenced his words with more kisses. Soon, they had satisfied their longing and were asleep in each others arms. Both were thinking that tomorrow would be time enough for talking.

Svanhild awoke first and lay there looking at the husband she had feared was dead. She realized, anew, how much she loved him. Even if she was forced to share him, she was going to show her love for him when she had the chance.

Harald awoke with a start and sat up in the bed. He looked around as if wondering where he was. Then he saw Svanhild and lay back down, cradling her in his arms.

"You are so thin I can see your bones!" she cried.

"Are you ready to hear my story now?" he asked.

"I think so," she replied hesitantly.

Harald started at the beginning. He felt he needed to tell her again the story of how Svase the Finn had first captured him as a boy...to help her understand how powerful his spells could be.

It was difficult to explain the part about Snofrid. He did not want to tell her about the burning yearning he had felt for her body. He knew now that his sexual desire was the greatest power she had over him. Harald just focused on the evil power Svase the Finn possessed.

When he told her about the four boys, she sat up and looked at him in surprise...or disgust...he could not tell which.

"How could you have done that? Made babies with a witch whose father was holding you captive?"

"It is hard to explain," Harald said gently. "Svase must have put that spell on me. He taunted me, just before I killed him, that he now had four Princes of Norway. I think he thought that would save him, but it did not!"

"Where are the boys now?" asked Svanhild.

"At first I was so angered when the Finn told me the boys were of my seed that I ordered them to be left in the hut to die. But Guttorm could not do it and brought them secretly to Borg. It was a good deed that he did, for Odin came to me and told me I must not punish them for their mother's evil, and that I should foster them as my sons."

"I hope I shall never have to see them!" she cried.

"No, they shall be sent to jarls in the north," replied Harald reassuringly.

He did not want to tell her that they might compete with her sons someday as Odin wanted him to recognize them as his legal sons. He would deal with that problem later. For now, he was just happy to be at Viken, being loved by Svanhild. She had accepted his story better than he had expected. He hoped Gyda would be as understanding.

Actually, Gyda was more understanding. She blamed Guttorm and Ragnvald for their inability to find and rescue him...and she blamed Berdaluke and his men for not protecting him in the first place! Harald decided not to tell her it was his own fault that Odin had let him be captured.

Saying that would make him seem weak and he wanted Gyda to always think of him as the mighty warrior chieftain who had won every battle and put all of Norway under his rule. It was enough that his mother and Guttorm knew of the message Odin had given him. They were the ones who understood his mission and his dependence on Odin for his success.

Gyda's response to his return was not quite as passionate as Svanhild's, but she let him know she was glad to have him back...in her own way. Despite the fact that they had five children together, she did not desire him in her bed in the same way that Svanhild did. Gyda got her loving reassurances from the children...who gave her their undivided devotion.

It was amazing to see how his children had grown in four years. He had his four boys by Asa, his three boys by Svanhild, his four boys and a girl by Gyda and now his four sons by Snofrid. It was hard to think how he could give them the same kind of life he had enjoyed as the only child of two loving parents.

As Guttorm traveled to Lofoten to collect Harald's four sons, he wondered to himself who he could get to foster the boys. Harald had made it clear at the time of his rescue that he did not want anything to do with the grandsons of Svase the Finn. Despite the fact that they were just little children, they possessed the blood of a witch as well as the blood of kings. Would anyone want to risk bringing evil spirits into their homes?

He decided he must ask men who did not have young children of their own. If there was any suspicious behavior on the part of these boys, he would be responsible. Yet, he could not bring them down to Tune to live with him and Gutt. Harald had promised Svanhild that the boys would not live anywhere near her sons.

The trip back from Borg was better than he had expected. The oldest boy seemed to be quite capable and he had obviously taken charge of his younger brothers. A young woman whose child had died was engaged to nurse the baby and she traveled with them down the coast.

Halvdan, the four year old, told Guttorm what names their grandfather,

Svase, had chosen for him and his brothers. He knew that he was named for his grandfather, Halvdan the Black. His three year old brother was named Gudrod for their great grandfather, the Hunter. His two year old brother was named for Sigurd, their other great grandfather, and their baby brother had not been named yet.

Guttorm decided to stop at More on the way back from Lofoten. Ragnvald was happy to see his old friend and a little curious about the witch's children.

"I think you ought to take the baby," Guttorm said to Ragnvald and his wife Hild. He has not yet been named and all the other boys have been given the name of someone close to Harald. I am sure the King would be pleased to have another Ragnvald as a son."

That was certainly the right thing to say, as Ragnvald felt he was second only to Guttorm in his close relationship to Harald.

"We shall take him and I will pour water over him this very day. You will stand as witness, Guttorm, and deliver the message to our King that another Ragnvald will be raised in this manor."

"We will take the child, but as soon as he is done suckling, the young woman must return to Borg," exclaimed Hild.

One thing she did not want was a pretty young woman around to tempt her husband. It had been a long time since he had taken those two concubines, and she wasn't interested in having another one in her house.

"You are indeed a great friend," replied Guttorm. "Can you think of another friend who might take one of the boys?"

"What of Thjodolf of Hvin in Gudbrandsdal?"

"Yes, that would be a fine choice. He is also a good friend of Harald and always entertains the King at his large estate when he is traveling from Lade to Tande. I will journey there after a brief stay in Trondelag."

Guttorm wanted to spend a few days at both Lade and Tande, but he was also anxious to complete his mission and get back to Tune. Malfrid came from Lanke to see him and Snofrid's sons but she refused to bring Sigrod along.

Thjodolf of Hvin was willing to take one boy, and Guttorm chose to give him the three year old, Gudrod, to rear. He decided to bring Halvdan and his two year old brother, Sigurd, to Stein Manor in Ringerike. He felt a preference for those two boys because they were named for his sister's husband and his own father.

He liked the idea of a Sigurd being raised on his father's estate. Halvdan was already taking responsibility for his younger brother and Guttorm made a plan to visit each summer to check on them.

Ring Dagsson, a younger cousin of Guttorm, had been managing Stein Manor in his absence. The cousin had no boys of his own, so he was happy to have two sons of King Harald to foster. His one child was a daughter named Ashild, a lovely young girl of seven. She was thrilled to have other children to play with...even if they were boys.

Halvdan and Ashild became good friends, despite there being three years difference in their ages. He was large for a boy of four and she was small for a girl of seven. She especially liked to play mother to two year old Sigurd, and he toddled along after the other two...wherever they went.

CHAPTER 26

THE OUTLAW

The next four winters passed with peace in the land. However, the peace was not to last. This time it wasn't an enemy from without that attacked, but an enemy from within. It was Harald's cousin, Hrolf, the son of Ragnvald of More.

Hrolf spent every summer plundering on the shores of the East Sea. He had ships and men and found much treasure...and caused much trouble. He was a big man and very frightening to the women of the villages where he raided.

One summer as he was returning from after a successful plundering expedition, he made the mistake of sailing in to Kaupang with the intent to raid the village there. The law of Norway was very clear, there was to be no raiding or pillaging of your own people and in your own country. Hrolf knew the law...but he thought he was above the law.

Unfortunately for Hrolf, Harald was at Viken, just up the coast from Kaupang when the raid took place. The lagman, who was charged with keeping the law in that area of Skiringssal, immediately sent a rider to inform the King. Harald and three hundred men in his largest dragon ships sailed quickly down the coast and caught Hrolf and his three ships full of men just as they were leaving the shore.

A Thing was assembled quickly and Hrolf was condemned as an outlaw before those he had just been raiding. He was given seven days to gather his belongings from his home in More and leave the country, or anyone would be free to take his life...and there were plenty of men who wanted to do just that.

When he arrived back at Borgrund and told his mother what had happened, she immediately sent word to Harald, pleading for him to rescind the sentence and reminding him that Hrolf was his kin. Harald responded by saying that the law was the same for rich man or poor, kin or no kin. He said there would be no mercy shown to a thief who would rape, kill, and steal from his own people.

Then Hild sent this message to Harald:

"Think'st thou, King Harald, in thy anger,
To drive away my brave Hrolf Ganger
Like a mad wolf, from out the land?
Why, Harald, raise thy mighty hand?
Why banish Nefia's gallant name—son,
The brother of brave udal—men?
Why is thy cruelty so fell?
Bethink thee, monarch, it is ill
With such a wolf at wolf to play,
Who, driven to the wild woods away
May make the King's best deer his prey."
Heimskringla

But, Harald was not moved by Hild's pleading or her threatening. The law was the law and Hrolf had been given the punishment he deserved.

He sent her a reply that said, "Shall mercy rob justice? I say, nay! My father, Halvdan the Black, had peace for twenty years, because he weeded out the outlaws, one at a time. We have no room in our country for someone who robs his own. He showed no mercy to the people of Kaupang and he will receive no mercy from me!"

However, there was one other person who would need mercy... that was Ragnvald the Younger. He had committed no crime, except to be the son of a witch and the son of a King who would not pardon Hild's youngest son. He had been just tolerated in her household for the last four years, but now he would be tolerated no more. She sent a curt message to Harald, telling him to come and get his bastard.

Harald sent the message on to Guttorm. His uncle had agreed four years ago to be responsible for Snofrid's children, and Harald did not want to have to take any responsibility at this stage. Now there were two people he felt bad about...young Ragnvald and old Ragnvald. He knew his friend Ragnvald would understand his position on the law, and he did not want to think about young Ragnvald.

Obviously, the issue with Hrolf bothered the King more than what he would admit, for he had a nightmare about him. Hrolf was plundering and raping at Viken instead of Kaupang. Harald was listening to Svanhild scream, but he could not get to her. He saw Hrolf's men stealing horses and house goods, but he was powerless to move.

Then, he saw Ragnvald come in to the great room and kneel down in front of him and beg for Hrolf's forgiveness. He was about to say he would pardon Hrolf when Odin appeared in the dream. He had a strong message for both Ragnvald and Harald.

"Hrolf shall remain an outlaw in this country. Do not pardon him. There is a purpose for Hrolf's exile, and that purpose will only come to pass if he is sent away from his home and family."

Odin's words were a comfort to Ragnvald, but they made no impression on Hild. She was not a forgiving woman in the best of times, and she certainly wasn't a forgiving woman in the worst of times.

Then the angry outlaw took leave of his home and family, having forever forfeited his right to live in Norway. He and his mother both seethed with anger...and vowed to seek revenge against King Harald. They said nothing of this to Ragnvald, but kept the pact in secret...and waited for a more opportune time to strike against their enemy!

CHAPTER 27

A SURPRISE IN JUTLAND

One night, as Harald was praying, Odin appeared to him and told him to take his dragon ships and three hundred men and travel down to Jutland. When he asked the reason for the trip, the God just said there was a surprise waiting there for him.

He wanted to ask more questions, but Odin was gone. Why was he being asked to go to Jutland? Was there trouble there? He hoped not. He was enjoying life in his kingdom of Norway and really did not want to add Jutland to it, but he dare not disobey Odin. He would never forget the hard lesson he had learned from four years in a hidden cave near Lofoten.

Harald was sure Odin would not ask him to conquer Jutland with only three hundred men. He would just have to do what he was told and find out the purpose when his God was ready to show him.

It was Svanhild's turn to have Harald at Viken and she wasn't happy when he announced he was traveling to Jutland in a fortnight.

"How long will you be gone? You will be home for the Yule celebration, won't you?" she asked with a frown.

"Do not worry, I'm sure I shall be back before then," he said assuringly. "What gift of gold shall I bring my golden girl?"

He hadn't called her by that name for a long while and it pleased her to hear it.

"I should like some golden goblets to toast at our yuletide feast," she answered with a smile.

"Then golden goblets it shall be!" said her husband as he kissed her tenderly.

However, both the promise to be back for the Yule celebration and the golden goblets were forgotten after the surprise Harald received in Jutland. He decided to sail his ships to the well sheltered harbor at Aalborg and pay a visit to Sverre and Trygve. If there was trouble in Jutland, they would surely know about it.

He sent a message to Guttorm and his mother that Odin had told him to travel to Jutland. He then set sail with his body guard of twenty five berserkers, led by Berdaluke, as well as two hundred seventy five trusted warriors.

The sea was fierce as they made their way and the waves were extremely high. Harald's ships were making slow progress. The closer they got to Jutland, the worse grew the storm. Finally, they spotted land and sailed into a small harbor.

As they were trying to take down their sails and pull their ships out of the water, they heard the sound of a battle cry and turned to see a small force of fighting men coming at them with spears in one hand and drawn swords in the other. His warriors instinctively grabbed their shields from the sides of the ships and prepared for battle.

The charging warriors obviously did not realize they were attacking a group of seasoned soldiers. Harald quickly singled out the leader. He thought it must be a young man as he watched him trying to wield his heavy sword with two hands and shout encouragement to his men at the same time.

The King admired the bravery of this young man in the face of overwhelming odds. Harald countered his attacker, but tried to keep from killing him. Suddenly, he felt a sharp blow to his right leg and saw blood pouring out. He was shocked and angry that he had allowed an opponent to injure him.

"Alright, enough games! Anyone who draws my blood must die!" he shouted as he attacked his enemy with a vengeance.

Within moments, the opponent was knocked to the ground. The King quickly put his foot atop the man's midsection and prepared to give him the death blow. Just at that moment, he heard someone next to him shout, "My Lady!"

As Harald turned to look, the man beneath his foot recovered his sword and sliced open the other leg, then jumped to his feet and began running for the woods. Determined to exact punishment on the person who was responsible for not just one, but now two open wounds, he chased after the man.

The young soldier was fast, but the bigger man had more muscle strength. Just as they reached the edge of the woods, the young man turned and charged with his sword. Harald was startled, but managed to step quickly to one side and the blade just pierced his left arm.

A furious Harald grabbed the man by the forearm and wrestled him to the ground. This time his enemy's helmet flew off and the King realized why he had been called, "My Lady." Lying beneath him was not a slight young man, but a beautiful young woman.

Her eyes were flashing with hatred as she reached to claw him with her nails. He managed to grab both small hands with one of his large ones and pull her arms above her head. She spit in his face and struggled in vain to free herself.

Finally, she stopped struggling and said in a low voice, "Honor me with death before you place your seed in me."

Harald looked into the deep blue green of her eyes and replied, "I have no intention of placing my seed in you. I have women who love me and want my seed. I do not need to squander myself on you!"

"Then why have you landed your ships on my shore," she shouted.

"We have sought refuge from the storm, nothing more. We travel to Aalborg, but were blown off course. It was you who attacked us!" he answered just as loudly.

She was silent for a moment. "Then get your big body off of mine!" she countered.

"Only if you hand me your dagger...carefully...and promise not to pick up your sword."

"I give you my word."

"Is your word worth anything?"

"My word carries the honor of Erik of Skagen! I am his only daughter, Ragnild!" she answered with a note of pride in her voice.

As she said her name, the very name that belonged to his beloved mother, Harald thought he must now know what surprise Odin had in store for him. He got to his feet and reached down to pull her up with his left hand. As he did so, he saw that his hand was red with blood. Both leather boots were also covered with blood.

"I have fought in thirty battles and have not shed as much blood as this! You are quite the warrior!"

"I am called Ragnild the Mighty," she said with a grin, "and whose blood have I spilt this day?"

"I am Harald Halvdanson."

She stared in amazement. "Is it possible I have fought with the great King of Norway and drawn his blood?"

"You have!"

"You must come to my manor house and I will see to your wounds. Call off your men and we will offer you shelter from the storm."

The fighting quickly ceased when the warriors saw their leaders were no longer contending.

"Svend, see what you can do to provide for these men. I will speak to their leader alone," she shouted.

Svend was reluctant to leave his mistress at the mercy of a strange man and Harald's bodyguard was concerned about leaving him at the mercy of a strange woman. They still remembered the time that he had fallen under the influence of Snofrid Svasedatter.

The two left their men in the courtyard and walked into the great hall, closing the door behind them.

"I should offer you the high seat, but my father's spirit seems to linger there and I would not cause it to leave."

Harald graciously turned to the seats at the opposite end of the room. He did not feel like demanding his rights in the presence of this fair maiden. She was more beautiful than any woman he had ever seen... even more beautiful than his red haired Gyda.

Or was it that she looked so different from his other wives. She had hair as blue black as a raven's wing and eyes that seemed as blue green as a calm sea. Her skin was as white as a dove and her lips were the color of mountain berries. He wondered how she would look when she changed to a woman's gown.

Ragnild sat down beside the tall, muscular man and wondered that she should feel so safe in his presence. Her experience had taught her that men were not to be trusted.

"Are you truly the great warrior chief, Harald Fairhair?" she asked.

"Fairhair is the name my friend Ragnvald gave me when he cut my hair following the celebration of our great victory at Hafrsfjord. I am the son of the powerful warrior chief, Halvdan the Black, and his is the proud name I bear."

"We must see to your wounds," she said as she ordered water and cloth to be brought to her. Harald watched Ragnild as she carefully washed and then wrapped his wounds. She spit her saliva into the cuts on his legs and arm before covering them with clean linen cloth.

"I can understand why you spit in my face before, but I do not know why you must spit on my wounds now," he questioned.

"It is something Witch Brynhilde taught me to do when my father was injured."

"Did it make him well?"

She looked up at him over the bandages and tears began to run down her cheeks.

"No. He died anyway," she said quietly, avoiding his gaze.

He wanted to tease her and accuse her of trying to kill him a second time, but he recognized that she was in no mood for teasing. Instead, he inquired gently, "What was the cause of your father's injuries?"

"Raiders and thieves had come in the night. They landed on our shores and crept through the woods and surrounded the house. They threatened to burn our home over our heads if my father did not open the door. My father and his men rushed out to meet them, but they were overpowered. Most of our men had gone south to Hedeby on a trading expedition and only fifty remained at home."

"The raiders killed our men and left my father bleeding to death in his own doorway. They stole all the gold and silver they could find, but that was not the worst part. They found my mother hiding in her bedchamber and carried her off with them in their ships."

"She screamed for my father to help her and he tried to rise, but they just stepped on him as they ran out through the doorway. I was hiding in a small cupboard in the great hall and I could see my mother kicking and fighting as I looked through a crack in the door."

"She had made me take a vow that I would not open the cupboard door no matter what happened. I kept my vow, but I hate myself now for being such a coward! When I knew they were gone, I ran to my father and dragged him back into the house. The serving maids had hidden themselves in the woods and they came back to help bury the dead."

"My father lived for only a short time and he spent those hours calling for my mother. When the rest of our men returned the next day, I dressed in my father's clothes and we went to sea looking for the thieves. We did not find them, but we found something else."

"As our ships came close to the shore, we could see that a body had been washed ashore. Svend said, 'Do not look, My Lady, let us take care of this,' but I could not. I had let my mother be taken prisoner from our home and had done nothing to help her. Now I needed to go to her and tell her of my love and beg her forgiveness."

"I dressed her bruised body in her marriage gown and my father in his best robes. We placed them side by side in my father's small ship. The men pulled it to the lake that lies beyond our manor house. The ship was sunk to the bottom of the lake."

"Svend thought we should burn their bodies, but I just could not do it. They are together in death as they were together in life. Now there is just me and a hundred men to protect our manor. Often, I feel like joining my parents at the bottom of the lake."

"My father always called me Ragnild the Mighty because he said I was as brave as any son would have been...but he was wrong. When I should have been brave and tried to save my mother and my father, I did not. I hid in a cupboard like a coward and I shall never forgive myself."

Harald listened in silence to the sad tale told by this lovely young woman. He wanted to comfort her and protect her and make her feel happy again. He could understand now why she and her small band of warriors had attacked him and his men.

All he said was, "You need not worry, My Lady, I have been sent to help you."

He tried to stand up but the loss of blood had weakened him.

"I think I must rest until morning and then we will talk."

Ragnild showed him to a bedchamber and left to get him some food. By the time she returned, he was fast asleep. She stood looking at this large, handsome man whom she had wounded. Somehow, she knew he could easily have killed her, but he chose not to.

He said he had been sent to help her. She was anxious to hear how he would do that, but she would have to wait until morning, for this fighting warrior had fallen into a deep sleep.

When he did not come out to the hall in the morning, Ragnild thought he must still be asleep. One of his men, Berdaluke, came to inquire about him at mid-day and she led him to the chamber.

After a few moments, the soldier called to her, "My Lady, the King is not well. He asks for water."

She quickly filled a flask from the barrel next to the fire place and hurried into the room. Harald was burning up with a fever. It got worse by the end of the next day. He asked his men to carry him to the lake behind the manor house and he lay in the cool water to soothe the burning in his body.

Ragnild felt bad that she had caused his injuries and tried to help him as best she could. There were herbs she gathered from the woods and applied to his wounds. She tried to feed him hot broth and wipe the sweat from his brow.

After seven days had passed, Harald became delirious. He wildly threshed about on the bed and did not know where he was. At times he would sit up and begin shouting someone's name, but Ragnild tried to calm him and get him to lie back down.

When a fortnight had passed with no improvement, she began to fear that he might die. His men were very anxious to hear about his progress each day and she wondered how they might react if she told them he was dead. They knew she had been the cause of his wounds and might feel she deserved to die also.

She decided to send her man, Svend, to the hut of Brynhilde the witch. Whenever there was a bad sickness that the herbs did not cure, the witch was called to the manor house. She had saved Ragnild's life when she was bitten by a poisonous serpent. If anyone could keep this powerful warrior from dying, it would by Brynhilde.

The witch made a potent potion and forced him to drink it each day. She burned leaves and bark near his bed and blew the pungent smoke toward his head. She spoke incantations over his weak body, but nothing she did seemed to help.

One night as Ragnild sat by his bedside, Harald suddenly raised his right arm and shouted, "To Odin be the victory! To Odin be the victory! To Odin be the victory'!" and then fell into a deep sleep.

As she was wiping the sweat from his brow the next morning, he quietly opened his eyes. Ragnild was so startled that she jumped back in surprise.

"Is this Ragnild the Mighty who wipes my brow so gently," he asked.

"Are you well?" she questioned.

"I will be," he replied. "Odin has come to me in my dream and commanded me to be healed."

"I have feared you might die and your men would take out their anger on me."

"It is not yet my time to die, My Lady. Is that the only reason you hoped I would live?"

"I have felt regret to have been the cause of your wounds when you had not meant to harm me."

"But...is that all?" he probed.

"Is that not enough?" she replied. "What more do you want?"

"I want you for my wife!"

"I thought you said you did not want to place your seed in me...that you did not need to squander yourself on me!"

"I did say that to the person who had just cut both my legs and my arm and spit in my face!"

Her face reddened at the thought of that day. She had pondered her actions many times during the days Harald had lain near death.

"I suppose the names you cried out in your sleep belong to the women who love you and want your seed!"

"I am not sure who I called for."

"Well, it wasn't me!" she retorted.

"But I am calling for you now."

"Why should I marry you?"

"Because Odin sent me to you," he answered with a smile. "He came to me in a vision and told me to take three hundred men and ships and sail to Jutland. When I asked him the reason, he only said there was a surprise for me. He has just come to me again and told me you are my surprise."

"Did he say you would be surprised that a mere woman would be able to wound you unto death?" she bantered.

"No...he told me I would love you more than any other woman until the day I died and beyond."

"How many women do you love?"

"I have loved three... and two of them are still alive."

"I would never marry a man who had other wives. I would hate them and they would hate me!"

"I think you are right, but Odin has planned you for me anyway!"

"Well, Odin had better take away your other wives then!"

Suddenly, he could see Svanhild's face flash before him. How would he explain this woman? He could not blame his feeling for her on witchcraft this time. He could not blame it on a previous vow...but he could say that Odin had sent him here. That was the truth.

CHAPTER 28

RAGNILD THE MIGHTY

Harald grew more in love with Ragnild every day. He tried to convince her of his love, but she held steadfast to her demands. He was not sure whether she had also bewitched him...or whether he wanted her for his wife, so desperately, because he could not have her. It was the first time someone had refused his marriage offer and he was determined to win this battle.

The King and his men stayed at Skagen Manor in Jutland through the Yule season. He felt guilty about his promise to Svanhild, but he was afraid to leave Ragnild alone for fear the raiders who killed her mother might return and do the same thing to her. He tried to convince her to come back to Norway with him where he could protect her, but she refused to come unless they were married...and she refused to marry him unless he would give up his other wives.

In his efforts to persuade her to marry him, he told her that they would live in a special place...a manor he would build just for her. He suggested a place along the sea coast, in a setting like her home in Jutland. There they could raise their sons to be great, seafaring men.

"But what of Gyda and Svanhild?" questioned Ragnild.

"Gyda and Svanhild will be far away from you. You will never have to see them."

"But I will know they are there. No! You must put them aside if you want me! You must promise never to see them again!"

"That is a hard thing you ask."

"It is the only way you will have me as your wife!"

"You know I could take you anytime I chose to," he challenged.

"And you know I would scream and fight and hate you for it!" she shouted.

"Yes, I know," he answered quietly.

214

Harald had heard the sad story of the way his grandfather, Gudrod the Hunter, had forced his grandmother Aasa to marry him. How Aasa's father had refused the marriage offer and how Gudrod had cut off the head of Harald Redbeard and his son Gyrd and then carried Aasa to his manor in Vestfold. There he had forced her into a sham wedding. He also knew that Aasa had planned the murder of her husband to protect his father Halvdan.

There was also the story of Hake the Berserker who tried to force his own mother into marriage. Those images were clear in his mind. He knew he could never force himself on Ragnild. No, she would come to Norway willingly, as his wife, or she would not come at all.

As he tossed in his bed that night, he prayed for help and Odin finally came to him. When he asked for counsel, he was told, "Be still, my son. The task before you seems hard, but it is my will. Svanhild and Gyda will miss your presence, but Ragnild was promised to you when your bodies were just spirits and she is destined to become your wife. The son I shall send to the union of your bodies will become a mighty man. He will be the strongest of your sons and you will love him as you love his mother. Be at peace, my son, and know that I am with thee."

After Odin left, Harald slept peacefully. He would do as Odin commanded and not question. He would try to explain about Ragnild to Svanhild and Gyda and ask for their understanding and forgiveness.

In the morning, Harald arose before the rest of the household and walked to the sea shore. Berdaluke insisted on walking with him, and the King shared the message of Odin with his bodyguard and friend.

"Do you want me to sail to Viken and give that message to Svanhild," he asked.

"No," Harald answered, "I must do it myself."

He walked along the shore, looking at the rocks. When he found a large one that shone in the sun's reflection, he picked it up and placed it in the pouch that hung from his belt.

"This will work for now," he said.

Berdaluke was not sure what he meant, but followed his master back to the manor house. The serving maids were building a fire as he entered the great hall.

"I will speak to Ragnild in her bedchamber," he told his big berserker. "It is up to you to call Svend outside and keep him there."

Berdaluke was successful in convincing Svend to talk with him outside in the court yard. When the two men were through the front doors, Harald walked down the hall to Ragnild's bedchamber. He opened the door without knocking and found her sitting on her bed, combing her long, beautiful black hair.

"Dare you enter my chamber without knocking?" she demanded.

"I dare to see how my future wife looks as she awakens in the morning!" teased Harald.

As Ragnild was about to call for Svend, Harald walked to her bedside and knelt on the step before her. He reached for her hands and set the comb down on the bed linen. He kissed both hands and looked at her startled face.

"I have come to propose marriage to you."

As she opened her mouth to offer the same conditions she had set before, he reached up and covered her mouth with his fingers.

"Before you say more, please listen to my proposal. I, Harald Halvdanson, ask thee, Ragnild Eriksdatter, to be my wife...to be my only wife. I promise to protect and love you, and only you, until we both shall die, and then I promise to love you in the halls of Gimli, for as long as Odin's Kingdom lasts. Will that be long enough?"

Ragnild slipped over to the edge of the bed platform and took his hands in both of hers. She kissed the fingertips of each hand.

"With these kisses, I accept your offer to love and protect me until your dying day...and beyond!"

"I have a gift for you, my love," he said as he placed his leather pouch in her hands.

"It is a very heavy gift," she said with a smile. "Perhaps it is a bag of gold coins!"

"It is better than a bag of gold coins," he answered as she lifted the large rock from the pouch. "It is a beautiful rock from the shores of Skagen Manor. Gold would come from another country, but this rock will sit by your bedside and remind you of the place where we first met."

That comment caused them both to smile.

"It will also remind you of your home here in Jutland...the home you agreed to leave because of your love for me," he added.

"Do you suppose that I love you more than the home where I was born...the home where my parents died while protecting me?" she questioned.

"You may not love me more, as yet, but I intend to make you love me more than anything else in this world!"

Ragnild laughed and put his hands around her waist, put her arms around his neck and gave him the first of many kisses. "It will be exciting to watch you try to make that happen," she whispered in his ear.

"I think I shall call you Rani," Harald told her.

"Why not Ragnild?"

"Ragnild is my mother's name, and though I love my mother dearly, I do not want to be calling her name with a body full of desire!"

"Then I shall call you Hara, and you will know for a certainty which wife is calling for you in the middle of the night!"

"Do you think I would be thinking of anyone else but you?" he asked with a sly smile on his face.

"Not if you know what is good for you!" she retorted.

"Ah, jealousy is a two-edged sword! I hope you do not intend to make my life miserable by becoming a jealous wife."

"That will be up to you! Will you do anything to make me jealous?"

"Never!" he insisted, but smiled at her frown. "Come here, my Rani, and I will show you why you need not be jealous of my affections."

"Well, Hara, I will come to you, as long as you promise to remember that I have not given myself to you in marriage...yet!"

"How could I forget? I have been dreaming about you every night and counting the days until we are wed!"

"Good! You will love me even better after having to wait!"

It was decided that they would have their marriage feast when the ice was gone and the pleasant weather had arrived. Ragnild wanted to spend the lovely spring days riding among the sand dunes along the sea shore and through the fields behind the manor house.

"I shall miss my home when you take me across the sea," she said with a wistful sigh.

"You do not have to look at me as if I was capturing you and taking you to some far off country against your will! I guess that look means you haven't yet come to love me more than Skagen Manor," he teased as they sat their horses on a hill overlooking her childhood home.

"What of my parents...sunk to the bottom of our lake?"

"You know their spirits have long since gone to the spirit world."

"I know...but it will be sad to never come to this hill again and look down at the lake. I love to sit here and see the sunlight and the manor house reflected in the still water."

"What if I say we can come back here, every spring, and ride up to this same hill, and think about your selfless parents? Will that make leaving more bearable?"

She turned her head and smiled at him. The wind was blowing her black hair around her shoulders and she looked wildly beautiful.

"I think you really do love me," she said.

He leaned across his saddle and kissed her soft lips.

"Do you doubt my love?" he asked.

"No...not really," she hesitated.

"Not really? What does that mean?"

"I was just trying to think if I loved you more than Skagen Manor yet!" she bantered as she turned her horse and galloped down the hill.

Harald's horse was not to be left behind and he arrived at the back of the manor house just minutes after she did.

The plan they made was to leave Svend in charge of the manor, plus all of the workers, the animals and the fields. Ragnild really wanted to have him come with her, but Harald had convinced her that he would be the best individual to take responsibility for her large estate. She knew she needed to have someone she could depend on, whose loyalty was unquestioned, and he was the person she could trust the most.

Harald had not told her that he did not want Svend to come to their new home with them. There was still something in his attitude toward him that Harald did not like. It felt like jealousy, although he knew Svend could not have expected to marry Ragnild. Still, there had been that time when they were close comrades, after her parents were dead and they worried about raiders returning. He must have enjoyed his role of protector and friend.

Planning a marriage without her parent's presence was very difficult for Rani. She felt sure that they would approve of Harald as a husband, but she had always thought her father would make the marriage agreement for her and her mother would help with her gown and other preparations. She had no living family members and felt really alone.

Just when she was about to break down and began crying with sadness, Harald would come striding into the great room, all full of life and excitement and cheer her up. Then she would think about how fortunate she was to have the opportunity for this new life with someone who really loved her...who had pledged to love and protect her for the rest of her life and beyond. Yes, she was glad she had not taken his life on the sea shore that day. It seemed so long ago.

She made plans to speak their wedding vows at the edge of the lake. That was as close to her parents as she could get. A covered pavilion was being built where she and Harald would stand while they exchanged their rings and drank from the marriage cup. Colorful spring flowers and branches with new leaves would cover the poles and decorate the railings. It would smell wonderful.

The wedding crown that her mother had worn for her marriage was among the few precious jewels that had escaped discovery by the raiders. Rani was thrilled to be able to wear the same crown that had been worn by the women of her family for many generations. The red stones set in the silver metal would sparkle beautifully in the bright sunlight.

A long gown of red silk was being made for her to wear for her special day. Berdaluke had ventured across the water to Gautberg to find the bolt of fabric in just the right shade. He seemed happy to please her, as she knew how much he cared for her future husband. She wondered what other treasures Harald had instructed him to purchase at the market there. Her father always used to bring back something lovely for her and her mother after a trading expedition.

As that thought crossed her mind, she pictured the gold rings that Harald wore on each hand. Probably he had given a gold ring to each of his wives. Well, she would not be content to have the same ring as all the rest. She would choose silver. Though it wasn't considered as precious as gold, it would be precious to her.

That night, after the evening meal, she broached the subject.

"Do Svanhild and Gyda wear gold rings like the ones you have on your hands?"

He had gotten so used to seeing the gold rings on his fingers that he did not even think about them anymore.

"Yes, they do."

"I hope you aren't planning to give me a gold ring like theirs!" she said with a raised voice.

"Gyda and Svanhild both wear a gold ring with my name on it. Are you saying you do not want a ring, or you do not want a ring with my name on it?"

"I am saying I refuse to be treated like just another wife of King Harald Halvdanson! Did you ask Berdaluke to have rings made for us in Gautberg?"

Harald paused. He thought they were the perfect gift. She was right. He had chosen to have matching gold rings made for each of his wives...except Snofrid.

"It seems to me that it is my right to choose the rings to be made for my wife and myself. May be things are done differently down here in Jutland!" he answered with a slight hint of sarcasm.

"I do not care how things are done in Norway or in Jutland! I will not be put in the pen with all the other cows!" she exclaimed.

He started to laugh, but he could see that she did not think it was funny.

"Do you think I consider you just the latest addition to my cow herd?" he asked, trying hard not to smile.

"I am saying I wish I was your first and only wife. I do not want to be like any of your other wives!"

"Believe me, you are not like any of my other wives," he said, trying to sound reassuring.

"I want a silver ring.....and I want you to have a silver ring also!"

"I am sure Berdaluke won't mind making another trip over to Gautberg," he said calmly.

"Do you think I am being childish?" she asked, suddenly unsure of herself.

The thought that he was forty and his bride just twenty crossed his mind.

"You are too much a woman for me to ever consider you childish! I think silver will be perfect for my dark haired beauty."

That comment softened her feelings and she walked over to where Harald was sitting. She stood close between his legs and put her hands on his broad shoulders.

"I think you know just how to make a woman love you!" she said as she gave him a big hug.

I ought to know by now, he thought, but he wisely kept the thought to himself.

The weeks of preparation flew by and soon the marriage feast day arrived. The morning dawned bright and sunny, with no rain clouds visible anywhere in the sky.

"I told you that Freya would not let it rain on Friday!" exclaimed Rani. "She is especially happy that we are saying our vows out by the lake."

"Are you saying that if we had waited until Saturday, the Godess would have made it rain?" he teased.

She just gave him a look and turned around to go back into her bedchamber.

"You shan't see me again until I come walking toward you in my bride gown!" she called as she pranced down the hallway.

Yes, she was going to be a handful, he thought, a handsome handful though.

Harald stood on the covered platform and looked out over the crowd of people who were standing in rows between the manor house and the lake. He saw the friendly faces of his men, who had spent the winter and spring, waiting with him for this moment. Berdaluke was smiling as boldly as he had ever seen him. He was standing close to the platform and would act as witness for his friend.

Svend stood on the other side as witness for Rani. He was the closest thing to family she had left. Her men and house servants were all assembled and waiting to see their mistress come walking out of the manor house. Then Harald saw a face that disturbed him. It was Witch Brynhilde. What was she doing here? Rani must have asked her to come. He knew she did not understand the evil that sorcerers could cause. Well, he was not going to let an old witch ruin his happiness this day!

It really was a beautiful day...he had to give Freya that. There were birds singing and the scent of fresh green grass and flowers filled the air. A slight breeze was blowing the leaves on the branches used to decorate the pavilion where they would speak their marriage vows.

He stood waiting, and waiting, until the crowd began to get restless. She could not have changed her mind, could she? Should he ask Svend to go back to the house and see if anything was wrong? None of his other wives had made him stand and wait like this! Just as that thought crossed his mind, he chastised himself. If he wanted to have a miserable life, all he would have to do is constantly compare Rani to his other wives...and she would probably divorce him! That was a chilling thought.

Suddenly, the door to the manor house opened, and out stepped the most beautiful bride he had ever seen. He did not think she would mind hearing that statement, but he decided right then and there, that he would never be guilty of comparing Rani to any of his wives...ever again.

The silver wedding crown sat on her shiny black hair and she walked like a woman who was already a queen. The red dress had turned out beautifully with long, flowing sleeves and a train that followed several feet behind her. He wondered if red was her favorite color, or if she had just chosen it because of the red stones in the wedding crown. Well, he would soon find out.

When he walked forward to help her up the step and into the pavilion, he thought his smile must match that of Berdaluke. Of course, Rani was smiling so brightly that it made his heart began to pound uncontrollably in his chest. Odin had surely blessed him once again!

As they stood gazing into each others eyes, an intense feeling of deep affection seemed to flow from one to the other. After a few moments spent in acknowledging the presence of those who were waiting to witness their union, it was time for the ring ceremony. Harald reached into his pouch and pulled out a wide silver band, complete with Hara inscribed on it. Rani smiled as he placed it on her right hand.

Then he reached into the pouch once more. This time he had a silver ring with a large red stone in the center. She gasped with delight as she saw it and Berdaluke noted her pleasure with a feeling of satisfaction. This ring was placed on her left hand. Rani was so thrilled and excited about the stunning ring that she reached up and kissed Harald several times, and even forgot about the fact that she had not remembered his ring.

"I do not think we are truly married until my ring is also on my finger!" he whispered in her ear.

"Oh yes... your ring! Where is it?"

"It is right here in my pouch."

"Well, let me have it!" she said impatiently.

He reached in and produced another wide silver band.....this one bearing the name of Rani. She quickly placed it on his finger and then stretched out her hands to admire her two rings again.

"Well, I guess Berdaluke made a good choice, did not he?" Harald asked.

"Yes, I love them! Thank you Berdaluke," she said as she turned to flash him a big smile.

"And what of our vows? Are you ready yet?" he teased.

"Of course I am!" she answered.

He carefully unsheathed his special sword, Frey, and held it out to her. Rani placed her delicate hand on the handle above his large one as they stood facing each other. With the rings on their hands and their hands joined on the sword hilt, the couple spoke their vows.

"I hope you are listening, Mother and Father. I am about to pledge my life and love to this King of Norway."

"And I am about to be joined to your Ragnild the Mighty!" he added.

With that, Ragnild vowed to love and serve Hara forever. Harald pledged to love and protect Rani, not just until death, but into the spirit world beyond. They turned and raised the sword between them, to all those who had come to witness this marriage. Next, they turned to face the lake and raised the sword in honor of her parents.

Harald sheathed his sword and took the handle of the silver mead bowl that Svend handed him. Rani took the handle on the other side and they carefully tipped the bowl to their lips. The sharing of the mead bowl sealed their vows in the presence of the witnesses, the assembled friends, and their God.

The happy couple walked hand in hand back to the door of the manor house. Here, Harald placed his sword across the threshold and lifted his bride up and over it. He handed her the keys to all of the doors and closets of Skagen Manor. Of course, this action was only symbolic, as Rani had been controlling the keys of her manor house for quite some time already.

A great feast had been prepared for the wedding couple and their guests. The mead flowed freely, and many kind toasts were offered for their marriage. Finally, the end of the day arrived and it was time for Rani and her Hara to make their way to the bedchamber. She left the group first, as it would take her longer to prepare. After some time, the men gave Harald one more toast and wished him well as he made his way down the hall.

Rani had decided to make a sleep robe out of the same red silk as her wedding dress. She knew she looked radiant in red and the smooth silk fabric felt soft against her skin. She had also decided that Hara and she would spend their marriage night in the master bedchamber, even though the bed had not been slept in since the death of her parents.

New bed linens had been woven and an extra thick eiderdown mattress covered the bed boards. It did seem strange to her to be lying in the big bed that her parents had shared, but she knew that she was truly mistress of Skagen Manor now and there was a new master.

He opened the door quietly and looked into the room. A single candle burned by the bed and there was a lovely, black haired woman, dressed in a red robe, lying on top of the linen sheets. As he walked slowly over to the bed, he could hear the soft, even breathing of his sleeping beauty. She must have gotten tired of waiting for him.

His wedding clothes did not take very long to come off his body. He was glad that he still had firm muscles and smooth skin under all his hair. He did not want to look like an old man for his lovely, young wife. She must have laid out the new linen nightshirt on the trunk for him to wear. He decided to put it on, in case she might be shocked at seeing the bare skin of a man in her bed for the first time.

Should he leave the candle burning so that he could enjoy looking at her, or should he blow it out? Maybe tomorrow night would be a better time to enjoy each other without their night clothes. He must keep reminding himself that this was her first time to lie with a man and he needed to be careful not to act like a man who had already enjoyed four wedding nights.

Harald climbed into the bed beside his sleeping wife and tried to decide what to do. Well, he would just begin with a kiss or two and see how she responded. Rani opened her eyes as his lips found hers, but the room was in total darkness. She could smell the mead on his breath, but it wasn't unpleasant. She had drunk her share of mead, as well.

After a few kisses, she asked him why he had blown out the candle.

"I wasn't sure if you wanted to experience your marriage night in the light or in the dark, so I chose the dark," he answered.

"Did you want to experience it in the dark," she asked.

"My first choice would be to see your lovely face before I kiss it."

"My first choice would be to see you looking into my lovely face before you kiss me!"

"Well, let's get that candle lit!" he exclaimed as he rolled to the edge of the bed.

When he turned around, he saw that she was smiling up at him.

"Do you like my red sleep gown?"

"I do. You look almost the same as you did walking toward me this afternoon...except you have removed your wedding crown."

"The sewing women said it was a waste of time to make a matching sleep gown, for you would take it off me as soon as you got into the bed!"

"Oh, they did, did they?"

"Do you want to take it off me?" she asked quietly.

"Yes, I want to take it off you...very much!" he answered.

"Have you taken off the sleep gown of your other wives on their wedding night?"

He sat up with a bolt, grabbed her body and set it down hard on his lap.

"Alright, that's it! We are not going to speak of this! I do not want to think about any of my other wives and I surely do not want you to talk about them. This is your first time to lie with a husband and I am going to act like this is my first time to lie with a wife. Do you understand?" he said with a frown.

She was so startled with his aggressive action that all she could do was to nod in agreement.

"No...I want to hear your voice! Do you agree that we are going to forget about everyone else and enjoy having just two people in this marriage bed?"

"Yes, I agree," she whispered.

"Good! Now let's see what is under that red sleep gown!"

She laughed as he opened the robe and gave her belly a big kiss.

"And what about your sleep shirt, my hairy husband?"

"Here, you can have it," he said as he lifted it off his head. "I do not like to sleep with a night shirt, anyway!" he exclaimed.

He set her gently back down on the bed and rolled on top of her.

"You once asked me to kill you before I placed my seed in you! Are you ready to die?"

"You do take my breath away!" she said laughing.

"I'll show you how to take your breath away!" he said as he covered her lips with his own.

It was easy to pretend that this was his first wedding night. He felt like he had never loved any other woman as completely as he loved his Rani. He hoped that she would feel his love fill her...that she would be able to have the joy that love can bring.

The bedside candle burned through the night and into the morning. Harald opened his eyes to see the soft pink skin of Rani's back turned toward him. How could he have been so fortunate as to have married this lovely woman? He wrapped his arms around her and she nestled back against his chest.

"I just want to ask you one question this morning," he said. "Do you love me more than you love Skagen Manor?"

She turned to face him and looked seriously into his eyes.

"I think I do."

"What do you mean, 'You think you do'?" he demanded as he began to tickle her belly again.

"Help! Stop! I give up!" she shouted as she tried to catch her breath.

"That's not good enough!" he continued.

"Okay, okay!" she laughed. "I love you more than Skagen Manor!

"That's good," he said, "because we have to get sailing for Norway soon."

"But not today," she whispered as she reached for his lips.

"No, not today," he mumbled.

A fortnight passed before they took their leave. Rani walked through the manor house, trying to fix it in her mind so that she could remember it when she was far away. Hara kept trying to reassure her that they could come back for a visit each year, but somehow, she had the feeling that was not going to happen.

She filled seven chests with clothing and bedding, plus her mother's silver goblets and chargers. She wanted to bring the tapestries from the walls also, but Hara said she would need to take those on their next trip. The special glittering rock he had given her when he proposed marriage was tucked away in a red leather pouch attached to her woven belt and the silver wedding crown was safely packed with the bedding. She still felt like there was something she was missing. Oh yes, it was her father's sword.

The morning of departure dawned bright and sunny. Hara had jumped up and was out of the bedchamber before Rani could even get fully awake. She knew he was anxious to leave, but she still felt a sense of dread. Was it just that she would miss the closeness of having her parents buried in the small lake behind the manor house? It seemed like it was something else, but what could it be?

The same friends and servants that had assembled to wish her well, just a short time ago, now assembled to say their farewell. She tried to speak to each one and press their hand. Hara was watching her and she wanted to act brave before him. It would not do to act the part of a child, especially now that she was a true married woman.

Finally, she came to the end of the line of well wishers and was about to walk the plank into Hara's great dragon ship, when she had a strange feeling that someone had touched the back of her neck. But her hair and head scarf were covering her neck so how could anyone have touched her? Hara was the only one close, and he was holding both her hand and her arm.

Suddenly, she turned and saw a dark figure standing at the edge of the beach. It was Brynhilde. Somehow, Rani knew the witch wanted to say a few parting words.

"I must go to her," she murmured.

Harald turned his head in the direction she was looking. He recognized the menacing figure of Brynhilde and tightened his grip on Rani's arm.

"No! I forbid you to go! Just get in the ship!" he demanded.

Rani looked up at him in surprise.

"You forbid me to go?" she questioned.

He could see the determined look in her eyes beneath the raised eyebrows.

"I plead with you not to go," he whispered.

She just smiled up at him and lifted his hand from her arm.

"I will be back soon," she said reassuringly.

He wanted to grab her and lift her into the ship, but he did not want to make a scene in front of her men and his. A feeling of dread crept over him as he watched his beloved walk slowly toward old Brynhilde. There was an evil smile on the witch's face, but Rani did not seem to notice.

The two women spoke for just a few minutes, and then Rani turned and walked back to the ship. Harald breathed a sigh of relief as she got close to him.

"What is that you have in the large pouch?" he asked.

"It is the parting gift Brynhilde wanted me to have. I am not to open it until we are on the water."

"That is fine with me. Let us get out on the water!" he exclaimed.

Rani watched as the figures on the shore got smaller and smaller. She could not hold back the tears any longer as she sailed away from the only home she had ever known. She tried not to let Hara see her crying, but he came over and sat down by her side.

"Let me kiss away those tears," he said as cheerfully as he could. "Remember, you told me that you love me more than Skagen Manor!"

She turned and gave him a weak smile.

"You are right. I did say that, didn't I?" she answered as she gave him a light kiss on his cheek.

In an effort to take her mind off the place she was leaving behind, he asked, "And what is in that big pouch you got from Brynhilde?"

She placed the pouch on her lap and untied the string from the top. As she looked at the contents, a strangled cry escaped her lips. Hara grabbed the pouch and stared inside. The witch had placed a dead black bird with a broken neck in the pouch.

"She said this gift had reminded her of me...of how I would look when I returned!" Rani screamed. "I must be going to die! I must be going to return as a dead woman!"

Harald grabbed her shoulders and shook her.

"You are not going to die! I will not let you! Odin would not have sent me to find you if you were just going to die! She is an evil old woman who does not want to see you happy... and leaving!"

With that, he grabbed the pouch and threw it into the water.

"There, she can have her gift back and maybe she will be the one to die!" he shouted.

Rani was sobbing quietly. She did not want Harald's men to see her behaving like this. She was a married woman now and she was expected to act the part.

"Just hold me," she pleaded. "Hold me and tell me again that you will love and protect me forever."

"I will love you and protect you forever...and ever!" he said as reassuringly as he could.

They sat with their arms around each other, holding on tightly, with his cloak wrapped around her small body as well as his broad shoulders. The rocking of the ship as it headed out into the waves comforted her. She did not know what to expect as they traveled to her new home, but she was going to think only good thoughts. She was happy to be sitting in the strong arms of a man who loved her so very completely.

The thoughts going through the mind of her husband were not so positive. I should have grabbed her and carried her into the boat, even if it made her angry. It would have been better than letting her get close to the foul influence of that witch! I thought she would be safe once I got her home with me, but Brynhilde probably put a curse on her! I think I will send word back to Svend to have her evil life ended. That is probably the only way to break the spell.

CHAPTER 29

OUT WITH THE OLD, IN WITH THE NEW

There were no storms to contend with on the return trip to Norway, and soon they were sailing up the Glama River on their way to Guttorm's home at Skjeberg Manor. The house was in a beautiful setting, just a short way down from the waterfall. Berdaluke had delivered a message to some of Harald's men who were stationed in Gautberg and they had traveled to Tune with the news of Harald's return.

Not only was Hara anxious for his uncle to meet Rani, he also needed a place for her to stay while he traveled across the fjord to talk to Svanhild. Even though he had gotten used to the idea, he still knew it was going to be a difficult thing for his second wife to accept.

Guttorm and young Gutt were pleased to see Harald and his new wife. Gutt's mother, Asa, had been dead for many years, so it did not bother him that his father was marrying yet another woman. His only thought was a feeling of envy that his father had found such a charming and beautiful young lady.

There was also a small amount of envy in the heart of Guttorm. He had long since given up on the idea of marrying, but the looks of love that he saw pass between Harald and Rani made him wish for such an experience.

"Where will you plan to live?" he asked the couple as they sat by the fire that evening.

"I have decided to build a manor in Rogaland, along the Norway Sea. Rani has grown up close to the water and I want to make her feel at home here with us," Harald explained.

"I hope you plan to travel to Tande Manor first so your mother can meet Rani," suggested Guttorm.

"That is our plan, as soon as I take care of another matter across the fjord," Harald replied as he gave Rani a knowing glance.

Guttorm wanted to ask about the impact this new marriage would have on Svanhild, but he was wise enough not to ask Harald in front of his new wife.

Maybe there would be time for a private conversation before they left for Ringsaker.

After he and Rani had spent three days enjoying the hospitality of Gutt and Guttorm, Harald decided he could put off the visit to Viken no longer. Berdaluke was left to watch over Rani as Guttorm planned to distract her with a visit to the markets in Tune. They were not as plentiful as those in Tunsberg, but they were further away from Viken Manor.

It was a short trip down the Glama River and across the fjord to his estate in Vestfold. His bodyguard sailed with him, but he walked alone from the shore to the manor house at the top of the hill. There was no joy in his heart this day as there had been on so many other returns. He prayed that Odin would guide him to say the words that would hurt Svanhild the least...if that was possible.

She was sitting in her usual place in front of the large weaving loom in a corner of the great hall when he walked in the door. She was startled to see him, but rose immediately and walked swiftly over to embrace him.

"You have been gone much longer than I expected," she commented as she struggled to keep an irritated tone out of her voice.

His embrace wasn't as warm as it should have been after a long absence. She tried to look into his eyes, but he was avoiding looking into hers.

"I have something to tell you," he answered as he held her at arms length away from him. "Let us sit here by the fire."

He led the way and she followed. She could feel a tension in his manner that worried her.

She wanted to demand an explanation for the time he had spent away when it was her turn to have him at Viken, plus she wanted to hear the apology he owed her for breaking his word and not returning for the Yule celebration. Guttorm had come to tell her that Harald was delayed, but he could not or would not say why.

Something about the look on her husband's face kept her from making those demands. He sat still for a few moments, struggling in his mind for the words to say to this wife of his youth.

"I do not know any better way to tell you this but just to say it out plain. I have a new wife that I married in Jutland."

"What? Is that your excuse for failing to keep your word and returning at Yule?" she stammered, quickly loosing what little control she possessed.

"Yes, that is my reason," he answered in a quiet voice designed to calm her anger.

"I guess two wives were not enough for you, you had to go seeking a third?" she cried, loosing more control by the minute.

"I did not go seeking a third wife. Odin has asked this of me and I must obey."

"I do not think I believe you! Why would Odin think you needed another wife when you already have two?"

Svanhild's voice was getting louder and louder and she could no longer sit still by his side.

"I swear to you that this is Odin's will," he exclaimed, looking up at her.

"So now Gyda and I must share you with this third wife?" she shouted.

"No, it will not be like that," he said hesitatingly.

She stopped in front of him and waited for him to finish his words.

"I have made a promise to my new wife that I would put aside my other wives and cling only to her," he continued as he raised his eyes to meet Svanhild's glare.

After a moment's shock, the meaning of his words struck her a blow like a dagger stabbing into her heart. She lifted her arm and slapped him across the face as hard as she could.

He tried to say he was sorry for hurting her, but she was beyond hearing.

"You will not put me aside! I will put you aside! You are a traitor! I hate you! I never want to see you again! Get out of my house this minute and never return! Do you hear me? I hate you! I never want to see you again!" she screamed as loud as she could through her tears, then turned and ran down the hall to the large master bedchamber they had shared for so many years.

She slammed the door behind her and the sound echoed back down the hallway to where Harald still sat by the fire. He was a little stunned by her angry outburst, but he wasn't really surprised. He knew she would take it hard, yet he felt sad to have their marriage end with those angry words. He thought he could hear her sobs through the closed door, but there was nothing he could do or say to ease her pain. He had given his word to Rani and so he must cause one wife's grief to please another.

He walked quietly out of the manor house and down to the water's edge where his men were waiting.

"Let us be off," he shouted, and there was a tone of resignation in his voice. He had done the deed he had come to do, but it had brought him no pleasure.

Rani was excited to tell Hara of the beautiful white fur cape she had seen at the market that afternoon. When she entered the great hall at Skjeberg, he was sitting alone, just staring into the fire. She walked over to where he sat and put her arms around his neck.

"Do you love me," she asked.

He looked up into her deep blue green eyes. "Yes, I do love you,"

"Then, do notlook so sad. You will make me think you are sorry you married me!"

"Of course I am not sorry that I married you. I shall never regret that."

"Then, let us depart tomorrow and leave this sad place behind!"

"Yes, I am ready for a nice visit with Mother...my other Ragnhild."

That night, after they had enjoyed their evening meal and spent some time visiting, Rani excused herself to retire to their bedchamber.

"I shall stay and discuss some matters with Gutt and Guttorm, if that will not displease you," he said.

"We have only been married a short time and you already choose to stay out here talking business with the men!" she said with a laugh.

"You get the bed warm for me and I will join you before you go to sleep."

"I will have a difficult time going to sleep tonight anyway. I will be thinking about that beautiful white fur cape you are going to purchase for me tomorrow!" she said over her shoulder as she turned and walked down the hall.

With Rani out of the room, Guttorm was quick to ask about Svanhild. He had been acting as guardian for her in Harald's absence for many years and he was concerned about her reaction to the news of a new wife.

"Had it just been the news of a new wife, we might have come away with some kind of an understanding," said Harald, "but I had to tell her that I agreed to set my other wives aside to please my new wife!"

"What are you saying? You intend to set aside both Svanhild and Gyda to please Rani?" questioned Guttorm.

"Those are the terms she gave me before she would consent to our marriage," he answered. "I knew it would be difficult, but Odin told me to go forward. He said Rani and I had been promised to each other from our time in the spirit world."

"Odin is still influencing your life. We know he protected you through all our battles, and he has blessed you with many sons. Of course, I think he gave you the best one first...do you not think so Gutt?"

Gutt laughingly agreed.

"I'll drink to that!" Harald said as he raised his horn of mead.

Gutt and Guttorm raised their drinking horns together. There was a great feeling of camaraderie between the three men as they sat by the fire in the great hall at Skjeberg.

Gutt watched his contented father walk gingerly from the room. Was it married life that kept him so virile and young looking? What a pleasure it was to sit in the company of the two great men who were the mainstays in his life. One, the father who had sired him, and the other, the namesake who had become his father in all but name.

These two would always seem like giants of men to him, no matter how much time passed between them. He would never forget seeing them disembark from their great warships on the shore at Lade Manor, fully dressed in their battle armor, with enemy blood spattered on their chainmail. Their appearance struck terror in the hearts of their enemies, but they always had a warm welcome and throaty laughter for him and his brothers.

It did seem strange to him that his father should have so many wives, and yet Uncle Guttorm should have none. When he was old enough and brave enough to ask his namesake about the difference in the two men's lives, he had been given a simple explanation.

Odin had given them different callings for their lives. His father was asked to produce a large posterity for the future leadership of the kingdom of Norway and his uncle had been asked to devote his life to assisting his sister's son with the great challenges in his life of destiny. Gutt had been taught early that one did not disobey Odin...at the peril of one's life.

It was a real treat for Rani to walk through the stalls at the Tune market. Skagen Manor had been too far from either Hedeby or Gautberg for her and her mother to visit very often. Mostly, her father would go and then bring them back some gift of cloth or precious metal. Looking at all the trade goods that filled the booths was much more exciting than having someone else choose for you.

When they came to the booth that had the white fur cape, she tried it on to show her husband. It had a lining of soft, black wool and looked wonderful with her long black hair.

"So this is the cape that you were dreaming about last night, is it? I think it looks as if it was made for you!" he said with a smile.

"Can I have it, then?" she asked with a tone of expectation in her voice.

"Only if you promise that I will be in your dreams from now on and not fur capes!" he teased.

She was quick to promise as she ran her hands over the soft fur of the beautiful cape.

"Perhaps I will also get a new cape for my mother. What other capes do you have?" he asked the vendor.

"How about this lovely black fur with the red wool lining?" he suggested.

When Rani heard him mention the word red, she turned to see the cape her husband was looking at.

"Well, red is my wife's favorite color, maybe she would like this one instead."

Rani stepped forward and let the white cape slip from her shoulders. She did love the red with the black.

"Now I am not sure. I love them both," she said hesitantly.

Harald watched his beautiful wife lovingly stroking the white fur and then the black.

"I think we will take them both!" he told the vendor.

Rani turned toward Hara with a surprised look on her face.

"Will you give the black one to your mother then?" she questioned.

"No, my love, these are both for you."

"Oh Hara, you are too good to me!"

"I am sure you will reward me in your own way," he said with a wink.

Rani just flashed him a knowing smile.

"Maybe you have a cape with a blue lining. Blue is my mother's favorite color."

"I have this thick silver fox fur with a dark blue lining."

"That will be perfect!" stated Harald. "Now I think I will make both of my women happy."

They stopped next at a booth filled with jewelry of many kinds. There were rings and bracelets, heavy belts of gold and silver, necklaces of colored beads and ornate brooches of many different shapes.

"I think my lady-love will need two strong fibula to fasten her new capes on her shoulders, what do you think?" he asked Rani.

"Oh, this is wonderful! I did not realize married life was going to be so enjoyable."

"Well, maybe we had better leave the market before I start thinking you married me for my riches!" he laughed.

"Of course I did not even think about you being a rich man when I said I would marry you, but now that I know you are, I intend to help you enjoy your riches!" she teased.

They left the market with their arms full of goods and his promise to her that they could stop at another market on another day.

Hara and Rani traveled up the River Glama until they reached the Vorma River and Eidsvold Manor. This was a place where the King held a yearly Thing, as his father Halvdan had before him. They spent the night with Jarl Bjorn and his family.

Bjorn always liked to tell the story of how Harald, as a boy of eight years, had cut off the small finger on his left hand and how his father, Torbjorn, had made him feed his finger to the dogs. During the telling, he would hold up his left fingerless hand to prove the deed had really been done.

As a fourteen year old, Bjorn had been too shocked and angry to want to tell of the incidence, but now that he was an older man, he liked to brag about teaching King Harald how to sword fight. It made him seem rather important.

"I have had a sword fight with the King myself," said Rani with a mischievous grin on her face. Harald shot her a warning glance, so she said, "Maybe I will have to wait to tell that story until another visit."

Harald made a mental note to make sure this was her only visit to Eidsvold Manor. Sometimes he wondered what had happened to the fearsome warrior that fought thirty battles without a death wound, yet received three wounds from a mere woman. Both love and war had been a part of his life the last thirty years...and he enjoyed them both.

The next day they set out again on their journey and traveled by way of the Vorma River. Harald was anxious to make Rani comfortable and impress her with the splendid scenery on every side. Just as the sun was beginning to set, they entered Lake Mjosa. From there, it was just a short distance to Tande Manor.

A warm feeling swept over him as their ships came in sight of his boyhood home. He had so many good memories of growing up there, despite some sad ones. It was undoubtedly one of the most beautiful manors in all of Norway. He had tried to make Lade Manor look as much like his Ringsaker home as he could, but there was just something about Tande Manor that set it apart.

Rani watched his face as they came close to shore. She could tell that he felt as sentimental about this home as she felt about her Skagen Manor. She was happy to think that he had a tender heart under his tough exterior. He was an only child, just as she was, but he was fortunate to have his mother still living.

Ragnhild was overjoyed to meet Rani. She could see, after only a short time, that her son was deeply in love with this girl. How very remarkable that Odin should keep planning women for him to marry. He now had so many sons that there would be no shortage of princes to rule after him. She, of course, favored the twins who were named for her husband. They had really filled a deep void in her life after Halvdan died and Harald and Guttorm were off fighting one battle after another.

"It is so nice to meet the mother of my husband. You have raised a tender and loving man."

"He has grown to be just like his father, and I could not have asked Odin to send me any better spirit to rear," replied Ragnhild.

"Well, it is good to know that the two women I love most in this world think I am so great!" Harald laughed.

"Tande Manor is such a beautiful place," Rani said. "I can see why Hara loves it so."

"It sounds strange to hear you call him Hara, but I think it is wonderful that the two of you have chosen to call each other special names. I can see that there is a good deal of love between you."

Harald put his arm around Rani's shoulder and gave her a hug.

"I have never been so happy, Mother. Odin has truly blessed me this time."

His mother felt like asking, "What about your other wives?" but instead she asked, "Would you like to stay here with me at Tande?"

"You know Tande Manor is one of my favorite places, Mother, but we shall build a large manor of our own by the Sea. I think I will leave Rani here for the winter months while I get things ready for her."

No sooner had they closed the door on Harald's bedchamber than Rani turned on him with a defiant look on her face.

"What do you mean by telling your mother that you are going to leave me here for the winter...and not even asking me if that is what I would choose to do?"

By now, Harald had come to know what to expect when she gave him that disapproving look.

"Are you saying that you do not want to spend the winter with my mother?"

"No, I am not saying that! I am saying I intend to spend the winter wherever you spend the winter. Do you think I am ready to be separated from you so soon?"

He reached down and lifted her up so that their eyes were at the same level.

"Do you love me so much then?" he teased.

"If I love you more than Skagen Manor, then I love you more than anyone or anything in this world!"

"And I love you more than Tande Manor...and I love you more than anyone or anything in this world, also."

"Then, why would you choose to leave me?"

"I thought it would be easier for you here. You know, we won't have our own home finished until next summer."

"Did you intend to leave me here until next summer?" she asked with a hurt look on her face.

"No, I could not bear that!" he exclaimed.

"Well, I do not intend to be left for even one day, much less one year, so you can tell that to your mother on the morrow. I want you to promise me you will never leave me!"

"I guess I did not realize how much you needed me!" he laughed.

She grabbed the hair on the back of his neck and began to pull.

"Do I have to resort to torture to get a promise out of you?" she asked.

"Torture won't work, but this will!" he said as he carried her to his bed.

He laid her down and covered her small body with his large one.

"I, Hara, promise never to leave you, not even for one day, and I seal the promise with this kiss," he whispered just before his lips found hers.

She could not respond with words, but she responded with her body and tried hard to express all the love that she felt for this special man.

"Rani will be coming with me to Rogaland when I leave," he told his mother the next morning.

"Are you sure that is wise?" she asked.

"Wise or foolish, that is how it must be," he answered with a smile. "We will stay for a fortnight and I will hold a Thing for Hedmark in Vang and one in Hundorp for Gulbrandsdal on our way to Nidaros. I must send Berdaluke and a group of men around with an arrow message-token today. Then we will set out for Lade."

Rani enjoyed her time with Ragnhild once she knew she was not going to be left at Tande. It was fun to hear the stories about the things that had happened to her husband when he was a boy. His mother chose not to mention the episode with Svase the Finn. Harald would have to tell her that story if he chose to.

It was exciting to ride in the hills above the manor and see the spot where the mother bear had almost killed Torda, Harald's dog. The horses raised at Tande were a superior breed, beautiful yet bold. The apple trees in the orchard were in full bloom and seemed to foretell a bountiful harvest.

"It would have been nice to have company here for Yuletide," Ragnhild said with a wistful tone in her voice. "The house has been painfully quiet since Halvdan the White and Halvdan the Black moved back up to Lade. I knew they would go sometime, but the time went so fast."

"Why not travel up to Lade after the harvest festival and spend Yule with the boys?"

"I do not know if I am up to that long a trip," said his mother with a sigh.

"Of course you are! And then you can come to spend Yuletide with us at our new manor the next year."

Ragnhild just smiled. She did not really want to admit that she was feeling old and tired and anxious to join her beloved Halvdan in Gimli. As long as Harald needed her, she knew Odin would not let her leave. She would just have to continue to deal with her loneliness.

CHAPTER 30

THE NIDAROS THING

After the Thing in Gulbrandsdal, Hara and Rani continued their journey, through the Uplands, then on to Nidaros and finally to Lade. Halvdan the Black and Halvdan the White were certainly enjoying being the masters of Harald's large manor on the shores of the Trondelag Fjord. They were very curious about their father's new wife. Rani felt a little strange to be introduced to sons of Harald that were older than her. Gutt seemed different, but these twin boys seemed just like that...boys.

The day after their arrival, Asa's mother Malfrid traveled over from Lanke Manor along with Sigrod. He was quieter than the twins and must have taken after his deceased mother. Rani could feel a coldness toward her coming from the older woman, who left after a short time. Sigrod stayed to visit with his father, but hardly said a word.

Rani was impressed by the very large and beautiful master bedchamber when they finally retired that night. She thought it must be the largest bedchamber she had ever seen. The walls were covered with beautiful tapestries and there were lavender hangings on the bed posts.

After Rani had fallen asleep, Harald lay awake staring at the beams above his head. This was not the first time that he had slept in this bed since Asa died, but it was the first time he had slept in her bed with another woman. He knew she had approved of his marriage to Svanhild, but he wondered if she could see him here with Rani.

It was the first night since their marriage that Hara had not made love to his wife. He had kissed her tenderly as she lay with her head on his shoulder, her black hair covering the pillows and intermingling with his still golden strands. They talked about the day's events and his three sons and then Harald got lost in his private thoughts. Rani had drifted off to sleep in the silence. As he looked down at her lovely face, aglow in the candlelight, his mind wandered back to the day he had vowed to love only her. Asa would hopefully understand.

As they walked out of the manor door the next morning, heading for the stables, Rani saw the large rune stone with Asa's name on it.

"I guess you loved her very much," she said as they stood before the stone.

"She was my first wife, and she taught me how wonderful it can be to have a special woman in your life," he answered, still looking at the stone.

"Do you still think about her after all these years?"

"Well, mostly just when I am at Lade...then the memories come back to me."

"Perhaps you love me less when you are here," she said matter of factly while looking up into his blue eyes.

"I love you with my whole heart, you know that," he protested.

"Then why did not you make love to me last night?" she countered.

The question made him feel uncomfortable. Did he dare tell her the truth?

"Just to show you how much I love you, I am taking you riding to see the beautiful Stjordal River today!" he said as he scooped her up and gave her a playful kiss. "The first one to the barn gets the fastest horse!" he said as he started to run.

She wasn't sure if he was just trying to avoid looking her in the eye, but she was always up for a challenge, so she took off running as well. It was more difficult for her to run in a long dress, so he got there first. He stood there, out of breath, and waited for her to catch up.

"I'm not as fast as I used to be, but I am still faster than you!" he panted.

"It's not fair! You started first. I want the fastest horse!" she pouted.

"I think all of the horses at Lade are fast, but you may have the first choice."

As it turned out, she chose a big black and Hara chose a white stallion.

"These horses were sired by the great war horses, Slepni and May Day, the horses my father and Guttorm and I rode into battle. I do not know what kind of training they are getting these days, but I am sure they probably know their way to the river.

It was a beautiful day for a ride. Much of the mountain snow had melted and the river was running very high. When they came to the spot where Asa and he used to stop, he did not even suggest that they dismount. He was working on keeping his first wife out of his mind and he was sure he wasn't going to miss another night of making love with Rani, his fifth wife, no matter what bed they were sleeping in.

A Nidaros Thing had been arranged for Harald's visit and this time Rani went along. It was a great gathering and people came out for the social event, even if they did not have a case to be settled. Fortunately, there had been no murders committed in the last year and the cases were mostly concerning laws that had been broken, animals that had been wrongfully killed and land disputes of prospective heirs.

Sunday was the day set aside to hold a Thing. Not only because it was a spiritual event, but because Saturday was the day for bathing and everyone wanted their bodies to be clean before they dressed in their best clothing for attendance at the Thing.

Rani wore a bright blue green pell velvet gown that brought out the color of her eyes. She had a narrow silver diadem on her hair with a large green stone in the center and a wide silver belt hung from her waist. Silver bracelets adorned her wrists and multiple strands of silver chains hung from her neck. She covered her dress with a red sleeveless cloak for the journey to Nidaros.

"It is a good thing you have chosen all of that jewelry in silver," said Hara. "If it had been made of gold, someone may have captured you for a ransom!"

"Is it too much?" she asked.

"The lovely wife of King Harald can wear whatever she chooses."

"I have never attended a Thing before, and I wanted to be sure you would be proud of me," she answered shyly.

"You would have been the most beautiful woman at the Thing, no matter what you wore!" he said as he lifted her into the carriage.

Harald's three sons accompanied them on the way to Nidaros, each riding a magnificent stallion. It seemed interesting to Rani that Halvdan the Black rode a black horse and Halvdan the White's horse was white. Harald was also on a white horse and Sigrod rode a black. The four men rode in front of the carriage and she thought she had never seen such proud men and horseflesh.

The young men were dressed in fine clothes as befitted the sons of the King. All three were wearing blue wool breeches above black leather boots. Their white linen shirts and cloaks were trimmed with a border of gold and silver threads that had been woven for them by their grandmother Malfrid. They wore cloaks of dark green pell velvet with blue silk linings.

They had their long hair parted in the middle and on their foreheads they wore broad silver bands. As unmarried men, they wore no rings, but had heavy silver fibula clasps used to fasten their cloaks on the right shoulder. Wide silver belts held short daggers and silver spurs completed their royal dress. The amulet around their neck was made of gold and bore the seal of their father, just as Harald wore an amulet given to him by his father.

Their father's dress was much more elaborate than theirs. A purple cloak of pell velvet wrapped his wide shoulders, held in place by a massive gold fibula pin.

His heavy crown and belt were also made of gold. The only piece of silver he wore was his wedding band from Rani. His black leather boots were covered by ornate gold spurs. Black linen breeches and a white linen shirt covered his still muscular body.

The Lade stallions were dressed to match their riders. Harald's saddle and bridle was richly ornamented with gold and his son's horses wore silver. Gold was considered to be the providence of the King and others were allowed to have limited gold added to the silver of their decorations. The horses that drew the carriage in which Rani rode were white and their harnesses and horse collars were oppulent with bronze gilt, silver and gold.

Harald always carried his special sword, Frey, in its gold and silver scabbard. It hung from a belt across his shoulder. The only weapons allowed at the Thing belonged to the King, his sons, the lagmen, his bodyguard and his hird of men. The fearsome twenty five of his bodyguard, lead by Berdaluke, followed behind the carriage riding on chestnut colored horses. The troop of seventy five men, riding bay horses, rode last.

The Thing was always held in a holy place, and the Temple location in Nidaros was the most holy place in the area. There was a large, open plain near a bend of the Nid River and people loved to gather there. Only the free men who owned land had a voice in the deliberations, but the landowners were followed by a large retinue, according to their rank or wealth.

The Thing plain was a sacred place which must not be sullied by bloodshed or any other impurity. Each gathering was opened with religious ceremonies, which included a solemn peace declaration over the assembly. From the time it was opened until it was dissolved, the meeting was under the protection of the Gods. It was a very special occasion when the King was present.

The area around the Nidaros Temple was filled with people by the time Harald and his entourage arrived. Booths were arranged around the perimeter of the plain and families had claimed theirs by placing a large tent over the standing walls. Between the sessions of the Thing there were various amusements offered. It was an ideal place for a scald to share his verse or entertain by telling a saga.

There were eight fylkes or districts in the Trondelag area, so the crowd was very large. Each fylke was responsible to provide twelve trustworthy lagmen to act as jurors for the cases that would be presented from their area. It was King Harald's responsibility to know the law and the punishment that was to be given to those individuals who were deemed guilty.

It was impressive to see how much the people loved and respected her Hara. They were also very curious and anxious to see his new wife from Jutland. It bothered her a little to be the center of attention, but once the Thing started people's interest shifted to the opening ceremony. Harald, sitting in his judge's seat, offered a prayer for the protection of the Gods and made a solemn peace declaration over all those assembled. Rani and the Princes of Lade sat in special chairs to his right.

The twelve lagmen from the first fylke sat in a special section directly across from the King. The first case under review was a man who had received a judgement in his local fylke Thing and was appealing his case here at the regional Thing. He was accused of having a dagger in his belt while traveling to the local Thing. His defense was that he needed it for protection from an angry neighbor.

The neighbor, who had been accused, testified that he had not been armed and was traveling peace-holy and would not have broken the peace of the Thing to settle an argument. The twelve lagmen jurors determined that there was not just cause for the carrying of the weapon. They referred to King Harald.

The King quoted the law as: "All men traveling to a Thing shall be at peace or peace-holy with each other until they come back to their homes. If anyone breaks the peace and wounds or maims a man, he must forfeit all loose property." He then ordered the guilty man to forfeit his dagger and pay a fine of four marks of silver. All fines collected during a Thing were given to the priests for maintenance of the Temple.

The next case interested Rani greatly, because it involved the rights of a woman. A man was charged with being caught in the act of kissing another man's wife. A neighbor had happened upon the two adults in the woods behind the woman's home. Nine neighbors were called as witnesses. Although just one person had witnessed the act, the other eight witnesses believed the one. The lagmen gave a guilty verdict to the charge and referred the case to the King.

Harald quoted the law as: "If a man kisses a woman belonging to another, secretly, with her will, he is liable to pay three marks of silver. If it is against her will, the man is liable for lesser outlawry."

Rani thought her husband rather enjoyed this case. He said he must secure additional information before sentencing and he called the woman to the witness chair.

"I have not been able to determine if this kiss was with or without your will," he probed.

The woman's face turned red, but she answered, "It was with my will, My Lord."

"Then the penalty for this secret kiss will be three marks of silver."

Just as the woman was about to step down from the witness chair, a man walked forward and asked to speak.

"What interest have you in this case?" Harald asked.

"I am the husband of the woman who is giving her kisses to another!"

"What is it you would like to say to this court?"

"I had supposed my wife was going to say she was kissed against her will, so the thief would be charged with lesser outlawry, but now I hear his penalty is only three marks of silver. Well, I have an additional charge. I charge him with making a song of love on my wife!" he shouted.

Harald looked at the woman still seated in the witness chair. Her face was even more red than it had been before.

"Has the man you willingly kissed made a love song on you?" he questioned.

The woman sat in the chair with her eyes cast down and seemed unable to speak. Suddenly, there was another man's voice heard over the din of the crowd.

"Yes, I admit to both the kiss and the love song. I plead with you to let her be and put me in the witness chair," he requested as he came close to where Harald was seated.

Harald agreed to let the man and woman trade places and asked the man to repeat his statement now that he was sitting in the witness chair. The man did so.

"Are you sorry for your crime?" Harald asked.

"I am not. I will pay whatever penalty the law demands," was his answer.

The King quoted the law as: "If a man makes a song of love on a woman who is married to another, he is to be outlawed. I guess I have no choice but to pronounce you an outlaw. Are you prepared to leave the country or risk being killed?"

Just as the man opened his mouth to speak, a women's voice cried out, "No! Please have mercy, My Lord. I have declared my separation from my husband two times in two places in the presence of witnesses, and now I declare it thirdly in front of these witnesses at this Thing. I choose to divorce my husband and marry this man I love. I beg you to show mercy," she pleaded.

Rani stared at her husband. The hundreds of people who had just observed the emotional scene were staring at him also.

Harald looked at the woman standing before him and then answered, "The law is clear that you have followed the steps needed to gain a divorce from your husband...and that divorce means you would be free to marry this man that you profess to love. However, if he is declared an outlaw, I would presume that your former husband might be inclined to take his life as soon as this Thing is pronounced finished."

"As your King, I have the right to moderate a sentence when I see good cause. As I sit here next to the woman I love, it is hard for me to think of denying the opportunity for another man to have that same blessing."

The crowd was silently holding its breath...waiting to hear the judgement of their King. Finally he said, in a voice loud enough to be heard, "I pronounce you a lesser outlaw and order you to pay a fine of ten marks of silver."

The woman fell to her knees and thanked Harald through her tears. The man stepped down from the witness chair and thanked him as well. Hara turned to smile at his Rani and she whispered the words, "I love you!"

A few days later, the newlyweds traveled on through the Trondelag Fjord, past Orkadal and on to More. Here they stopped at Borgund Manor, the estate of Jarl Ragnvald and his wife Hild. There had been hard feelings between Harald and Hild since Hrolf was judged an outlaw, and he wasn't sure what kind of reception there would be in her home. Actually, Hild had told her husband that she would not receive Harald...until Ragnvald told her that Harald was bringing his new wife along to meet them.

Hild begrudged any happiness that Harald might have, but her curiosity about this woman from Jutland took precedence over her anger. She was disappointed to see what a beauty Ragnild was, and even more disappointed to see how happy Harald looked. There was only one thing that she was happy about, and that was that her husband was now too old to attract a young woman like that.

Ragnvald had sired several sons by two concubines before they married, and it always made Hild slightly nervous to have an attractive woman around. The sooner this loving couple paid their visit and then continued on with their trip, the happier Hild would be. She decided it was in her best interest to be civil...at least she could try for a few days.

"You know, Harald asked us to raise one of the four sons he had by that witch, but we had to get rid of him," Hild stated as they were eating their evening meal. "Has he told you about his wife Snofrid?"

There was silence as Harald and Ragnvald looked at Hild in disbelief.

Rani turned to look at Hara. Seeing the shocked look on his face and the smug look on Hild's face, she cleverly answered, "I do not care about any of Hara's other wives. He is mine now and that is all that matters!"

Ragnvald glared at his wife and then added, "Harald tells me Odin says you two were promised to each other in the spirit world. I guess he just had to wait until you were of marrying age."

"That is right," added Harald with a sigh of relief.

In fact, Harald had not told Rani about Snofrid and he wasn't sure he wanted to, but now he knew he had to.

The guest bedchamber at Borgund was right next to the master bedchamber, so Rani spoke in a whisper. She surely did not want Hild to have the satisfaction of knowing she may have been the cause of the first argument between this loving couple.

"Were you really married to a witch?" she asked quietly.

"Yes I was, but at least she was not an old hag like Brynhilde!"

"Oh, so you loved her then?"

"Not really," he answered, unsure of how to explain his time with Snofrid. "I will tell you about that experience, but not here and not now."

Rani was silent for a few moments.

"I think you gave just the right answer to Hild's question. You knew I had other wives, but I agreed to put the others aside for you. I love you and only you... surely you do not still question that."

"And what about Gyda?" she asked.

"I will tell Gyda...just as I told Svanhild."

"I will be anxious to have that done with," she said and turned her back to her husband.

It was the second night since they had been married that the lovers did not make love.

Much as Harald appreciated and respected his Uncle Ragnvald, he could not understand why he chose to put up with a woman like Hild. She had always had a sharp tongue, but after he refused to pardon Hrolf, she had turned into a quarrelsome, ill-tempered shrew. Three days in their home would be all he could tolerate. Of course, it had the effect of making him realize how fortunate he had been in his choice of wives...or rather, Odin's choice of wives.

Ordinarily, Harald would have stopped next at Eidsvag, but not this time. He would have to go back up there after he got Rani settled. He had decided that Norheim would be a good choice of manors to house them until their new home was completed. He had taken it as a king's ransom after the battle at Hafrsfjord.

It was one of the largest and loveliest estates in Rogaland. Like his Viken estate in Vestfold, it had been deserted after the former owner took his family and moved to the western islands rather than bow to the new system of laws and taxes. Jarl Odd Tolleivsen had been managing the estate for Harald for a number of years.

As exciting as seeing all of these new places and meeting all of these new people had been, Rani was ready for a prolonged period of time off a ship. The family living at Norheim was very anxious to make her feel welcome. Odd's wife was named Ingeborg and they had two sons, Tolleiv and Bjorn. Birgitte, who looked to be about her age, had married Tolleiv in the spring.

Birgitte, they told her, was named after a grandmother who had come from Jutland many years earlier.

"I hope we can be friends," she told Rani as she showed her to the master bedchamber. "This side of the hall is always kept for King Harald when he visits. I trust it will suit your needs."

"The carvings in here are indeed beautiful. I have only seen one bedchamber that was larger, and that one is in Hara's manor at Lade," Rani replied.

"You call the King Hara?" Birgitte asked in surprise.

Rani smiled. "We have special names for each other. I call him Hara and he calls me Rani, though my parents named me Ragnild."

Birgitte answered, "That is very nice. I hope we can be friends."

"I hope we can be friends, also," said Rani.

The two young women were about as different in appearance as two people could be. Where Rani had very dark hair and blue green eyes, Birgitte's hair was a very light gold color and her eyes were pale blue. Other than that, they were so alike in size that they could have passed for sisters.

With Rani settled in at Norheim, Harald left for his trip up to Eidsvag to talk with Gyda. He was sure she would not react with the loud outburst that Svanhild had, but he was still not looking forward to giving her the message he had to give. As his ships landed on the beach outside the manor, there was the usual excitement of his arrival. Several servants ran up through the gate to tell their mistress that her husband was disembarking.

He greeted a number of the men who were stationed at Eidsvag, as a protection for the wife of King Harald. He would need to make sure that she still felt protected, despite her change of status. His sons were the first to come running out of the manor house...excited at the return of their father. They shook his hand and wondered why he was so late coming this year.

His daughter, Alov, was in the great hall with her mother when he entered. They both came to greet him with the usual hugs and kisses.

"You look more like your mother every year, Alov."

"Thank you Father. That is high praise, as you have always said that Mother is the most beautiful woman you know."

"Yes, I have said that, haven't I?" he answered with a slight twinge of guilt. "Could you leave us alone for a time? I need to speak to your mother in private."

"Well, alright, but I want some of that private time, also," she said as she left the room.

"I know you do, dear, I know you do," he answered quietly.

"Something must be wrong," Gyda said, "You aren't quite yourself."

"You are right, I am not quite myself. I have something to tell you and I am afraid it is not good news."

"Say it quickly then."

He hesitated, but forged on. "I have married a new wife..."

"And..."

"And, she has insisted that I put my other wives aside and cling only to her."

"And you have agreed to that," Gyda stated with resignation.

"Yes, I have."

There was silence in the room. Harald was watching Gyda's face for some clue to her feelings, but her head was bowed and she was looking at the floor so he could not see her eyes. After what seemed like a long space of time, she raised her head and stared at him. The look on her face was more stoic than angry.

"You know, I do not need you anymore, now that you have given me five children. If you no longer love me or want me for your wife, then you may divorce me. It will not break my heart. One thing that I insist on, however, is that you continue to provide for and recognize our children as your heirs. They do not deserve a divorcement from their father!"

She never looked more beautiful to him than she did right then, standing there with her head held high...refusing to act the part of the shunned wife.

"It really is not that I no longer love you or want you for my wife. I would have been satisfied to add Rani as a wife, together with both you and Svanhild, but she would not."

"Well, I thank you for that," she replied. "Will you declare our divorce at the Gulathing?"

"You may divorce me, if you would like, but I am not counting this as a divorcement. It is more like a separation, a rather permanent separation."

"Then, will you continue to let our children be a part of your life?"

"Yes, I will. I will not be living here for half of the year as I have in the past, but I will visit."

"You just will not be sharing a bed with me when you visit," she said quietly...and he saw the first glimpse of pain in her eyes.

"No, I will not be sharing your bed when I visit," he answered just as quietly, with a similar amount of pain.

"I think we need to bring the children in here so you can tell them of your decision," she stated firmly.

"Yes, I think we should."

Telling his five children about this decision and the change it would make in their lives was more difficult than telling Gyda had been. Alov, the oldest at nineteen, cried softly into her hands. Rorek and Sigtrygg, seventeen and fifteen, were angry. Frode and Torgils, thirteen and eleven, were hurt.

Even as he said he would still be their father, he knew in his heart that life at Eidsvag would not be the same. He decided it might be best if he left quickly rather than to stay and argue or defend his position. He was sure he could count on Gyda to smooth things over as best she could.

Hara arrived back at Norheim in time for the evening meal. He began to tell Odd and his family about his plans to build a home for Rani and him near Haugar. He wasn't sure of the exact location yet, but he knew Odin would show him the right place when he found it. He planned to begin his search on the morrow.

"You are planning to take me with you tomorrow, aren't you?" she asked her husband when they were settled in bed.

"I thought you might want to stay here and rest after all of our travels."

"It bothers me when I hear you announcing your plans when I haven't heard them first. It makes me feel like the night you announced to your mother that you were going to leave me at Tande for a year!"

"Now, you know I never intended leaving you there for a year," he protested.

"Well, I am just telling you, I want to go where you go. Do you understand?"

"Well, I am telling you that I want to make love to you. Do you understand?" he answered as he picked her up and laid her down on top of him.

"Are you trying to change the subject?"

"Of course not! You just make me aroused when you get that determined look on your face."

"Am I coming with you tomorrow?"

"Are you making that a condition of our lovemaking?"

"Yes!"

"Alright, you win!" he said as he wove his fingers through her hair and pressed his lips to hers.

CHAPTER 31

A NEW HOME...A HOLY PLACE

Rani was anxious to see this special place where Odin wanted them to build their new home. Hara was right...it would please her to be near to the sea, although this sea was much larger than the sea by Skagen Manor. Here you could smell the salty air as the wind blew water drops into your face.

The area around Haugar had numerous islands just off the shore. Hara had an idea that one of the islands would be an ideal spot for their home. He liked the location of Lade because it had water around it on three sides. This gave ample room for his ships and allowed an unobstructed view of any enemy ships that may be invading. An island should be even better.

When Odin had told him to make his new home here, he said there was an area that had been the place of great spirits. Hara wanted to find that exact spot. The old tales told of a King Augvald who lived on an island near Haugar and called his home Avaldsnes.

They started their search along the shoreline, going in a southwesterly direction, accompanied by Berdaluke and the body guard. There were so many islands and they all looked like possibilities to Rani, but Harald did not feel a sense of inspiration about any of them. The second day they rode toward the north and looked over the islands lying there, but none of them seemed right either.

That night, Harald knelt by their bed and said a fervent prayer, pleading with Odin to guide him to the place where he wanted them to settle. Rani had never seen him pray like that before. It made her realize that he really was a very spiritual man who expected Odin to answer his prayer.

The next day they rode out again, searching the shoreline and waiting for Odin to speak. They rode home at the end of the day, no closer to a decision that when they had left. Harald repeated his plea for Odin's help again that night, but the next day's search was just as fruitless as the last three had been. This same pattern continued for another five days with no success.

On the morning after the seventh prayer, Hara awoke with a start and jumped out of bed. He pulled the covers off a still sleepy Rani and shouted, "Arise, my beauty! I have just seen our new home in a dream."

As they were getting their riding clothes on for the day, Rani asked Hara if Odin had told him why it took seven prayers to get an answer.

"Yes, my dear, he did. He was unhappy that I had not asked for his direction before riding out the first day. He was disappointed that I still had not completely learned the lesson he has been trying to teach me for years."

"What lesson is that?" she asked.

"He has said to me many times, 'In all thy actions, acknowledge me, and I shall direct thy path.' I thought I had learned that lesson well after four years in a cave at Lofoten, but I needed to spend seven nights on my knees to be reminded that Odin is in charge of my life."

Harald could hardly wait for the morning meal to be finished and the horses saddled. He led the group in a southwesterly direction again, but this time he knew where he was going. As they came to the area next to Haugar, he rode right to the beach and looked across the Karmsund waterway. There was a long narrow island, lying parallel to the shoreline, with a high point at the far southern end.

In his excitement, he urged his mount into the water and soon the horse was swimming toward the far shore.

"Come! Follow me!" he called over his back.

Berdaluke moved his horse in front of Rani's and led it into the deep water. Soon, they had joined Hara on the other side. He was so impatient to ride up to the high point of the island, he could hardly wait for everyone to get across.

"This is the place! We shall build our castle from the rocks of our island!" he shouted into the wind.

"But, all of your other estates have manor houses of wood," said Berdaluke.

"That is true, but no enemy shall be able to come here and burn us in our beds at night. We shall have a castle so strong that no enemy shall penetrate its walls!"

It was hard to contain Harald when he got his mind set on something. Rani was testament of that. All she could do was to follow him around and marvel at the energy and enthusiasm he showed...now that he knew what Odin's will was.

While exploring the island, they happened upon a group of upright stones that had been placed in the form of a dragon ship on the sea side of the land. In the center of the stones was a large stone box-like structure made out of flat slabs, with the two end slabs placed on the north and the south. The stone box was mostly covered by an earthen mound, but it was obvious that the wind and sea had removed part of the covering.

When Harald saw the stones, he immediately reined in his horse and dismounted. As he walked closer to the largest stone, he could see that there was a name carved into the surface. Without hesitation, he dropped to his knees and bowed his head. The rest of the group sat mounted on their horses, watching the scene before them.

After he rose, he turned to them and declared, "Here lays the great chieftain Augvald, a true disciple of Odin. His body lying here has consecrated this soil and he is but one of the mighty chiefs who have been buried on Karmr. It is a sacred island and I know here we shall be blessed. Our God has reaffirmed to me that the name of our estate is to be Avaldsnes in honor of Augvald.

As they reached the highpoint of the island, Harald once again dismounted and knelt to thank Odin for the blessing of this island. From the top of the hill, you could see for miles out to sea from north to south. On the west side of the island were rocky cliffs and turbulent waters. This would make it very difficult for any enemies to land their ships safely on that side.

A great old ash tree stood majestically near the highpoint, with its craggy branches reaching out to accept the powerful wind that blew in from the sea.

"This will make a pleasant place to rest and eat the food that Ingeborg has sent with us," declared Harald.

It was indeed an awe inspiring spot. Only Hara and Rani sat on the quilt that had been sent along with the lunch. Berdaluke and the other men of the bodyguard sat a little ways off. When they were done eating, Hara lay down on his back and glanced up through the leaves of the giant tree. The white blossoms had already turned to white berries.

"This ash reminds me of the Yggdrasil tree I saw in vision when I was but a boy. Odin has said that when the world ends in almost total devastation, that tree will still stand...and provide seeds for the next generation of people who will inherit the earth. I want this to be our special Yggdrasil tree. We shall build near to it, but take great care not to disturb it."

"It will also be a good spot for Odin's two ravens, Muninn and Huginn to visit and keep watch on us. Then they can fly back to Odin and tell him what we are doing. Why don't you come and lie down beside me under this magical tree and we will give the ravens something to talk about," he said as he reached for her.

"Not now with Berdaluke and your guard just down the hill!" she exclaimed.

"Maybe we will have to come back on another day when we can be alone. I think Odin would send a powerful spirit to a child that was conceived under the Yggdrasil tree!"

Rani wasn't sure she wanted to have the ravens spying on her, but she did like the handsome tree. On the southeast side of the high point was a natural harbor, with a flat plain perfect for the location of the large buildings that would house the three hundred warriors that Harald kept with him permanently.

There seemed to be only one main farm on the island, located on the far northwestern end. The group stopped there on their way back to the crossing. The bonde who owned the farm was named Steig Olavson. His farm, Ferkingstad, had been in use on the island for countless years. Steig had made his home of rock from the island and Harald asked him for the name of the person who had built the building.

"I am the man who has designed and built this house," Steig answered proudly.

"We are building a castle on the highpoint of the island and will need someone experienced in working with stone. Are you such a man?"

"I am. It would please me greatly to have a hand in the building of a castle for you, King Harald."

"We shall come by tomorrow and discuss my plans for the estate," said Harald.

"I shall be honored to receive you," Steig replied.

With that, the King bid farewell and turned his horse toward the Karmsund.

There was great discussion about the wonders of Karmr Island during the evening meal at Norheim that night. All agreed it sounded like the perfect place to build a fine estate.

"It was Odin's choice...and that is mostly what makes it so perfect," said Harald.

Travel to Karmr came to be an everyday experience for Hara, Rani, and Berdaluke. Steig turned out to be a very skilled worker with stone and Harald's three hundred warriors became an army of workers. Even though building of stone took more time than just wood, the castle was rising fast. The wooden frame and the roof, covered by slate, were completed by the end of harvest season.

Harald had said he would give each worker a gold mark if he and his queen were able sleep in their own bedchamber by spring. A flat raft was built to carry wagon loads of materials from the mainland to the island. Many of the trees were cut near Tysvaer and sailed down the Fordesfjord to the harbor below Avaldsnes.

As it turned out, a rich deposit of copper rock was discovered on the northern end of the island, near to Steig's farm. Plenty of it lay on top of the ground as light green stone. Blacksmiths were hired to work in copper trim for the castle and they created ornate gates and fire grates, plus trim for the doors and windows. The island was full of activity every day except Sunday. That was a day to rest one's body and give thanks to the Gods who had given guidance and protection throughout the week.

There were skilled wood carvers from Haugar who had been hired to decorate the thick wooden doors and window arches, plus the interior walls of the castle. Other men, skilled in woodworking, were building the high seat, the bedsteads and other furnishings for their home.

The first piece of furniture they were asked to make was a beautifully carved bench. This was to be placed under the Yggdrasil Tree so that Rani would have a place to sit and watch the building...yet be a safe distance away so she would not get injured. The tree gave such nice shade from the afternoon sun and Hara could walk over and consult with her whenever he wanted.

On the last Sunday of the summer, Hara said he wanted to spend the day at Avaldsnes. Rani was anxious to see the progress on their home, as she hadn't made the trip to the island for a number of weeks. After they mounted their horses, Berdaluke handed him a large bundle.

"What is in your bundle, my husband?" she asked.

"You will know soon enough," he answered with a smile.

The body guard planned to travel with the pair only as far as the island. Harald told them he wanted to be alone with his wife on this day, but he knew it was safest to have Berdaluke and his twenty five close enough that he could summon them if there was trouble.

They had almost reached the castle when Hara told Rani she must close her eyes for a surprise. He took the reins of her horse with his and rode up to the Yggdrasil tree.

"Do not open your eyes yet!" he called. "Wait until I take you down from the saddle."

He lifted her down and kissed her eyelids to make sure they were closed. Then he turned her around and told her there was a surprise just in front of her. She opened her eyes to see a giant, beautifully carved bed sitting in the spot under the tree where her bench had been.

"Is this our new bed?" she asked.

"The carvers finished it just yesterday," he answered.

"But, why is it sitting out here under the tree?"

"I will show you," he replied and opened up his bundle. Inside was a thick eiderdown quilt that he placed on the bed. He wrapped his arms around her and tipped her head up so he could look into her blue green eyes.

"This day, on this bed, under this noble tree, on this sacred island, I am going to place a very special seed within your body."

Rani asked teasingly, "Are you saying, My Lord, that in all this time, you have never placed a seed within me?"

Hara smiled and said, "Those were indeed my seeds, but today you shall receive the seed of the special son who Odin has promised will be born to us!"

With that declaration, he picked her up and set her gently on the soft quilt. He climbed in beside her, wrapped his arm around her shoulder, and stared up at the holy tree.

"Do you see the white berries our tree has produced? So it will be with you. Your body will produce a sweet fruit."

She looked up at the tree branches above their heads and then turned to look at her husband. "Then why don't you kiss me?" she said.

He turned to her and began to kiss her forehead, then the tip of her nose, then her chin, and next her neck. She put her hands under his chin and pulled his head up. Her eager lips sought his through his smile.

I hope you are watching, Huginn and Muninn, this is going to be a lovemaking to remember, he said to himself.

Work on the outside of the castle slowed with the onset of colder weather, but the men kept busy inside. Despite the fact that it was taking extra time to complete, Harald was glad he had decided to build out of stone. He was sure the rock facing would make their home safe from raiders or enemies who might try to kill him by burning his house down around him.

The great hall was going to be large enough to seat three hundred guests and he was going to enjoy having great feasts in their new home. Yuletide had always been a favorite time to make merry with friends, just as his parents had always done. This year he and Rani would celebrate with Odd and his family, but next year they would be in their own home, and there would be much to celebrate.

Despite the fact that winter was upon them, there was only a dusting of snow covering the ground. The warm winds that blew from the southwest kept the weather from turning excessively cold. The Karmsund water was not even frozen and they could still use their raft to carry goods across. The winters at Lade and Tande had been much colder than Avaldsnes would be.

The market town at Bergen was busy with traders and people purchasing Yule gifts when Harald and his bodyguard sailed into the harbor the Sunday before Yuletide. He wanted to find some special gifts for his wife and he knew that some trade ships had just passed through the Karmsund a few days before. The men enjoyed looking at the merchandise and Hara purchased gifts to be brought back to Norheim. Then he decided to choose gifts to be delivered to Eidsvag.

When the day for exchanging Yule gifts arrived, Hara presented his gifts. To Ingeborg, he gave a set of twelve blue glasses. To Birgitte, he gave a set of silver spoons. But to Rani, he gave an ornate silver brooch and a silver loop bracelet. She thanked her husband warmly.

"But, that is not all," he told her, "How would you like this fine red pell velvet to be used for bed hangings on our new bed?" he asked as he uncovered the large bundle.

"Oh, I love it! Thank you," she said and reached up to give him a quick kiss.

"One more present is in my pouch," he continued.

"What is it?" she asked.

He handed her the pouch and she withdrew a small silver horse with wheels attached to the hooves.

"That is the first gift for the son you will carry for me one day!" he answered boastfully.

Rani's face was flushed as she looked first at Hara and then at the others sitting around the room.

"I have a gift for you, also, but it is not here. We shall have to travel to find it tomorrow," she said quietly.

"Ah, a secret. I love secrets!" he shouted.

The next day, Rani told Hara she wanted to ride to Avaldsnes. It was a Sunday afternoon and there were no men working on the house. Berdaluke and the twenty five rode with them to Haugar and crossed the Karmsund, but Rani had told them she wanted to have Hara alone by the castle. The men stopped several miles away and the two of them continued to the top of the hill.

As they rode up to their favorite spot by the Yggdrasil tree, Rani asked Hara to help her dismount. She reached for his hand and led him to her bench under the tree branches.

When they were seated, he asked, "Where is my Yule gift?"

"It is right here," she said as she guided Hara's hand to her belly.

"Are you telling me our son now lives within you?"

"If Ingeborg and Birgitte are correct, yes, there is a child growing in here," she smiled as she looked down to the area where his hand rested.

Hara jumped up and lifted her up into his arms. He swung her around a full circle and then hugged her to him. Next, he reached for her lips and his lips lingered against hers for a long moment. This kiss was more intense and powerful than any she had felt before. After he released her lips, he tipped her head back and said, "You have made me the happiest man on Karmr!"

"That shouldn't be hard. Who is on Karmr besides you, Steig, and your men?"

"You have made me the happiest man in Rogaland...nay, the happiest man in all of Norway!"

"I am sure there are many wives who are also giving this good news to their husbands this Yule season."

"Yes, but they do not have the most beautiful woman in Norway for their wife."

"Only Norway? What about Jutland?"

"Alright, I am the happiest man on the earth!" he answered as he gave her another long, slow kiss. His emotions swelled as he lost himself in the thrill and power of the kiss.

"Can we make love again here, under the Yggdrasil tree?" he asked with a coy smile.

"If I thought you were going to ask that, I should have had Berdaluke move our bed back out here for this day!" she replied.

"Are you saying you prefer a bed, my dear, versus the hard ground?"

She just smiled at him and shook her head.

"That is answer enough," he shouted and swept her up into his arms. "Each time I have seen our finely carved bed in the master bedchamber, I have pictured the first night I shall see you lying there waiting for me. Now, I shall wait no longer."

He carried her quickly across the cold ground of December and into the unfinished castle. With the swift stride of his long legs, they were in the master bedchamber minutes later. He set her down in front of their bed, and saying nothing, removed the fibula clasp from his fur cloak and carefully laid it down on the bed platform. Then he picked her back up and set her gently down on the soft, thick fur.

"I love you, my Rani, more than anything on this earth. I am so thankful that Odin gave you to me. Let me fill you with my love," he said as he began to kiss her gently. His touch was more tender than usual, and he made love to her as if she would break or the precious seed in her belly might be crushed.

As he carried her back out to the horses standing tied at the tree, he whispered into her ear, "You know, you have given me the best Yule gift ever."

She snuggled against his chest and answered, "Yes, I love you, my Hara, even more than Skagen Manor."

He just smiled. Life was good. No...life was great. He could not ask for anything more from Odin. He had been given every blessing he could imagine and now he would have the son of Ragnild the Mighty. How could this son be anything but mighty also?

The days were getting colder and Rani chose to stay inside the warmth of Norheim Manor more now. Ingeborg and Birgitte fussed over her and tried to make her comfortable. They occupied the long winter nights by sitting in front of the fire and knitting caps, socks, and other clothing for the new baby. Birgitte wished there was a child growing in her belly also, but there wasn't.

Soon it was spring, and despite the fact that the castle was not completely finished, Harald decided to move them into their new home. He was uncertain as to when his son would be born and he was determined that the child be born at Avaldsnes. May Day had always been a special time for him, and he and Rani celebrated it together, sitting on her bench under their Yggdrasil Tree. The sun was warm and the tree was full of beautiful white blossoms.

Twin towers were built on the south side of the castle, with open windows facing north, south, east and west. The placement of the windows allowed an unobstructed view of the sea on all four sides of the island. Stone steps curved up from the bottom of each tower and led to the very top. An inside balcony, around the great hall that led to guest bedchambers on the second story, was the last feature to be completed. Rani was relieved when the sound of pounding finally ceased.

Harald had never seemed happier than he was to finally be living in their new home on Karmr Island. Each morning he would be up early and anxious to be about his business. The warrior halls were being built down on the plain below the castle, and he would run down the hill in his eagerness to see those buildings completed. Berdaluke would run after him and the two men would race to see who could reach the beach first. Then they would take a wade in the Karmsund.

Things weren't quite as pleasant for Rani. Her body was swollen and she had a difficult time sleeping. She missed the company of her friends Ingeborg and Birgitte, even though she now had a full staff of servants to help her. The rooms in the castle were so much larger than her home at Skagen Manor and she longed to have the beautiful tapestries that her mother had sewn. Unfortunately, there had not been room to take them when she left. She wondered when she would visit her dear Sagen Manor again.

There was only one regional Thing that Hara attended that spring. The Gulathing was held in Gulen, north of Bergen, and he had traveled there for just a few days and hurried back to Avaldsnes. He hadn't always been present at the birth of his children, but he was determined to be there for this one. He was sure Odin had sent the special spirit he had promised...and having a son born at Avaldsnes would make him even more blessed.

Aside from that reason, Rani was not feeling at ease about the birth. She was naturally apprehensive because this was her first child, but she seemed to feel a sense of pending doom that Hara could not talk her out of. Any time he left the castle, she questioned him as to where he was going and when he would return.

CHAPTER 32

THE TIME HAS COME

A loud scream pierced the air of the master bedchamber and woke Hara out of a deep sleep. He felt for Rani, but she had rolled out of his reach. He found her arm and tried to shake her awake, but the screams continued. Her body was wet with perspiration and she was trembling uncontrollably. He quickly lit the candle by the bed and hurried around to the far side where she lay.

He sat down on the bed and lifted her quivering body onto his lap. Rani stopped screaming and began to sob. He held her tightly and rocked back and forth.

"What causes you to scream so, my love?" he asked, but she could not stop sobbing.

"Are you in pain? How can I help you?" he questioned soothingly, but she could not get the words to come out.

He rubbed her back and kissed her tangled hair and finally she spoke.

"I was dying!" she cried. "I was dying and no one could save me!"

"You aren't dying. You are right here on my lap. Do not worry! I won't let you die!" he comforted.

"I am afraid. I do not know how to have a baby. I need my mother here. I need Brynhilde here. That's it! I need Brynhilde to come. She was with my mother at my birth and she will help me too," she sobbed.

Her statement gave Harald a sickened feeling in his gut. Hadn't she remembered the gift Brynhilde had handed her as they were about to leave Skagen Manor? Had that dead blackbird been a curse on Rani's life? Did he dare mention the bird to her now?

"I think Ingeborg and Birgitte will be enough help. I do not think we need Brynhilde here, do we?" he pleaded.

"Yes, yes! I need Brynhilde! If Brynhilde is here when our baby comes everything will be all right," she insisted.

"But Brynhilde is near Skagen Manor. How can she get here?" he reasoned.

"You must send Berdaluke to go and get her! He must hurry! He must leave as soon as it is light!"

"I do not know if he can get there and back before our son is born."

"Please send him this day! Please!" she cried and began sobbing again.

"Shush now, I will send him this day. You must not cry so or you will cause our son to start his journey now," he comforted.

"Thank you, Hara. I love you so much."

"And I love you, my Rani. Let us lie back down and sleep until the sun rises."

"Yes...everything will be all right now. Berdaluke will bring Brynhilde and everything will be all right," she whispered as she fell asleep in his arms.

Harald did not sleep, however. He sat and held his precious wife as she slept...peacefully at last. What was he going to do? He knew everything would not be all right if the witch Brynhilde was at the birth of their son, but how could he tell Rani that without making her more distressed than she already was.

That morning, Harald and Berdaluke walked down to the beach, side by side. Their conversation was too serious to indulge in their usual light hearted race.

"Rani has it in her head that Brynhilde should be here to assist in the birth of our son. You remember what the witch gave to her as we were leaving Skagen Manor, don't you?" he asked.

"I do remember. Do you think the bird was a curse put on Rani?"

"I do not know. I just know that Snofrid's curse did not leave me until she and Svase were dead. I need you to take a ship and travel to Skagen Manor. I promised Rani that you would leave today. You must find Brynhilde and kill her so that she will have no more power over my wife!"

"You know you can trust me"

"Yes, I have always trusted you, my friend."

Berdaluke traveled to Jutland and searched around Skagen Manor for Brynhilde. He finally found her in a hut in the woods. He told her he was sent to bring her back to Norway at the request of Ragnild the Mighty.

The witch looked at him and asked, "But what of the request of King Harald?"

Berdaluke seemed surprised by her question, but answered, "The King wishes you to come with me also."

"It is a lie! He has ordered my death!" Brynhilde screamed and quickly closed the door to her small abode.

"Open this door!" shouted Berdaluke. "Open this door or I will break it down!"

No answer came from within the small dwelling. Berdaluke, as good as his word, raised his axe and chopped at the door. Two blows were all it took to break the bindings and the door crashed into the hovel. Brynhilde stood with her back to the wall and a staff in her outstretched hand.

"If you harm me, you will be sorry," she cried.

As Berdaluke raised the axe over her head, she cackled, "Death to your mistress and sorrow to your master."

The axe was already in motion and came down to split open the old witch's head before her words could penetrate Berdaluke's conscience and stop the motion of his arm.

He turned to the men standing behind him and shouted, "Burn this filthy hut and its evil contents!" as he hurried to be rid of the ugly sight.

Surely, the witch did not have the power to take Rani's life, he thought to himself. Her death should have wiped out any curse she had placed on Rani at the time they departed from Skagen Manor two years before. Besides, he had just carried out the orders of his King. He did not want to think that his action might have signaled the death of his Queen.

Rani laboriously climbed the rock steps of the east tower each day when Hara left to run down the hill to the flat area where his men had their hall. He loved to wade in the Karmsund when the weather was fine. He said it made him feel close to Odin's son, Thor, who was said to wade there on his way to help the sun to rise. The water was so gentle, and it was even warm when the air was cold.

If only Berdaluke would return with Brynhilde soon, she thought, then she knew this baby would be ready to come forth. Because the witch had been present at her own birth, Rani trusted her magic to see that all would be well. After seven days of waiting and watching, her effort was finally rewarded. The ship she saw heading toward their beach was flying Hara's flag, so she knew it had to be Berdaluke.

She could not make out the figure of Brynhilde in her black garments, but she felt relief to know that the witch would be with her during this birthing time. Rani hurried to descend the circular stairs. There were over one hundred steps, but the pain in her legs was ignored in her excitement to reach the bottom.

Less than half the way down, a new pain started. This pain was not in her swollen legs, but in her belly. Sharp, intense pains came with each step. Her mind told her that this must be the pain the women had told her to expect when her child was beginning its descent. She was so relieved to think that Brynhilde had arrived just at the right time.

With about twenty steps to go, Rani's foot slid off the narrow step and she lost her balance. As her body began to tumble, head over heel, she gave out a loud scream for help. Though her screams echoed off the stone walls of the stairwell, there was no way for the sound to penetrate the thick walls of this fortress.

Her body landed in a heap at the bottom of the last step. Her final scream wasn't more than a whimper, but a serving woman had heard it. She came running to help her mistress, but the efforts to raise her just resulted in a shriek of pain.

"Send for the King! My Lady has fallen from the tower stair!" echoed through the hall. A servant ran for the castle door and was quickly down the hill to where Harald was greeting a returning Berdaluke. The berserker had just told him that the deed was done.

"My Lady has fallen from the tower stair and is screaming in pain!" shouted the breathless thrall.

Both Harald and Berdaluke raced up the hill to the castle with a feeling of dread at hearing the awful news. As they rushed in through the doorway, they could hear Rani's pitiful cries coming from the other end of the great hall.

"Rani, my Rani!" Harald cried as he reached her.

She sobbed to see him. "Our baby," she whispered, "Our baby is coming. Brynhilde got here just in time," she said and fainted.

Harald and Berdaluke exchanged a look of panic and guilt. Rani's face grimaced with pain through her delirium as Hara gently raised her into his arms. He carried her swiftly to the master bedchamber and tried to lay her down on the thick eiderdown mattress.

"No! Hold me!" she cried. "Please hold me."

Thus sat Hara, with his wife in his arms, while the women of the manor helped to deliver their son. His relief that the pain of childbirth was over was overshadowed by the pain that Rani experienced when he tried to move her from his arms. He kissed the perspiration on her forehead and cheeks and whispered into her ear, "We have a little black haired boy, my black haired beauty."

She was barely conscious, but smiled in relief at his words. The baby's lusty cry was further proof that she had accomplished the ultimate act in a woman's life...that of giving her husband a son. Now she could rest, she thought, if only this pain in her back would go away. In her confusion, she thought she saw her mother, standing far off, but smiling at her. Yes, she had proven herself a real woman.

Rani waivered between consciousness and unconsciousness for the next three days. If Harald tried to lay her on their bed, she woke with a scream of pain. He was beside himself. He did not know what to do for her except to hold her as she pleaded. He could not eat or sleep, but just watched her lovely face for any sign that the pain might be lessened.

He prayed, pleaded and begged Odin to help her...to help him...to bless their child. The God seemed to be absent, for he sent no answers and no improvement in Rani's condition. On the third night's vigil, Hara's body shook with the sobs that he tried to hide in the cold light of day. As he looked down at his love's face in the golden glow of the candlelight, she opened her eyes.

"Are you crying for me?" she whispered.

"My Rani! I have begged Odin to bless you, to take away your pain and make you whole again."

"It is of no use. Odin has sent my mother to take me to Gimli," she said with quiet resignation.

"No! I will not let you go!" he cried, holding her limp body even tighter.

"It is of no use to try and keep me, my love, I must leave you."

"No! Please do not go! Please!"

"Will you promise me....?"

"Yes, anything, but...."

"Promise that you will never marry another wife and forget me."

"I could never forget you, never!"

"Promise that you will make our son King after you...that he will rule over all the sons of your other wives."

"Yes, of course, I promise."

"No, you must take an oath. A promise is not enough."

"I swear to you, by Odin, that I will make our son the King that will rule over all my other sons."

"And what of other wives?" she persisted.

"I also swear to you, by Odin, that I will never take another wife to my bed."

"Please kiss me once more," she said with a faint smile.

He lifted her head up and tenderly touched her lips with his. The kiss seemed to last for an eternity. Finally, she released his lips and whispered, "That is all...and now I must leave you."

"No!" he cried, but her eyes had closed and he could feel the spirit slipping from her body. "No!" he cried again, and held her body closer to his chest. This time, her body felt like an empty vessel. He stared down at her beautiful countenance and began to sob in earnest. He knew in his heart that her spirit had already left the flesh and bones that he was holding, but he just could not let go.

He eased the fragile body down into the eiderdown of their bed and laid his large frame next to it. The King who had sat awake for three days and nights, finally slept beside his Queen. Rani's spirit, looking down on her beloved from her place above the bed, smiled with love at the peaceful scene in the master bedchamber of their castle at Avaldsnes.

Harald could hardly think. People were asking him what they should do to prepare for Rani's burial, but he had no answers. He did not want to think about a burial. He just wanted everyone to leave him alone with his grief. Rani still lay on their bed, covered by her red pell bedspread. He knew, in the back of his mind, that he could not leave her there for too many days, but the thought of putting her away and never again being able to see her beautiful face was more than he could endure.

Finally, it was Ingeborg who was able to convince him that he needed to let his wife be placed in her mound. When she suggested to Harald that he place their new bed under her in the cairn and use the red pell bed hangings for her tent, he agreed. He had told Berdaluke that the mound should be close to the Yggdrasil tree, and his orders had been carried out exactly.

The night before the burial feast, he wrote a poem to be read to her and then placed under her hands, so she could read it when she arrived in Gimli.

From my wet eyes in that sad hour of parting,
There fell my tears, they bathed thy cheeks
And laying upon thy loveliest neck, a circle of silver
Set in stones as red as thy sweet lips
I know not how it chanced that the fierce flame
Of that all consuming grief consumed me not.
Mad with sorrow, I asked, "Where is my light of life?
My heart's sole treasure, where?" Yet, there in truth,
There didst thou lurk, there in my heart of hearts.
Where thou wilt ever be, the pole-star of my life
Soul of my soul! Mine own! Mine own Rani.

Harald knew he had to get through the next day somehow, but he wasn't sure how. He did not care that his men and his friends saw that he cried, that he had been crying for days. His eyes were red and swollen, but he minded them not. All who knew him knew of his deep love for his Rani and could understand his equally deep sorrow.

Once their bed was moved out of the master bedchamber, Harald avoided going in there. He slept in one of the guest rooms near to Berdaluke's room. He did not think he could ever again look in the bedchamber that he and Rani had shared. It would be empty of its lovely bed and empty of his lovely wife.

He poured water over his little son and named him Erik for Rani's father. He was sure she would be pleased with that. Ingeborg and Birgitte had taken the baby home with them to Norheim. He was relieved that the child had lived, but he did not want to think about him right now.

CHAPTER 33

THE WILL TO LIVE

Harald slipped into a deep depression within weeks after his wife was buried. He cried out to Odin, "Why? Why did you take my Rani...you have just given her to me. I need her! I am an empty man without her. Let me follow after her. Take me, too! I do not want to live without her. Have I not lived long enough? Have I not done enough? Why are you punishing me? Just let me die!"

His days were spent walking aimlessly though the empty rooms of his castle. After crying out in a loud voice to Odin, he would become subdued and seem not to know where he was. He would not eat. He could not sleep. Berdaluke watched this behavior with concern. He tried talking to him, but Harald would not be consoled.

"Where will your spirit go if you take your life and Odin will not allow you into Gimli?" Berdaluke asked.

"Do not speak of that to me!" Harald shouted.

Finally, Berdaluke traveled by ship to Tune to tell Guttorm that he feared Harald might kill himself.

"I plead with you, My Lord, come to Avaldsnes and talk to the King. I fear for his life. This time the enemy is within the walls and not without!"

"Thank you for coming to me. I shall prepare to leave at once. Gutt, you must take charge of the affairs here while I am gone. Berdaluke, you have to travel to Tande Manor and tell this story to Harald's mother. If anyone can reach both his heart and his mind, she can."

Guttorm left for the West Coast the very next day. He took two ships and one hundred men. After three days on the sea, they arrived at Avaldsnes. As soon as the ships reached the shore, he climbed up the steep hill to the stone fortress Harald had built there. He walked into the great hall and saw the forlorn figure of a man, slumped over in the high seat, staring into the fire.

The King looked up as Guttorm walked toward him and cried, "I can not live without her! I just can not!"

Guttorm walked over and embraced his nephew and friend. He wasn't sure what to say. Harald looked like a mad man. His hair was uncombed and there was a desperate look in his eyes. Guttorm could feel the ribs of his back through the woolen shirt. Obviously, Berdaluke wasn't exaggerating when he said Harald hadn't been eating.

"And what of the child?" questioned Guttorm.

"Erik...his name is Erik after Rani's father."

"Yes, that is good. Did it please Rani to have a son to carry on her father's name?"

Harald just nodded, gazing back at the fire.

"Where is Erik now?"

"He is at Norheim. Odd's wife and daughter care for him there."

Guttorm wasn't sure what to say next. Should he get Harald to talk about Rani or avoid talking about her? He decided it might be good for Harald to talk, so he asked, "Was Rani happy here at Avaldsnes?"

Harald winced as if the very hearing of her name brought him pain. He paused for a moment and then smiled.

"Rani loved Avaldsnes. She loved the smell of the sea and the sound of the waves lapping the shore. I do not know if she loved it more than her Skagen Manor, but I know she loved me more than her Skagen Manor."

Harald seemed to be talking to himself, but Guttorm was glad he was talking and not just staring at the fire.

"I will never forget how you looked when you first brought Rani to meet Gutt and me at Tune...when you two were newly married," he continued.

"Yes, my friend, I think I was more happy then than at any other time in my life."

"Do you regret the fact that Odin gave you Rani to wife?"

"Oh, no! I loved every moment I had with her. That is why I want to follow after her."

"Yes, but if you had to chose to have never met her, or to have had her in your life for just two years, which would you choose?"

Harald looked up into the kind, wise face of his uncle and began to cry again.

"You have not yet told me how you would choose," said Guttorm patiently.

After a few moments more, Harald answered emphatically, "Of course I would choose to have her...even for just one year... or one month!"

"And do you have the hope of seeing her again?"

"You know I do. I have more than a hope. I promised her that I would be her husband for this life and for all eternity!"

"Yes, I understand Odin has told you that is true."

"He has. He has told me that if I follow him and do my best to obey, I shall be blessed for eternity."

"Would he think you were obeying him while you sit here and cry for what you have lost...lost only for a short time?"

The logic of Guttorm's sensible words began to sink in to Harald's mind.

"I see what you mean. This is hard, but I must do it," he answered.

"Yes, you must. And if you should begin to start feeling sorry for yourself again, you might think on this. You have enjoyed the loving companionship of four different women, not counting Snofrid, while I have not had even one wife. Would you trade lives with me?"

Harald looked at Guttorm with astonishment. Never before had he heard his trusted friend complain about the life Odin had planned for him. With a feeling of shame, Harald began to see his actions for what they were...selfish and pitiful...and hardly worthy of a man whom Odin had blessed so abundantly.

"I feel Odin will bless you with a special woman with whom you might spend eternity!"

"I hope you are right, my friend, I hope you are right," sighed Guttorm.

The pained expression had left Harald's face and a more peaceful feeling came over him.

"Your counsel is as good as ever it was," said Harald. "What would I have done without you in my life?"

"Odin would have sent you someone else, no doubt!"

"I can not imagine anyone else who could have been to me as a brother and counselor the way you have been," Harald said and embraced his uncle once more.

Both men were equally as tall and similar in appearance, although Guttorm's brown hair was now peppered with grey. Despite being fifteen years the senior, the Duke's back was straight and his bearing erect.

"Your mother is on the way here to see you also. She comes by wagon over the hills of Hadeland and on through Hordaland to Haugesund."

"That is too hard a trip for her."

"Yes, but you know she would come to you in your need...if she had to walk all the way!"

"You are right. I have learned much from the great example of my parents. I am sure she has often longed to be rid of this life and depart for Gimli to join father, yet I have never seen her cry and wail as I have done. Thank you, Guttorm, for helping me to move forward from that pitiful state before my mother had to see me and feel ashamed of her son."

"I do not know if she could ever feel ashamed of you...but I could!"

"You really are a true friend...and now I am getting ashamed of myself!"

"Let us forget our sorrows and order a great feast to be prepared. I have journeyed here with one hundred good men who would like to drink to the health and long life of their King."

"Do we have to drink to a long life?" asked Harald with a frown.

"We will drink to a good life, then," said Guttorm as he threw his arm around Harald's shoulder.

Ragnhild arrived within a week, very tired after the long journey. Harald felt bad that she had had to endure the trip on his account, but he was happy to see her. They sat together and talked into the night.

For the first time since he was a boy, his mother shared with him the desperate feelings of sorrow she suffered when her Halvdan had drowned. She told how she had wished she had been in the sleigh with him, so she could have drowned also.

She told him how Odin had advised her that her son would need her to help guide his life. She also reminded him that he had those same obligations to care for and guide the life of his little Erik, especially now that his mother wasn't there to show him love.

"I have wondered how Odin expects me to give all of my children the kind of a life that you and father gave to me."

"It may not be possible to offer that amount of time to each of your children, but you must try to let them know you love them, despite whatever changes come into your life. Erik will need you the most."

"I will try to give him love enough, but I do not know how I could ever replace Rani in his life."

"You can not, but you must always let him know how much you loved his mother, and that will help him feel her love."

They traveled to Norheim the next day to see little Erik. Ragnhild agreed that he looked very much like his mother, with a head full of dark hair. Birgitte had taken charge of him and was acting as if he had been born from her body. Harald asked her if she and Tolleiv would be willing to move to Avaldsnes for a time to help him with his son. The excited look on her face showed her answer before she could get the words out.

Her husband was in agreement, so they planned to move their things within a fortnight. Harald decided they would be the ones to occupy the master bedchamber, for now, so Erik could stay with them. Tolleiv seemed not to mind the extra attention his wife was paying to another man's child. He and Birgitte had grown fond of Rani and Hara during the time they stayed at Norheim...and he felt sympathy for the bereft husband.

In an effort to show his repentance for questioning Odin's taking of Rani, Harald decided to build a temple to honor his God. He spent the fall and winter months overseeing the great building that was to be placed near the edge of the cliff on the east side of the Yggdrasil tree. The building faced the rising sun and would be clearly visible from across the Karmsund to Rogaland, as well as from the sea.

The rectangular building had an alter area placed on the south with an opening that let sunlight shine in. Sheets of copper covered the roof tiles and only the beautiful green stone of Karmr was used in the construction. There was a cross-beam of silver placed near to the front as a memorial to Rani. The high seat that was made for Odin was covered with the most intricate carving anyone had ever seen. The high seat created for Harald was smaller and plainer.

The arched door in the front was made of heavy wood, covered all over with copper. A large gold ring was placed in the very center of the massive door. The doorway was extremely tall and finely carved with scenes of the battles Odin had helped Harald win. At the very top was shown the final battle for Norway at Hafrsfjord

When the temple was completed, Odin came to Harald and gave him this reassurance. "Death...there is no fear in death. Death does not bring about the end, but a glorious beginning to the next life. You will see your Rani again and you will be joined together as man and wife. Your existence in the eternities will be more marvelous than anything you could imagine. Now go forth and live the rest of your life in full obedience and never fear."

This was just the message Harald needed. It sustained him through the many joys and sorrows he had yet to experience before his life would come to an end and Odin would tell him he had accomplished all that he had been sent to the earth to achieve.

Harald began to spend a few quiet moments there every day. He would sit in his high seat and talk to Odin. Sometimes he talked about the past and sometimes he talked about the future. He wanted his God to know that he was very grateful for all the experiences he had in his life...both the good and the bad.

He hoped those experiences would give him the wisdom he would need to deal with the problems that were yet to come. He had finally understood what was meant by the words, "There must needs be an opposition in all things." He had definitely grown in wisdom and understanding from the things he had experienced in his life thus far... and he expected that he would yet learn many useful things.

CHAPTER 34

A LOSS AND A GAIN

Svanhild knew that Harald would be coming to Viken for the summer solstice. He came through Vestfold every year and held the Haugathing near Tunsberg. She was desperate to see him again. Maybe, now that Rani was dead, he would want to be with her again. She knew he had loved her once...could not he love her again? She had told him she never wanted to see his face again, but she had not really meant it. She had been so angry...angry and hurt.

He had promised to be back for Yuletide after a short trip to Jutland. She had not wanted him to go, but she knew she could not have stopped him. He said Odin had told him to go...and Harald always obeyed Odin's commands. Why could not Odin have just left things the way they were? Had she not done her part by letting her husband marry beautiful Gyda? Of course, she had complained some, but she had wanted to complain much more. It just was not fair!

When Rani died after her baby was born, Svanhild had been so relieved. She was sure things would get back to normal again. But her husband had promised to stay faithful to his black haired wife, even though she had left him. It just wasn't fair! At least she hadn't made him vow to refuse to see his children. Svanhild thought, If only she could think of a way to get Harald back again...then she would be happy.

Harald had continued to visit their sons each year, but Svanhild refused to see him and went to her brother's home at Borre while he was at Viken Manor. She always wished he would come and beg her to see him, but he did not. She knew she had been too hasty to tell him that she never wanted to see him again...but she was too proud to admit it and tell him that she had forgiven him.

Svanhild finally thought of a plan to get Harald to come and see her. She knew he was planning to be at Viken two days prior to the Haugathing, so she left for Borre manor just before he was to arrive. As part of her plan, she was helping her brother's wife cut the meat for the evening meal and intentionally made a deep cut in her forearm. Blood came gushing out and she told her brother to hurry to Viken and summon her sons to her before death came to claim her. She was sure that Harald would come with them when he heard that she was near to death.

Then, when they all arrived, she planned to tighten the linen wraps on her arm and stop the bleeding. Harald would see that he still felt love for her and wanted to share his life with her again. Everything proceeded according to the plan Svanhild had made, except for one thing. Harald's ships got caught in a storm as they were traveling from Rogaland and they had to pull in at Agder to wait for calmer seas.

By the time her sons arrived at Borre, their mother had lost a lot of blood and was barely able to maintain consciousness. She told them how much she loved them and how much she loved their father. She expected them to ask her if Harald could come in to see her, but they did not. When she finally asked them to have their father come in to say farewell, they told her that he had not yet arrived.

Her plan was foiled. She tried to tighten the cloths around her arm in an effort to stop the blood flow, but she did not have enough strength left to do it. She asked her son Olaf to help her and he rushed to her side, but she lost consciousness.

Svanhild's sons stood by helplessly and watched as the blood seeped from their mother's arm and the life slowly drained from her body. Her plan had been foiled by an angry sea.

Had Odin tricked her? Did he not realize how desperate she was to see her Harald again and hear him call her his golden girl?

As her subconscious mind was asking Odin these questions, he appeared to her and told her she would have to wait now to be with her Harald until it was his time to leave the earth. As her spirit left her body, she looked at her three sons standing around her lifeless form lying on the bed. She was glad to see their sorrow at her parting.

Her mind turned to a remembrance of the loving moments she had enjoyed as the wife of King Harald Halvdanson and the joy she had felt at the birth of each of their sons. She had taken much pleasure in watching them grow into strong men, despite not having the constant presence of their father. She realized that this was the legacy she was leaving behind and she was pleased to think that her life had been of worth.

Harald arrived two days later. His sons had waited for him to take charge of the death ceremony for their mother. He felt bad that Svanhild had died with an angry heart toward him. He hoped she would find peace in the next life.

He walked down the long hall toward the master bedchamber in his former home at Viken. His other trips down this same hall had been filled with pleasant anticipation as he returned to see his ever faithful Svanhild. This trip down the same hall was filled with sadness.

As he quietly opened the door, he saw his second wife's body lying peacefully on their bed. She was dressed in the golden gown she had worn on the day of their marriage. The gold highlights that danced through her hair had dulled years ago and the golden brown eyes were now closed. She wore the heavy gold chain around her neck that he had brought her from Tunsberg all those years ago....it seemed like it had been another lifetime since those days.

He walked to the bed and knelt by her side for the last time. He was flooded by memories of their early days together and of the happiness they had found in each others arms. He had been proud of the way she had struggled to overcome her jealousy of Gyda...but then there had been Rani.

His marriage to Rani had really ended his relationship with Svanhild. He could not actually blame her for being so angry and hurt, but he wished he could have spoken to her once more before she died. Then he did the one thing that she had been willing to die for, he bent close and gave her a farewell kiss.

"I did love you, my golden girl," he whispered in her ear.

As he said those words, he thought he felt her arms around his neck for just a fleeting moment. Yes, her spirit would go to join those of her mother Dagny and her father Eystein in the spirit world. How comforting to know that death was not the end of one's existence.

Just then, his sons walked in and joined him around the large bed. They were pleased to see the loving gesture being made by their father to their mother. Harald ordered a mound prepared and they all chose items that they thought she would want to take with her to the next life.

Harald chose the beautiful tapestries that were hanging in the master bedchamber at Viken when they had taken it over. Svanhild had always loved them and now they would surround her as she lay on her eiderdown mattress in the small ship that would be prepared for her.

The carved cradle that had been made by her father to hold each of their baby sons would lay next to her bed in death as it had lain by their bed in life. There was one additional thing that Harald chose to include in his wife's death mound, but he would have to travel to get it.

The trip to Tunsberg was just a short one by sea. He hoped he would be able to find what he was looking for in the trader's market that thrived along the waterfront. In the third tent he found what he sought... a set of twelve golden goblets. Maybe these would help make up for the ones he had never brought back for that Yule gift so many years before.

Harald asked his sons what message they would like to see on their mother's rune stone. They all agreed that he should choose the saying, as long as it included the words that would recognize that she had been the mother of Princes. Harald had these words carved for his second wife:

> Svanhild Eysteinsdatter
> child bride and wife of
> King Harald Halvdanson
> and mother of three Princes
> Olaf, Bjorn and Ragnar.

After the unhappy ending of Svanhild's life, Harald decided he did not want his relationship with Gyda to end in the same way. As he traveled back from his round of holding Things, he stopped at Eidsvag Manor to see her.

When he arrived, she assumed he was there to visit with their five children and was about to leave the manor house. Then a serving maid found her and told her the King wished to speak with her. She was guarded in her manner as she entered the great hall. Harald was sitting in the high seat where she had not been privileged to see him for several years past.

"This is an unexpected visit," Gyda said as she walked toward him.

"Sit down here next to me, will you?" he asked tenderly.

Gyda was not used to her former husband acting so submissive. She sat down and waited for him to continue.

"I have some sad news to report. Svanhild is dead. She cut her arm in an accident and bled to death in front of her sons. It made me think of you and realize I did not want to see you the next time on your death bed."

"Are you saying that you wanted just one more look at me while I was still alive...or are you saying that you desire to come back into my life?" Gyda asked with a slight hint of sarcasm in her voice.

"I guess I am saying I would like to come back into your life. I will not be able to be back in your bed, but I would like us to be friends."

She was tempted to say she did not care if she had him back in her bed again, but it was nice to see him again...and having him stop by and visit her would be enjoyable.

"Yes, I would like to be friends. I would like to be able to talk about our children...and see you again."

And so it was, from that time, Harald made it a point to stop at Eidsvag Manor each time he traveled up the coast as he held Things at the sacred places. It seemed they had more to talk about now than ever before. Their children were growing up and it was pleasurable to remember when they were small...and talk about happy days from the past.

CHAPTER 35

AWFUL REVENGE

Three long ships sailed up to Eidsvag Manor, bearing the flag of Ragnvald of More on their mast. A tall man dressed as Harald's uncle disembarked from the lead ship and walked with five of his men toward the gate in front of the large estate. He called out to several thralls who are working outside the fenced enclosure.

"Tell your mistress that Ragnvald of More has an important message for her from King Harald. Ask her to come to me in haste. I shall wait for her here by the gate," said the large man at the head of the group.

Gyda donned a cape and hurried to meet her visitor. She hoped there was not bad news from Harald. She walked through the gate and called to Ragnvald. The tall man in the rich clothing of a jarl had his back to her. When he heard her voice, he turned to face her.

"Hrolf!" was the only word she was able to utter before his dagger sunk deep into her chest.

The six men hurried off to their ship as the thralls shouted for help. Rorek was the first to reach his mother. As he bent over her blood soaked body, she whispered, "Hrolf, Hrolf." Gyda's other sons and some of their men ran to the shore, but the ships had been prepared to pull out quickly and were already heading toward the open sea.

"Get the men! Get the ships," shouted Sigtrygg.

By the time the Eidsvag ships were launched, there was no sign of the three enemy ships. The men spent the day trying in vain to find Hrolf Ragnvaldson, their mother's murderer. As darkness set in, the Eidsvag ships carrying Sigtrygg, Frode and Torgils returned to their harbor.

Alov had taken care of her mother's body and Gyda was laid out in a white linen dress on her bed in the master bed chamber.

"We must send word to Ragnvald. He will know where to find Father...and he will also want to find Hrolf," said Rorek.

"Send me, Rorek," pleaded Torgils.

"You are too young. Sigtrygg will go. Besides, I need you here to help in case Hrolf should decide to return."

"But I want to be the one to tell father," Torgils insisted.

"Why not let him go with Sigtrygg," spoke Frode. "I will be here to help you...and he is too young to be of much use."

"Very well, Torgils, you may go, but Sigtrygg will be in charge and you must stay out of trouble."

Sigtrygg and Torgils left with the outgoing tide and sailed swiftly up the coast to More. The wind was full in their sails and they made it to their destination by nightfall. They beached their ships at Borgund Manor and hurried to get through the fence gate before it was closed for the night.

Ragnvald was shocked and angered to hear that his son had committed yet another lawless act. This one was definitely intended to take revenge on Harald for branding him an outlaw. He wondered why his son had decided to commit this murder now, after so many years had passed. It seemed as if revenge never left the heart of the one who felt wrongly judged.

For a few moments, Ragnvald wondered how Hrolf had succeeded in making Gyda think it was him and not his son who had sailed in to Eidsvag. Had someone helped him in his plotting? There was one person in his household that hated Harald almost as much as Hrolf did, but he did not want to think that his wife would take part in murder for revenge.

Early the next morning, Ragnvald sailed up to the Trondelag Fjord, along with Sigtrygg and Torgils. As they rowed into the mouth of the Nid River, they could see all of the ships lined up along the water's edge. This meant the Thing was in progress. Harald was seated in the high seat near the front of the building, across from the twelve lagmen.

Torgils wanted to rush up to the front where his father was sitting, but Ragnvald held him back.

"This is a sacred duty your father is performing, and we must wait until he sees us standing here and is able to finish hearing the case."

It did not take long for Harald to notice Ragnvald standing with Gyda's two sons by his side. He knew they would not have come to Nidaros unless there was trouble. Within a short time, King Harald called a recess and walked over to where the three were standing.

"What has happened that you have come to see me here?" he asked.

"Mother is dead," shouted Torgils. "Hrolf has murdered her!"

"What do you know of this, Ragnvald?"

"I know only what your sons have told me," he answered.

"How is it Hrolf could get through the gates of Eidsvag Manor?"

"He told the servants he was his father, Ragnvald, who had come to deliver an urgent message from you, and Mother walked out of the gates unaware!" spoke Sigtrygg.

"I knew nothing of the matter and I would surely have stopped it if I had known," Ragnvald answered defensively.

"We shall deal with Hrolf at a later time. Right now, we must leave for Eidsvag and place the mother of my children in her grave!"

Harald made arrangements for Halvdan the White, Halvdan the Black and Sigrod to take his place on the high seat and left the Thing swiftly. With a hundred men maning his dragon ship, they reached Eidsvag in time for the burial feast.

When all the other guests and her children had had a chance to speak about their love for Gyda, Harald told the story of the first time they met. Most of the people had heard the story, but his children enjoyed hearing, once again, about the influence their mother had on their powerful father.

Gyda's mound was placed within the walls of Eidsvag Manor. The beautiful tapestries she had sown over the last 20 years, showing the conquests of her great warrior husband, were being used to cover the walls of the wooden tent that protected her body.

"Mother wanted you to have some of these tapestries to place on the walls of your castle at Avaldsnes," said Alov.

"She did not say anything about that to me," Harald remarked.

"She wasn't sure if you would want them...if they weren't sewn by your wife, Rani."

Harald looked into the green eyes of his only daughter. "Are you sure she wanted me to have them?"

"Well, they are all sewn to show the great battles you won while you were working to put all of Norway under your control. She was always proud to think that you had taken her challenge and then succeeded."

"Did she tell you she was proud of me?"

"Of course, she always spoke well of you. Even when you put her aside for Rani, she would not speak ill of you."

"She really was a great woman, besides being a great beauty. I think the thing that gave her the most pleasure was having you five children. She felt blessed to have my only daughter, as well as having the most children of all my wives. Do you know she told me that she did not need me anymore now that she had five children?"

"That is not true. She only said that to keep you from seeing how much you had hurt her. I saw how she cried when she thought no one was watching. She was a strong woman, but she had given you her heart, and she did not want you to give it back," said Alov.

Harald sat silently thinking about the wife he had just lost. Memories of their loving times filled his heart and mind.

"If you think it would please your mother to have me take this work of her hands to my home, then I will do so. I will take the tapestry that shows the defeat of my enemies, including her father, at the Battle of Hafrsfjord. I will place it in my bed chamber, and think about her when I look at it. Will that please you?"

Alov walked over and put her arms around her father's neck. He held her and caressed the beautiful long red hair that hung down her back. Suddenly, the tears she had been holding in check began to flow. They stood in the great hall of Eidsvag Manor and comforted each other...both thinking about the loved one they would not see again until it was time to be reunited in the next life.

"And God shall wipe away all tears from their eyes; and there shall be no more death, neither sorrow, nor crying, neither shall there be any more pain; for the former things are passed away." **Revelations 21:4**

CHAPTER 36

THE MANHUNT

After every detail was taken care of at Eidsvag, Harald asked Ragnvald to travel with him to Avaldsnes. There was something he needed to discuss with him...and he did not want Gyda's children to hear what he had to say.

"I am going to gather forces and go in search of Hrolf," Harald told his uncle. "I am telling you this because I intend to find him and kill him. This time the revenge will be mine. As his father, you have the right to know of my plan."

Ragnvald wasn't surprised at the declaration, and he was sure Hrolf was guilty of Gyda's murder, but his father's instinct made him cringe at the thought of it. Maybe if he went along, there might be a chance of warning Hrolf to stay out of Harald's way.

"I hope you will take me with you," Ragnvald said with a pleading tone in his voice.

"I intend to leave Guttorm in charge of keeping the peace along the East Coast and I was planning to leave you in charge of things here in the West."

"I will do whatever you command," stated Ragnvald, "but I feel it is my duty to help you find Hrolf. His actions are a reflection on my family name...and I would like to be present at his punishment. I shall ask Thorer to watch over the West Coast while we are gone."

"You want to be present...even if the punishment is death?" asked Harald.

"Yes...even if the punishment is death," assured Ragnvald.

"Then we leave in a fortnight. We must gather enough forces to overpower any resistance we find, and I intend to start at the Shetland Islands and keep looking until I find him. While we are there, we will rid the Islands of the others who have been raiding our shores in the past and take control of them once again."

Ragnvald was reluctant to tell his wife that he was going on a manhunt. He thought she might guess what man they were searching for and he did not want to take the chance. He still wondered if she had been a part of the scheme to get Gyda out of the gates of Eidsvag Manor so Hrolf could give her the death wound. Otherwise, how would his son have had access to his jarl robes.

Many men of influence and power had left Norway rather than accept Harald's Code of Law and protection taxes when he was trying to unify the country. A number of them sailed for Iceland and made new lives for themselves. Those that refused to give up and accept the fact that there was now just one King in Norway, settled in the Shetland, Orkney, Faroe and Hebrides Islands.

There they could have started a new life, but their pride and anger would not let them. Instead, they used their new location as a base of operations from which they would send out raiding expeditions to plunder the coasts of Norway. In that way, they thought they could prove that Harald's system of levying taxes in exchange for the benefit of protection was not working.

Hrolf was afraid to come back to Norway himself, but aided many other angry outlaws who had turned into raiders...and carried out raids on Norway's Western Coast. It seemed they always planned the raids when Harald was making his rounds of the Things that were far away from the coast.

Thus, revenge became a never ending quest. Six years after being outlawed, Hrolf decided to take one last raid on Norway before leaving the Islands for Ireland. His plan was to kill Gyda, because as Harald's last surviving wife, her death would be the most painful form of retaliation he could commit against the King.

Harald and Ragnvald gathered a fleet of one hundred ships and sailed to the Shetland Islands and then on to the Orkney islands, and others in the West Sea...all the while looking for Hrolf. Each place they stopped, it seemed he had just left. While they were in the Islands, they sought for information on other pirate raiders who had been attacking Norway's coastline. They found and killed all those who were judged guilty.

When Aethelstan, King of England, heard about Harald's quest, he traveled north to Caithness and asked to meet with him. The two powerful men met at the Bard Castle on the Northern Coast of Scotland. At first glance, it seemed that both men held the other in high regard. As they sat down at either end of a large oak table, they seemed to be taking each other's measure.

"Can I ask you some questions?" requested Aethelstan.

"You may," answered Harald.

"How is it that your law prohibits raiding in Norway, but allows or permits it in other countries?"

"It is your responsibility to defend your own borders...victory goes to the swift! If you do not have the power to defeat these Norse raiders, then you must give them what they seek...riches. You can pay them to leave your country and people unharmed or you can fight them. If you came to my country, I, of course, would never pay gold or ransom. I would fight! But then, I have trained warriors, many fine weapons and great battle ships. You lack enough of all three to be the aggressor," stated Harald matter of factly.

"We are very grateful to you for getting rid of the Norse raiders in the Islands and here in Northern Scotland," Aethelstan replied.

"I have not come to rid them of raiders for your sake...I have come to seek revenge on a kinsman who had been branded an outlaw in my country and left. In the last six years, he has continued to send others to do his dirty work. That was not revenge enough, however, and he has attacked my wife...and left her to die in front of her children. He knows I am searching for him and he also knows I will find him. There is nowhere he can hide from me. I, also, will have my revenge."

"It is said that you have more wives than one...and yet you loved her enough to undertake this quest?" asked Aethelstan.

"I love all of my wives, or I have. She was the last wife still living. I have outlived them all."

"You look to be still a fit man. Will you marry again?"

"Nay, I shall wait to spend eternity with Odin and the wives he has already given me," replied Harald with a smile.

"You speak so confidently of Odin as if you know him personally. But is he not a God?"

"He is my God and he is my protecter. I am sworn to do his will, not my own. He has guided my life from the time I entered my mother's belly. He had a work for me to do, and I have tried to follow his will throughout my life."

"It would be interesting to have such a God in one's life. Do you mean he actually speaks to you?" asked an incredulous Aethelstan.

"Yes, he does. Sometimes he comes to me in a dream and sometimes I hear his voice, or see him riding his horse Slepni across the sky, proclaiming that we have won the victory over our enemies. But what of your God? Doesn't he speak to you?"

"Well...not exactly. He speaks mostly to the priests and they tell me what he says. But you have more than one God, do you not?"

"Odin has other members of his family that help him rule the world, but he is the Allfather."

"Very interesting! I have always been led to believe that the Norsemen were heathen because they refused to believe in our Christian God. We, of course, consider Him far superior to Odin or any other heathen Gods."

"You may have your God and I will have mine. We both have the freedom to choose. Let the Gods decide who is superior!" With that statement, Harald rose from the table.

"I would like to give you a gift...as a reward for destroying those Norse raiders who have also been attacking our shores."

Harald was about to protest that he needed no reward, but at the end of Aethelstan's outstretched arm was the most beautiful sword he had ever beheld.

"That sword looks as if it has never seen battle!"

"No, it has never worn a drop of blood. It was made for me by the best sword maker in all of Britian. There is not another like it."

"It may be too beautiful to use," replied Harald as he held the sword and admired the jeweled handle and the gold inlay on the blade.

"I give this as a sign of friendship between us. I think this will never happen, but if you ever need anything from me, you just have to send this sword as a token and I will know it is a true messenger." said the English King.

Harald placed his hand on the hilt of the weapon at his side and replied, "I would not trade my sword Frey for even the most beautiful of swords."

"I am not suggesting that this sword replace the one you carry by your side. I would presume it has served you well."

Harald pulled his special sword from its scabbard. "Not only does this sword contain the names of the mighty ancestors who have carried it into battle, but it has protected my life through more than thirty battles."

"I still would like you to take this sword as a token of my high regard for you."

At that last word, Harald graciously took the sword and touched the hilt to his forehead in a sign of respect for a fellow ruler.

"I have also heard that you have many sons to follow after you. Is that true?"

"It is true indeed. I have fifteen fine sons, although some may be more worthy than the others."

"Alas, I have no sons. Your God has blessed you more than my God has blessed me."

Harald smiled and nodded his head. He did not know much about Aethelstan's God, but he was sure there could not be another God who was as powerful and all knowing as Odin.

From Scotland, Harald's fleet moved on to Ireland and beached their ships along the seashore, near the village of Dublin. There they would continue their search for Hrolf. The King, along with Ragnvald, Berdaluke and his bodyguard, called at the estate of Olaf the White Ingjaldson. They knew if the outlaw was hiding in the area, Olaf would know about it.

Olaf had been King in Dublin for some time and controlled not only Ireland, but also the Irish Sea. He had heard of Harald's quest for revenge and word had come telling of his ridding the Islands of the raiding pirates. Very few pirates tried to raid in Ireland, for Olaf had a large standing army and fought hard to protect his own.

"Do you know why we have traveled so far from the shores of Norway?" Harald asked.

"I do," Olaf replied, "Nothing happens in this part of the world that does not come to my attention."

"Have you seen Hrolf then?" asked Ragnvald.

"Your son has come here, trying to use another name, that I would not recognize him. But he is foolish in his attempt, for there are not many others who stand as large as Hrolf Ganger!" Olaf laughed.

"And do you know where he is now?" the father questioned.

"Are you as anxious to find him as your King is then?"

Ragnvald's face did not betray his emotion as he looked over at Harald. "He has dishonored my family name and I owe a loyalty to my King," was his answer.

"I think he will not go far in the angry winter seas," Olaf declared. "There are a number of fine harbors and settlements along the coastline. Hrolf could be hiding at Wexford, Waterford, Cork or even at Limerick. I invite you to spend the cold winter days here at my castle. We will feed both you and your men and you shall see how we live here in Ireland.

"Thou hast spoken well, my friend," replied Harald, "We will see what winter life is like in this part of the world!"

On the south side of Olaf's castle was a flat plain, stretching out to a wide river that flowed quietly past on its way to the sea. Here Harald's army would camp in tents made from the ships sail, their dragon ships pulled from the water and upturned on strong pole stakes. The hill above, where the castle stood, provided shelter from the strong winter winds that whipped along the seashore.

Dublin was a settlement full of Norsemen, and there were many activities that the men used to pass the time. Indoors, there was chess, dice throwing, backgammon and saga telling. Jumping and wrestling competitions as well as throwing the ash pole occupied the men for outside exercises. Hours spent in sword practice and spear throwing kept the warriors skills sharp for the next encounter.

As the weather began to moderate, Harald sent Berdaluke with a ship of one hundred seasoned warriors to search the islands and the shores for the whereabouts of Hrolf. He was sure the outlaw would have found a safe harbor to overwinter also.

After just a fortnight, Berdaluke returned with the message that Hrolf was hiding among the hills on the southern shore of the island. The area was called Cork and it had a wide harbor that would accept many ships.

The mighty Army of the North quietly prepared to leave Dublin and travel southward. The warriors were sworn to secrecy and no one knew of their destination except for the King and his trusted leaders. Only Harald, Ragnvald and Berdaluke knew the exact day of their departure. They knew if Hrolf got wind of their sailing, he would head for another place to hide.

Harald was uncertain if he could trust Ragnvald with the information, but the jarl denied any intent to warn his son. Berdaluke threatened death to the men who had sailed with him if word got out where the large armada was planning to travel.

Harald's army silently departed Dublin in the early dawn and headed toward open waters. Prayers had been offered to Odin for a safe journey before launching the ships, but there was also a prayer in the heart and mind of the ten thousand men who were sailing off into an angry sea. None wanted their dead body left in a watery grave.

There was great danger in travel on the Irish Sea when the winter weather was still upon it. Fierce wind storms blew in from the south where the sea opened to the larger body of water. Lashing rain, along with the wind, could threaten to sink even the best of ships...and that was not the only danger. Overcast skies and rough seas created dense fog that could challenge even the best of navigators.

The armada of one hundred ships threaded its way carefully through the thick fog along the shoreline, trying to avoid getting too close to the rocky coastline while avoiding the heavy currents in the deeper waters. They passed the settlements of Wexford and then Waterford and finally came to the place which looked to be the harbor at Cork. The men were deadly quiet and only the sound of oars softly rowing could be heard.

Odin must be guiding our path, thought Harald, for just as the ships entered the harbor, the fog lifted enough for him to see clearly. Hrolf's ships were not staked on the beach as he had expected, but he saw the mouth of a river that flowed into the inlet from the east side.

The King's ship was in the lead and headed toward the river. A long line of dragon ships soon filled the water of the large river. Around a wide bend, Harald spotted Hrolf's camp off in the distance. There were many tents and camp fires sending smoke drifting slowly into the foggy air. He signaled for his ships to head for the river's edge. The men, who were skilled in covert attacks, could disembark and quietly go ashore without being discovered by the enemy.

The trees were thick along the water's edge and kept the army hidden until they were very near the tents. Suddenly, the barking of dogs alerted the sleepy camp. Berdaluke was quick to signal the men who were following him to rush the camp. By the time Hrolf and his men hurried out of their tents they were totally surrounded by Harald's large army.

Hrolf's men had come from their tents with swords drawn, but they made no move to use them when they saw the huge numbers of the foe. To Harald's dismay, Ragnvald hurried forth to embrace his son.

"Step aside Ragnvald!" Harald shouted. "This is no happy reunion for which we have braved the winter seas!"

The jarl looked pleadingly into his son's eyes...as if begging for forgiveness for the deed that was about to be done.

"Hrolf Ragnvaldson, murderer and outlaw, I, Harald Halvdanson have come to claim the life of the man who gave the death blow to my wife Gyda...and left her to die in the sight of her children! What say you?"

Hrolf knew he could not fight his way out of this situation, so despite being shown a coward to his men, he chose the only option open to him. He dropped to his knees and began begging for mercy.

"Did you show any mercy to Gyda?" Harald growled, "A woman who had done you no harm? No! You are too much of a coward! If you were a real man, a brave warrior, you would have come against me, man to man! It was me you hated because I pronounced you an outlaw, a sentence you truly deserved. And now you will get the death blow you also deserve!"

Then Hrolf thought of another option he might try and appealed to the King's pride. "Will you act the part of the coward and strike me down as I am kneeling before you...or will you take my life as a true warrior, with sword in hand, and allow me the chance to defend myself man to man?"

"The King does not stoop to fight with cowards, but I do!" shouted Berdaluke as he stepped between Harald and Hrolf.

"Nay, this is not your fight...and it shall not be your revenge, my friend," said Harald as he pushed the berserker aside.

"A man who acts the part of a coward, and kills a woman, does not deserve a warrior's death! But never let it be said of me that I denied any man a warrior's death...that he might have to dwell in Helveti instead of Valhalla for the eternities!"

"Stand back and give us room to fight. It will be to the death!" said the King as he drew Frey from its scabbard.

"Do not risk your life on such a coward as this!" pleaded Berdaluke.

Harald glanced at Ragnvald, who was torn between his loyalty to his King and his love of his son. The jarl offered no advice. While the King was looking away from his opponent, Hrolf lunged forward with a swiftness that was surprising for so large a man. Only pure instinct brought Harald's sword up to deflect the blow that would have taken his life.

"So, that is how cowards fight, is it?" Harald shouted as his sword slashed open the front of Hrolf's vest.

Hrolf looked down to see blood staining his clothing as it trickled from the wound. Anger welled up in his throat and he gave an animal growl as he lunged again for the older man.

"Take my shield," cried Berdaluke in anguish as he tried to help his friend, but the King just pushed it aside.

"I will take no unfair advantage!" he shouted as he took another swipe with his sword. This one drew blood on Hrolf's right arm.

It was obvious that Hrolf was no match for Harald. As the fight progressed, the King was able to deflect each blow while his opponent sustained a wound on not just the chest, but both arms and both legs. It was obvious to the stunned crowd that Harald could have struck the death blow at any time, but he was giving the younger man every opportunity to defend himself.

Finally, the King began to tire of the charade and he knocked Hrolf's sword from his hand. With his sword to his enemy's throat, Harald shouted, "It is over!"

In true cowardly fashion, Hrolf dropped to his knees and began to beg again for mercy. When Ragnvald saw this, he ran to his son's side and added his voice to the cry for mercy. Harald looked at the pitiful scene before him.

"You do not deserve mercy!" Harald shouted.

"I will make a solemn oath that I will never again set a foot in Norway, nor in any of the Islands, or in any place where you reign! I will live my life far away from you and yours and you shall never have to see my face again!" Hrolf cried.

Harald raised his sword high above his head and was about to strike down this cowardly outlaw when he heard a voice in his ear saying, "Spare the life of Ragnvald's son. I have a greater purpose for his life." It was not hard to recognize this voice. He had heard it many times before. It was the voice of his God...and he knew he must obey.

To the astonishment of all the men watching this contest, who were waiting for the King to end the life of the man he had hunted, Harald lowered his weapon and thrust the handle of the sacred sword in front of his enemy.

"Kiss this sword as a sign that you have made an oath...and may Odin strike you dead if you break that oath!"

Hrolf readily kissed the handle of the King's sword and turned to embrace his father. Harald turned and shouted to his men, "To the ships...our work here is finished!"

He did not look to see if Ragnvald was coming or staying. It made no difference to him. Much as he loved and respected his uncle, there was even more of a question now as to whose side he would choose to fight on. When the King and his body guard had filled his dragon ship he told Berdaluke to cast off from the shore.

"Are we not waiting for Ragnvald?" the berserker asked.

"I do not think he is returning with us," was the curt reply.

"But...he is hurrying toward the ship."

Harald turned to see his breathless kinsman heading toward the gang plank.

"Hold up, we are waiting for Ragnvald," Berdaluke ordered.

Gasping for breath, Ragnvald walked up into the ship and went over to where Harald stood.

"You will never know how grateful I am that you spared the life of my son."

"It was not my will but Odin's that I obeyed. You know I would have easily given Hrolf the death blow."

"It grieves me to think I have lost your good will over this sad incident, but I wonder what you would give to save the life of one of your sons," spoke the jarl.

The King answered not but went to sit in his seat in the prow of the ship. May be his uncle was right...for he had yet to be called on to defend one of his sons against a charge of murder...and he hoped he never would.

The vast armada of ships returned to the sea and headed north for another stop at Dublin. They would wait now until the waters were calm enough for a safe trip back to their homes in Norway. The goal of this journey had been accomplished, even though the outcome was different than had been expected. There was at least one person who was relieved that he did not have to ever admit to his wife that he had participated in the death of their son.

"For rulers are not a terror to good works, but to the evil. Wilt thou then not be aftaid of the power? Do that which is good, and thou shalt have praise of the same. For he is the minister of God to thee for good.

But if thou do that which is evil, be afraid; for he beareth not the sword in vain: for he is the minister of God, a revenger to execute wrath upon him that doeth evil."   **Romans 13:3-4**

CHAPTER 37

FAREWELL GUTTORM

The year 896 was one of mourning. Guttorm Sigurdson, uncle and friend, warrior and Duke, died while making a visit to his boyhood home at Stein Manor in Ringerike. The situation that caused his death could not have been more tragic, for even at the end, he was trying to do what would be best for Harald.

In the time that Guttorm had been responsible for Snofrid's sons, he had visited Ringerike twice each year to make sure there were no problems with Halvdan and Sigurd. The boys had gotten on well and been good company for Ashild...that is until Ragnvald the younger arrived.

After Hrolf was declared an outlaw for raiding and pillaging at Kaupang in Vestfold, his mother Hild refused to allow Ragnvald the Younger to live with her and Ragnvald at Borgund. Guttorm traveled to More to get the four year old boy and brought him to Stein Manor.

Young Ragnvald was excited to meet his brothers and wanted to live with them, but Ring Dagson thought one more child would be too much for his wife, Olaug. He asked Guttorm to take the boy somewhere else, so he brought him to live at Aas Manor in Toten.

Aas Manor was very near to a holy place, and Guttorm thought that could be a good influence on a witch's son. Mads Elenson and his wife Marit had no sons, only a six year old daughter named Margaret. They felt honored to be asked to foster a son of the King.

This should have been a place where Ragnvald could forget about the harshness of Hild, but the scars were very deep. He was mean to Margaret and seemed to enjoy hurting her. The older he got, the worse he got. When he was ten, Mads gave him his own horse, thinking he would practice better treatment of his own property...but to no avail.

The horse did, however, give him the means to travel to Ringerike to see his brothers. At least, that is why he came at first. Ragnvald became infatuated with their foster sister, Ashild, and it was in her nature to be kind to him. As the months went by, he spent more and more time at Stein Manor...and more and more time with Ashild.

She was sixteen winters when he first took an interest in her...in the very blush of womanhood. Ragnvald was just ten winters, but like his father, was very large for his age. He seemed to have a strange hold on Ashild, and his brothers could not understand why she was willing to give so much attention to their younger brother.

After several years had passed, he convinced her that he was in love with her and asked her to run away with him. She knew that the plan sounded dangerous, but there was something inside that made her decide to say yes...a decision she would later come to regret.

On a Sunday morning, when most of the household were still asleep, Ashild crept, with her bundle of clothing, to the barn. She saddled her own horse and rode to meet Ragnvald outside the gates of the manor. He was excited to see her and relieved that she had come. He wasn't yet sure of his power to influence a person continually. Once she was in his presence he knew he could control her.

Ragnvald led the way as they traveled northward. He knew enough to stay off the main roads and instead, led her to some mountain trails he had discovered. She really was an easy prey.

By nightfall, they came to the mountain saeter of Aas Manor. The cattle had already been brought down from the mountain pastures to the lowland meadows in preparation for the winter. He had been to the lonely cabin before and he knew there would be no one around.

Ashild wasn't sure what Ragnvald had planned...she just urged her horse along and followed behind him. Ragnvald knew what he had planned, but he wasn't about to let her in on his secret.

Shortly after he began riding to visit his brothers at Stein Manor, it became obvious to him that they had gotten the best of the situations. They hadn't been beaten by their foster mother, they hadn't been lonely and forced to play with a sister they hated...they had found love and acceptance at Ring Dagson's home.

Ragnvald had never felt either love or acceptance. He knew no one wanted him...Hild had told him that enough times. When he asked Guttorm if he could live at Stein Manor with Halvdan and Sigurd, he had been told no. The reason had been that they already had two boys and did not have room for another one. He knew that was just an excuse...because they did not want him. Nobody wanted him.

His father never even came to see him, he just sent old Guttorm to do his dirty work. And why did he have to pick a place like Aas Manor to put him? He did not like Mads Elenson or his wife...and they did not like him either. He knew they just kept him to please their King. But the King did not care whether he liked it in Toten or not...the King did not care about him at all.

Well, he would show them...he would show them all. He knew how to control people, especially people who were kind, like Ashild. She said she had kept their leaving a secret from everyone, so it should take them a while to find their hiding place. It was just too bad it had rained the previous night, for their horse tracks would probably show in the mud.

The plan he had for Ashild would not take him more than one night, just one night to ruin their precious Ashild and show them his power. Then they would all be sorry they had been mean to him...all of them, even the King.

When they arrived at the saeter, Ragnvald helped Ashild to dismount and tied the horses to a stake. He brought her into the dark interior of the cabin and lit a candle. As he led her over to the small bed in the corner of the room, he spoke to her softly and told her he loved her. He said he wanted her to be his wife. She said nothing, but just stared blankly at him. This was going to be even easier than he thought.

He opened a box that sat on the table by the bed and asked Ashild to set out the cheese and bread for their meal while he went out to gather some wood. Soon, he had a nice, warm fire going in the fireplace and they ate by the firelight. When the meal was over, Ragnvald started whispering his soothing words into her ear.

He led her back to the bed and began to loosen her hair from its braid. All the while, Ashild just looked at him with a dazed expression on her face. Next, he began removing her clothing, one item at a time. She was like a woman in a trance...and he knew he had full power over her. He covered her with the blanket while he removed his clothing, and then climbed into the bed and under the cover with her.

She was so much under his spell that it was no longer even necessary for him to lie and tell her he loved her and wanted to marry her. He realized now that she was powerless to resist his advances ... and he climbed on top of her soft, supple body.

The next thing he knew, there was a cold draft of air coming from the open door. There stood Ring Dagson, with Guttorm, Halvdan and Sigurd standing behind him. The glowing embers from the fire place cast an eerie glow on the faces of those at the door...and those in the bed.

"Ashild!" Ring shouted and grabbed her by the arm. As he reached for his daughter, he shoved Ragnvald to the floor and kicked him out of the way. He wrapped the blanket around his daughter's bare body and demanded, "Where are your clothes?"

Ashild was shocked out of her spell and looked at the scene around her. There was her father's angry face and behind that was Ragnvald standing naked and laughing. His brothers rushed past both father and daughter to get their hands on him, but they could not stop his laughing.

"Now I have stolen what is most precious from your daughter, Ring Dagson, and you have paid for rejecting me when I came here as a boy of four winters. Yes, you have all paid...you my happy brothers, our old uncle Guttorm...and even our mighty father, King Harald!"

The evil laugh began again. Halvdan and Sigurd seemed helpless to stop it. Ring grabbed Ashild's clothes from the floor and carried her out the door of the cabin. Before he shut the door, he instructed his foster sons to keep their wicked brother captive until he could get Ashild safely home.

Guttorm advised the brothers to take Ragnvald to Tande Manor and let their father know what evil deed he had committed. They did not want him to ever go to Stein Manor again...or even Aas Manor. If he had done this to Ashild, he might also commit this crime on Mads' daughter Margaret.

Fortunately, Harald was visiting at Tande Manor and quickly took charge of the situation when the boys and Guttorm arrived.

"We shall not hold a public Thing for this crime, because that would just further injure the innocent person who has been violated. But, we shall wait for her father to attend, for he deserves to hear the sentence that is handed down."

Ring rode to Tande Manor the next day and sat with Guttorm, Halvdan and Sigurd as witnesses. Harald had already heard most of the story from them, but he wanted to make Ragnvald hear what the four witnesses had to say. After they described finding the two of them in the cabin bed, stripped of their clothing, and repeating the words that were said, it was the prisoner's turn to speak.

What a sad tale he told...of being beaten by Hild...of being told he was a worthless son of a witch...of being sent to a second home where he was not wanted...of having to see what a nice life his brothers led, while he did not matter to anyone...least of all his father.

As he started telling of when and how he began his plan to make them all pay...to make them all sorry...to practice his control on sweet Ashild, all Harald could think about was Snofrid and Svase...and how they had worked their evil spell on him. He also felt some shame to hear Ragnvald tell of feeling unwanted and alone. His father was indeed guilty of not wanting him.

Although forcing a woman was against the law, there was no provision for a woman who was taken while under a spell. The law was also lenient with those who were under the age of thirteen, and Ragnvald was now just twelve winters old.

Despite the fact that there were four people in the room that would have liked to take a knife to the throat of this offender, Harald decided on a different punishment.

"You will not be put to death for this evil deed, my son, even though you do deserve it. You can never repay to Ashild what you have taken...and I hope one day you will feel sorrow for that crime. Because of your age, I hereby declare that your punishment will be banishment. I banish you back to the land where you were born...to Lofoten...and there you must stay for a period of twenty years."

"So, I am to be sent out to strangers once again, am I? Well then, so be it. I care nothing for you...no, not any of you!" he shouted. "And you, old man, you have deemed me to be the least of all my brothers, and I hate you the most!" he growled as he lunged toward Guttorm and spat into his startled face.

Guttorm clutched at his chest...a look of anger and anguish flooded his face as the spittle ran down his thick beard. The group stood in stunned silence for a few moments.

Harald and Berdaluke reacted almost simultaneously, reaching to catch the Duke as his large body slumped to the floor. Halvdan and Sigurd both grabbed an arm of Ragnvald, but he just glared back at them. They had never developed a brotherly affection for him, and now that he had ruined Ashild and shown such disrespect for Guttorm, they had nothing but disgust and hatred for their brother.

The berserker lifted and carried the limp body of Guttorm into the nearest bed chamber. Harald followed behind his great friend and kinsman. After being gently placed on the soft eiderdown cover, he reached his hand toward Harald and struggled to speak.

"Return to the hall and finish with Ragnvald. I will not rest until he has been dealt with."

Harald gripped the once strong hand and nodded in agreement.

"You rest here and I shall return when the judgement has been made," the King responded and turned to leave the room. He ordered a serving maid to find Ragnhild, who had been spared attendance at the Thing, and tell her to hurry to Guttorm's side.

It bothered him more than he could have imagined, to see mighty Guttorm lying there in that weakened condition. The thought of losing the man who had stood and fought at his side through more than thirty battles, and had given him the counsel he needed to keep his kingdoms intact and peaceful, made him cringe.

Seeing his three sons standing in front of the high seat brought his mind back to the unpleasant business at hand.

"You have heard the judgement pronounced on your head and you have had the opportunity to respond. I feel the urge to spit in your face as you so dishonored your great-uncle, but I refuse to drop down to your low level of behavior. You will leave immediately for Lofoten and have twenty long years to repent of your evil acts!"

Ragnvald stood silent, his arms held by the two brothers who despised him. But, there was no attitude of repentance from the offender. His head was held high in defiance and the look on his face was one of hatred for those standing around him.

Berdaluke and one hundred men were sent, by ship, to deliver their prisoner to his place of banishment. Harald did not say farewell to his errant son. He knew Ragnvald would relish some show of caring from his father, but Harald had no feelings of caring to give to him.

Faithful, loyal, uncle and brother, Guttorm took his last breath sometime during the night. His nephew and his sister spent the last few hours of his life, sitting by his side and sharing sweet memories of their time together. The Duke had lived a good life…a long life of sixty two years.

"Guttorm is fortunate to have the opportunity to now spend his next life associating with our parents and others who have preceded him to Gimli. He certainly was a righteous spirit. I hope my time comes soon. I do not think you need me anymore, my son, do you?" asked Ragnhild with a sigh.

"I still have my son Erik to rear," replied Harald.

"Yes, but he is now five winters old and enjoying life with you at Avaldsnes. He is large for his age, just as you were, and can travel to the Things with you in the summer season. I remember when your father first said he was taking you with him on the journey through his seven kingdoms. I was so afraid to let you go...and you were already eight winters old."

"I am very glad you relented. I really needed those two years riding with father and Guttorm to learn from their example."

"You have become the great man that was prophesied in the two dreams your father and I had before you were born. We are very proud of you, and I think Odin must be as well."

"I hope so, Mother, I hope so!"

Mother and son sat together beside the bed of their dear departed, lost in thoughts of years gone by. The room was totally quiet, but they could feel the presence of the spirits who had come to claim Guttorm and usher him into the next life. It was a special time...a special time indeed.

CHAPTER 38

LIFE AND DEATH

The next four years passed in peace. Harald's oldest son, Gutt, could now claim his birth name and the name of his beloved foster father Guttorm, but he was content to continue as just Gutt. He had married Anne Iversdatter of Halvorsrud Manor and was managing the southern kingdoms of Vingulmark, Gautland, Vermaland, Raumarike and Vestfold.

Harald and Erik lived together in the castle at Avaldsnes on the island of Karmr. He was relieved that this son, who had his mother's dark hair and strong spirit, did not die with her. In many ways it was a lonely life, filled with memories of the short time Rani had been the mistress of this home. But Harald had Berdaluke and his personal body guard that lived in the castle with him and he knew Odin expected him to continue to live out his life in a meaningful way.

In the summer of the year 900, Harald was at Tande Manor for his yearly visit. He was sad to see that his mother was in failing health.

"It is finally time for me to join your father in Gimli. I have waited many years for this blessing, but there is one more thing I must do before leaving this mortal existence. Are you willing to honor your dying mother's last request?"

"Of course, mother, ask whatever you will."

"I wish you to take Ashild to wife."

"But mother...you ask the one thing I cannot do! How can I make a vow to you that will break my oath to Rani? You know I said to her, at the moment of death, that I would never wed another."

"What about your obligation to Ashild? She feels she is not worthy to wed because she was ruined by your wicked son Ragnvald. She deserves the protection of marriage and at least one child to love."

"But I am too old for her. Is there not someone else who could take her to wed?"

"What about the law that says a kinsman must care for the women of his family? Ashild has no other close kinsman to look to for support. Remember, she was an only child, just as you were. She has cared for me, faithfully, since that awful situation with your son. She deserves a husband...and I think it must be you."

Harald was mentally torn between his love and respect for his mother and the oath he had taken to his dead wife. How could he fulfill both of his obligations?

"What is it that you always do when you come to a crossroad in your life and are uncertain which path to take?" his mother asked.

"You are right. I must ask Odin for his direction as I always ask him for his protection."

Just before the sun was about to rise, the Allfather appeared at Harald's bedside. It was a relief to be able to ask Odin for guidance and know that he would answer.

"O Great One, thou knowest my dear mother is about to join my father in Gimli. She has waited many years for this blessing...and i am happy for her...though I will miss her loving counsel. She asks but one commitment of me before she leaves this earth, that i would take to wife the woman Ashild, who has served my mother faithfully these many years."

"I am told it is my obligation, as close kinsman, to give her a chance to bear a child. You know about the oath I gave to my wife rani. I told her, on her deathbed, that I would never marry another. How can I please both of these women that I love?"

"You are indeed a worthy son and a worthy husband. I have come to tell you that it is my will that you take Ashild to wife. Rani knows your heart and she knows that she will have you with her when you are called home to join us in Gimli. I have told her that your work is not yet complete on the earth and she has agreed that my will must be done. Give your mother your vow and let her leave in peace. Ashild will give you more sons."

Harald wanted to ask why he needed more sons, but Odin was gone. He walked slowly to the bedchamber that had been shared by his parents. His mother lay so still he wondered if her spirit had already left her body, but as he knelt on her bed platform, her eyes opened slowly.

"You are right, dear Mother, Odin does want me to marry Ashild. Rani has also given her blessing, so i do not have to worry about breaking my oath to her. Odin said Ashild will bear me more sons! Does it seem strange to you that Odin wants me to have so many sons?"

"The blood that flows in your veins is noble blood, my son. Odin will bless many nations because of the influence of your seed. Thank you for honoring your mother's last wish."

"Thank you for being the best mother a son could hope to have," he said as he kissed her furrowed brow.

That kiss made his mother smile...the last smile she would give him on this earth. Harald looked at his mother's wrinkled face and thought about what a beautiful woman she had been. He thought about his own life and wondered how many years he would need to keep living until he could join the rest of his family waiting in Gimli. His life was not going to be the same with the loss of his great comrade, Guttorm, and now his mother. Maybe Odin would take him soon.

As that thought crossed his mind, he heard the door open quietly. He turned to see Ashild standing in the doorway. He wondered if she knew about the promise his mother had extracted from him.

"She is gone," he said in a low voice. Ashild walked to the bedside.

"She was a very spiritual person. I would wish to be such a woman. She was loved by everyone who knew her. I am sad for you, My Lord, to have lost both your uncle and now your mother."

Harald turned his head and looked at the person kneeling beside him and his heart was pricked with sympathy for this young woman who had devoted herself to his mother.

"Do you know how much I appreciate you for taking such good care of my wonderful mother?" he asked.

"Spending every day in her presence brought great joy to my life. It is going to be very empty now that she is gone," said Ashild with a sigh.

He took a deep breath and reached for her hands. He rose to his feet and pulled her up beside him.

"How would you like to substitute me for my mother? I could use someone to care for me."

She looked up at him with a questioning look on her face. "Are you ill, My Lord?"

He tipped his head back and let out a great laugh. So, his mother hadn't told her about the last request.

"I am not ill, but I am in need of a wife," he said with as much conviction as he could muster.

"But...you do not want me for your wife," she stated with downcast eyes. "I am not worthy to be the wife of a great man. I am not worthy to be the wife of any man."

"I know your story, Ashild, and I know what Ragnvald did to you. He has been sent far away and you do not ever have to worry about seeing him again. He carried the blood of an evil man, and that evil rested in his heart until he is undeserving of the company of good people."

"But...I still do not know why you would want me for your wife."

Here he was in that difficult situation again. Why did Odin keep choosing wives for him? That was dangerous thinking, he told himself. Maybe he should have waited for a better time to bring up the question of marriage with Ashild. Was he going to go with the truth again? Yes, at the risk of offending her, he would tell her the truth.

"I will tell you the reason I am asking you to become my wife, and I pray that it will not displease you," he said, searching her face for the emotion hidden there.

"My mother has asked me to make a vow, before she died, that I would take you for my wife."

The room was silent for a moment. Ashild's eyes were staring up at him as she tried to comprehend the statement he had just made.

"It is not necessary," she said as her eyes looked down to the floor. "I am prepared for a solitary life."

His heart went out to her as he heard the sadness in her voice. He knew he needed to try a little harder.

"I will not accept no for an answer," he said with his boisterous voice. "Please tell me you are not rejecting a proposal of marriage from your King!"

With that, she looked up at him and a slow smile crept over her face. She could be very attractive when she smiled.

"I do not suppose the King is accustomed to having his offers refused," she said with a laugh.

"Certainly not!"

"Well, if it really was your mother's dying wish, I guess we must honor it."

"That is more like it. You know I am old enough to be your father," he said.

"Are you saying you are too old to father a child?" she asked with a concerned look on her face.

"I do not think so," he said and thought about the woman in Dublin. "Is that the only reason you agreed to marry me...so that I could give you a child?"

"Well, that is one of the main reasons women want to marry!" she said with a larger smile this time. "Why do men want to marry?"

"That is an interesting question. I shall have to ponder that and give you my answer at a later time. Do I have your word that you have agreed to become my wife?"

"I am tempted to say I shall have to ponder that and give you my answer at a later time, but I think your mother's spirit must be waiting to hear me give my promise before she leaves this room."

"I think you must be right," he said and looked over at his mother's still smiling face.

"Do you have a daughter named Ragnhild after your mother, as yet?" she asked.

"No, I do not. Are you planning our first child before we have even shared the marriage bed?" he asked with a raise of his eyebrows.

"I have wished for a child of my own for a long time. I would not want to wait too much longer!"

This was going to be an interesting marriage, Harald thought to himself. He hoped he would not disappoint her.

"I think we shall marry on Friday, Freya's day, the same day as the death ceremony. Then my mother's spirit can truly leave in peace. I know she is anxious to join my father as soon as possible."

"Your mother has shown me the lovely dark blue dress she wore at her own wedding many years ago. It lies right in the chest at the bottom of her bed. I had thought to send her to Gimli wearing that very dress. Do you think she would like to see me wear it for our marriage before we dress her for her departure?"

"I think that would please her about as much as our promise to marry," he answered enthusiastically. "Will you have time to prepare?"

"I will ask the servants to arrange for a large feast. We shall mark the passing of your mother and the beginning of our marriage on the same day!"

"Would you like to seal our promise with a kiss?" he asked as she turned to leave the bedchamber.

She stopped, paused, and turned back to face him. "No, I can wait. I have waited this long, I can wait a few days more," she said with a saucy toss of her head.

Harald sat down on the edge of his mother's bed. He was a little shocked at his own behavior. It hadn't been as hard to get a new wife as he had thought it would be. Not that he wanted Rani to look down on him and think he was going to enjoy this wife, but he knew it was his obligation to give her a child, or children, and certainly Odin would not begrudge him enjoying the process...at least somewhat.

He turned to his mother's silent body lying peacefully on her bed linens. "You have been a powerful influence in my life all the years you lived and now you are still influencing me in death. Please give my greeting to Father and my Rani when you get there." Then, as an after thought, he said, "And greet my Asa, Svanhild and Gyda also, will you?"

What a life he had lived. He had loved and been loved by four women besides his mother, and now he would have another wife. Perhaps he would even grow to love her as he had with Asa, Svanhild, and Gyda. Then there had been Snofrid. He was certain he would not see her in Gimli! Helviti was the place for her and Svase.

Rani was a different matter. He had loved her passionately from the beginning. If only she had been allowed to live longer... but he had learned not to question the plan Odin had for his life. Odin had indeed planned a full and interesting life for him.

A rider was sent to Ring Dagsson at Stein Manor in Ringerike with two messages. The first was an announcement that their relative, Ragnhild

Sigurdsdatter had died. The second message was an announcement that Ashild was to be joined in marriage with King Harald Halvdanson. The first message was expected. The second message was completely unexpected.

There was something in the second message that mentioned the marriage would take place before the burial. Ring could not really understand the message, but he did understand that his only daughter was going to be married. Regardless of what the issue was, Ring was determined to get to Tande Manor as soon as he could.

Ashild looked almost as beautiful as Ragnhild had in the dark blue wedding gown. The dress had been lovingly packed away in a trunk all those years ago. It was only taken from its resting place each year at Yuletide when Ragnhild took it out as a sentimental act to remember the time she had been joined to the man who had saved her...Halvdan the Black.

Both Ashild and Ragnhild had long, golden hair and they were close enough in size that the dress fit well. Of course, Harald did not know how his mother had looked on her wedding day, but he had not really noticed Ashild's appearance until today. When she came walking down the hall into the great room, Harald's mind went back to all the times he had stood and waited to see his new bride come walking toward him. He had watched Gyda come down that same hall...thirty years earlier.

Ashild did not look anything like Gyda, with her long, curly red hair and piercing green eyes. Gyda had worn a green dress that had just matched her eyes, he remembered that. No, Ashild looked more like Asa, with her pale golden hair and her soft blue eyes. Had Odin planned for his first wife and his last wife to look and act alike? He was sure this would be his last wife. Well, he thought this would be his last wife.

Harald was standing before the high seat, enjoying the sight of Ashild walking slowly toward him, when the pleasant moment was interrupted by an evil sounding laugh. All eyes turned to see his son Ragnvald standing in the doorway to the great room. His hair was a stark white in contrast to the dark clothes he wore and there was a menacing look on his face.

His eyes had the piercing blackness of his mother and Harald felt, once again, the prickly sensation on the back of his neck that he experienced whenever he thought of Svase the Finn.

"What is this?" he jeered. "Is my mighty father taking to wife the women I ruined when a mere boy?"

The group of friends and neighbors who had gathered at Tande Manor to witness the marriage stood in shocked silence. Ashild's face turned from ashen white to flushed red as the meaning of his words spread throughout the room.

Harald was the first person to react to this invasion of their happy gathering.

"Seize him!" he shouted to the men who stood near the door.

Fortunately, Berdaluke was closest and had his dagger at Ragnvald's throat before any more foul words could be uttered. The King strode swiftly across the room as the guests backed away from the intruder.

"How dare you show your face in this company!" he shouted.

"I guess you would prefer that this son of your flesh stay banished to his birthplace in Lofoten so you can forget that he is a legal Prince and heir of the great King Harald," he spat out.

"I have many legal Princes and heirs, but none have acted as you have done and still lived! I should have killed you myself after you ravaged this lovely woman...instead of just sending you away!"

Ragnvald laughed at his father's words. Harald was so angry he could hardly speak. Suddenly, he thought of something he wanted to do.

"Berdaluke, take this wicked man out of this home and tie him to the large tree that stands next to the horse barn. Svase the Finn, his evil grandfather, spent time awaiting his punishment in front of that very tree. You will wait there for your own judgement, Ragnvald. You will not ruin this marriage day for Ashild. You have done enough damage to her in the past!"

With that pronouncement, Harald turned to the stunned young woman who still stood where she had stopped just moments before. He lifted her trembling hand and placed it on his arm as he guided her faltering steps to the front of the hall.

Berdaluke effortlessly lifted the unwelcome guest and carried him from the room. With their backs to the doorway, Harald and Ashild did not see the two additional men who also left the room. Ragnvald's brothers, Halvdan and Sigurd, had been just as shocked to see him again as the others had been.

Harald did his best to proceed calmly through the marriage ceremony, but the pleasant atmosphere had been ruined for everyone. He had decided they would borrow not only his mother's marriage dress, but also her marriage ring for his oaths with Ashild. They would exchange rings later, when there was time to have another gold band set made with Ashild's name and his name inscribed on them.

At the end of their interrupted ceremony, the couple proceeded to move forward with Ragnhild's death ceremony. Each person who desired to, was offered an opportunity to express their love and respect for the special woman who had lived in their midst for so many years. Ashild spoke first and then Harald said his final words at the end.

A grand feast had been prepared for the guests to enjoy after the two ceremonies and it was dark by the time people started leaving the manor. It had been a physically and mentally exhausting day for the couple. Even though they hadn't spoken about it, they both knew that Ragnvald still had to be dealt with.

"I think it is time for me to change out of Ragnhild's dress and prepare her for burial," Ashild said to her father and her new husband as they stood by the door talking.

They quickly agreed with her, and she walked back toward the same hall she had come down as an unmarried woman just hours before. She knew Harald did not want to sleep in his parent's bed, even after his mother was placed in Halvdan's mound. She was fine with that. The bedchamber he had used as a boy was where they would meet later that night.

Both Harald and Ashild's father, Ring, had been anxious to have her leave them alone. Ring wanted to finish their conversation about Ragnvald, but he did not want to say anything in front of his daughter.

"You would not let me take revenge on that scoundrel four years ago, but I hope you have changed your mind now," whispered Ring.

"As Ashild's father, you had a right to want him dead, but, because of his young age, I wanted to give him another chance to change his ways. As I heard that evil laugh today, it was like looking at a younger Svase the Finn, and I knew Ragnvald hadn't changed any. I took his grandfather's life and, as Ashild's husband, I claim the right to take the grandson's life also."

"You are the King as well as the judge, so I must defer to your decision."

"I will not commit a murder on my marriage day or on my mother's burial day. He must wait for his judgement day to come... but it will come," assured Harald as they walked out of the manor house and down the hill toward the barns.

When the two men came close to the large tree, Harald ordered Berdaluke to bring a torch over so he could have a word with the prisoner. As the light from the torch lit up the trunk of the tree, the men were surprised to see the head of white hair drooping forward and a trail of red running down the front of the captive's shirt.

Harald rushed forward, grabbed the white hair and lifted up the head. There, projecting from Ragnvald's chest were two matching daggers.

Ring immediately accused Berdaluke. "Did you take away the pleasure of our revenge?"

"Not me, My Lord, I act only at the King's command," he responded.

"Then who has done this?" Ring demanded.

Harald was strangely silent, for he recognized the twin daggers as the gifts he had given to Halvdan and Sigurd for honoring Guttorm during his death ceremony.

"The deed is done! He was judged an outlaw at the Thing four years ago and, as an outlaw, anyone could take his life!" retorted Harald. "Cut him down, Berdaluke, and hide his body. Ashild shall not be made to see this deed!"

With that statement, Harald turned to walk back up the hill to his childhood home. "I have dealt with enough for one day... and now I go to finish this night in my marriage bed."

As he washed his face and hands before entering the bedchamber, he felt as if he was washing off the stain of Svase and his daughter, Snofrid. He thought about the fact that he had wanted to leave her four boys to die in the hut in the forests of Lofoten. He would have too, if Odin hadn't ordered him to give them a chance. He had obeyed Odin, but maybe he should have done more.

Odin said he should foster them in good homes, and Guttorm, faithful Guttorm, had found them good homes. Ragnvald had been in a good home in More until the problem with Hrolf. Would his son have turned out differently if he had been able to stay in the home of his trusted friend Ragnvald? Did Snofrid's youngest son turn wicked because he had too much of her blood in him, or did he turn wicked because he was rejected as a young boy?

Harald knew he probably would not have the answer to that question...unless Odin told it to him. He could have given them more of his time instead of just turning them over to others, but he hadn't wanted to. He knew he still saw a part of Snofrid in them. Maybe he should just be grateful that Halvdan, Sigurd and Gudrod seemed to have turned out alright...or had they. What of those twin daggers?

He would have to deal with that tomorrow. He was tired tonight...too tired to think about it. And he wasn't free to just fall into his boyhood bed and drown his thoughts in sleep. No, he would be expected to go in to his marriage bed and make love to his new wife. Maybe he was just getting too old to be a new husband. He had lived fifty long years and married six times. He hoped maybe Odin would let him rest after this one.

It wasn't quite the marriage night that Ashild had wanted. It wasn't quite the same as the marriage nights Harald had enjoyed in the past either. She was waiting for him in his bedchamber when he walked in. She had been lying under the fresh linen sheets and thinking about the events of the day.

Would she ever be able to hold her head up in the neighborhood now that Ragnvald had told everyone her dark secret? She had gotten through the marriage ceremony only because of the strength that Harald had given her. He really was wonderful. No wonder his mother had wanted her to marry him. She would try hard to be worthy of him...and even make him happy if she could.

When he entered the bedchamber, she saw the deep creases in his face, made deeper by the shadow of the candles she had lit next to the bed. She thought he looked like an old man. He had said he was old enough to be her father, but that hadn't seemed to bother her in the light of day. Now, he looked old...old and tired. She made her first kind decision as a married woman.

"I pray you will not be angry with me, My Lord, but I am so tired after the many experiences of this day. Would you mind if we just lie together and sleep?"

Harald gave his new wife a slow smile and answered, "I thought you were anxious to get started on a little baby Ragnhild!"

"I think we should wait until your mother is buried, so she can go into the spirit world and pick out just the right spirit to send down for her namesake."

"I think you must be wise beyond your years, my new wife. Sleep sounds like just what my body wants this night," he said as he climbed into the bed beside her.

He blew out the candle and lay back with a sigh as his body sunk into the soft folds of the eiderdown mattress.

"Do you think your body is up to just one kiss?" she asked as she moved closer to her new husband.

"Yes...my body is not that old!" he countered.

One long kiss led to another, and then another, and soon he realized that his body was not as tired as he had thought.

When he awoke the next morning and looked over at Ashild, still sleeping peacefully, his mind went back to the morning after his marriage to Asa. He remembered thinking then that Odin must have planned for man and woman to complete each other. It was a good plan. It was certainly one of the great pleasures of life.

Ragnhild was buried in the same mound as the head of her beloved Halvdan. She looked beautiful in her dark blue wedding gown, even though her golden hair had turned to a soft white. A crown of gold filled with blue stones held the thinning hair in place. The supple silver fox cape with the blue lining that Harald had given to her years earlier was wrapped around her shoulders. Gold and silver chains adorned her neck and gold and silver bracelets were on her wrists. She had asked Ashild to make her look as beautiful as possible so she would look her best when she met her husband again.

Many of the items she had cherished during her lifetime were chosen to be buried with her. There were three chests filled with her favorite beautiful gowns, complete with the jewelry that matched them. Some of the tapestries she had sewn depicting the heroic deeds done by Halvdan were used to cover the bed where she lay and also decorate the tent that protected her body. Harald was sad to see the mound close over his mother, but he knew she was happy to be reunited with his father.

The ornately carved sleigh that had carried her to Tande Manor from her captivity by Hake the Berserker, had been lovingly cared for all these years, and now was going to carry her to Gimli. There she would join her wonderful Halvdan and her loving parents... while they waited for Ragnarok to mark the end of the earth's life.

CHAPTER 39

THE TWIN DAGGERS

Two days after his mother's burial, Harald traveled to Stein Manor in Ringerike to confront Halvdan and Sigurd. They were a little apprehensive to see their father riding through the manor gates, along with Berdaluke and his twenty five man bodyguard. Their foster father, Ring, had detained them in the great hall after the evening meal. Only Berdaluke and the King entered the building.

When he was seated, Harald reached into his pouch and drew out the two daggers. He threw them on the table in front of his sons.

"I believe these daggers belong to the two of you!" he said in a low voice.

Halvdan turned to look at Sigurd and then back at their father.

"You should know whose they are...a gift from you."

"I know whose they are, and that is why I am here."

"Do you blame us for taking the life of an outlaw?" Halvdan questioned, "an outlaw who dishonored our sister and deserved death?"

"It was the first right of Ashild's husband or her father to avenge her. It would have been better if it had come from one of us. There are some who are murmuring against you for the death of your brother."

"But, did we not have the right, under the law, to take the life of one who had harmed our sister?" asked Halfdan defensively.

"That would have been true...if Ashild had been your blood sister...but she is not. It is being called a secret murder because you left your daggers in Ragnvald's chest...and also murdered in the night."

The King reached into his pouch once more and withdrew a second pouch filled with coins and threw them on the table.

"I think it would be best if you two took a trip somewhere outside the country and stayed away until next summer. It will be good, both for you and for Ashild. The sooner all of this controversy over Ragnvald quiets down, the sooner things can get back to normal."

The brothers agreed and left within days of their father's visit. They rode their horses to the north end of Lake Mjosa and up the Gulbrandsdal Valley, heading toward the North Sea. Their father had told them to stop at Borgund and ask Jarl Ragnvald for some men and a large ship capable of a long sea voyage.

When they reached the jarl's home, a serving woman ushered them into the great room. The brothers asked to speak to Ragnvald, but his wife Hild came quickly into the room.

"Who is it that asks for my husband?" Hild demanded.

"We are Halvdan and Sigurd Haraldsson, sons of the King," they responded.

"What business do you have with my husband?" she asked with an even more irritable tone in her voice.

Her overbearing manner offended them and Halvdan said, "We have business with Ragnvald! Is he here or is he not?"

His high-handed tone just made matters worse.

"My husband is not here and I do not appreciate being treated in such a manner...especially by two men who were bred by a witch!"

This comment made Halvdan seethe with anger. He thought of the worst comment he could make to this irate woman...and made it.

"My father has often spoken of the pity he feels for poor Ragnvald...tied to a woman who acts like a witch!"

Hild's fury rose up to a fever pitch. She unlatched her belt with the keys hanging from it and began to beat the boys where they sat. They got up and hurried to the door with Hild chasing behind them. As he bolted through the front door, Halvdan turned and shouted, "You will be sorry for this, mark my words!"

Hild just stood on the front step of her manor house and shook her belt and keys in the air. Who did they think they were, calling her a witch? Well, she would not even tell Ragnvald they had been there. They had no rights over her!

Halvdan and Sigurd were thinking just the opposite. They were the sons of King Harald and they had rights over jarls, especially jarls' wives. They tried to think of what they could do to teach Hild a lesson...one she would never forget...and then the idea came to them.

They would wait until dark and creep back to the manor house. The best punishment they could think of for Hild was to start her house on fire. If the fire only burned a small portion of the house, that would be fine, but she would guess who had started it...and then she would be sorry for treating them as she had.

It was a good thing Ragnvald was not at home. They would not want anything to happen to their father's good friend...but Hild...that was a different matter. Ragnvald might even reward them for freeing him from a wife such as she was.

The boys did not wait around to see how large a fire their torch had started. There was a strong wind blowing and they had decided to travel down the coast to Eidsvag Manor and get a ship and men from Rorek. He would certainly help them when he was told that their father had ordered it.

Eidsvag Manor was where Harald found them...a fortnight later. He had sailed quickly down through the fold and around the tip of Agder on his way to attend to matters in More. Word came that there had been a fire at Borgund Manor and both Hild and Ragnvald had perished. As sad as he was to hear of the death of Ragnvald, he also hoped that Halvdan and Sigurd had not still been in their home at the time of the fire.

Harald was relieved to see them...and told of his fears for them. The brothers looked at each other as their father told of his sorrow over the death of Ragnvald. Unfortunately, the boys had told Rorek about their plan to teach Hild a lesson for her terrible treatment of them. Rorek looked at his half-brothers and then his father.

"I think Halvdan and Sigurd have something they need to tell you, Father."

Harald turned to his sons and said, "Well, what is it you need to tell me?"

The boys told their story, complete with the words of Hild, and their assurance that Ragnvald was not at home. Their father had to suppress a smile when they said they thought Ragnvald might even reward them if Hild died in the fire.

"Does anyone know about this except Rorek?" Harald asked.

"I do not think so," they replied.

"Which one of you threw the torch?"

"It was me," Halvdan answered.

"Then you must leave Norway for a time. Go to the Shetland Islands and stay there for a year. Rorek will give you a ship. Sigurd, you will go to Agder and stay there...and say nothing about this to anyone. I will travel to More and see what is being told about in that area. Remember, say nothing of this to anyone...that means you also, Rorek."

"This was a foolish act you have committed, but I am convinced you did not mean to harm anyone, except maybe Hild, and she has done her fair share of harm over the years. I hope you two have learned a good lesson from this. You will have to meet Ragnvald in the next life...and I hope he will forgive you."

Halvdan met Ragnvald in the next life much sooner than anyone had expected, for he ignored his father's direction to go to the Shetland Islands and stopped at Orkney first. Orkney Island was ruled by Einar, a son of Ragnvald. Somehow, the word had gotten out that the fire that took the life of his father may have been deliberately set...may be even by King Harald's sons.

When Einar challenged Halvdan and asked him if he had set the fire, Halvdan foolishly said yes. Einar was a small man with just one eye and Halvdan was sure he could best him in a fight. However, Einar's men overpowered Halvdan's, and soon Halvdan was face down in the dirt and Einar was astride him.

In Einar's mind, only the blood eagle would be punishment enough for this young man's foolish act. With his sharp dagger, he cut apart the ribs on either side of Halvdan's backbone, pulled the ribs open to expose the lungs, and then pulled the two lungs out through the opening...to form two bloody wings.

Halvdan's screams were ignored. It had taken only minutes to perform the awful deed...for this was not the first time Einar had killed a man with the blood eagle. The screams did not last very long, and soon Halvdan's body lay limp in a pool of blood.

Halvdan's men took his body and hurried to their ship. Einar thought about stopping them, but he reasoned that he could justify his actions, even to King Harald, as revenge for the death of his father Ragnvald. The law was clear...it was the duty of the nearest relative to avenge the death of a kinsman.

When Halvdan's body was brought to his father at Avaldsnes, there was both sorrow and anger. Many, including Sigurd and Gudrod, thought they needed to travel to Orkney and, as the nearest relatives, avenge their brother's death. Harald, fearing the loss of two more sons, claimed the right to get revenge for his son's death.

After Harald arrived on Orkney, he ordered a Thing be held to hear the case against Einar.

As Einar met King Harald, he said this verse:

> "Many a bearded man must roam,
> An exile from his house and home,
> For cow and horse; but Halfdan's gore
> Is red on Rinansey's wild shore.
> A nobler deed – on Harald's shield
> The arm of one who ne'er will yield
> Has left a scar. Let peasants dread
> The vengeance of the Norsemen's head:
> I reck not of his wrath, but sing,
> 'Do thy worst!' – I defy thee, King!"
> **Heimskringla**

The King wanted to do his worst, and condemn Einar to the same bloody death he had performed on Halvdan. But he knew that the only way he could count Einar's actions as murder versus revenge would be to deny that Halvdan had anything to do with Ragnvald's death.

Instead, he used the punishment that would be the most painful, second to death. He charged Einar to pay sixty marks of gold. Though this was a heavy fine, Einar paid it...and was glad to avoid receiving the death penalty.

Harald gave Gudrod and Sigurd each thirty marks of gold, as payment for the life of their brother. Halvdan's remains were buried at Stein Manor, next to Guttorm, the man who had saved him from certain death in a dirty hut at Lofoten many years before.

As he pondered the death of Halvdan, Harald asked Odin if this was the curse of the Finn coming in to his life again. Odin answered thus, "There must needs be opposition in this life. It is for your growth and wisdom. Peace comes temporarily, but permanently only in the next life."

CHAPTER 40

THREE MORE SONS

Ashild had proven to be to be the kind, gentle and loving wife his mother had predicted, and he was happy to have her. The difference in their ages seemed to be less of an issue now that they were husband and wife. Harald continued to travel to Tande Manor each year for the winter months...to spend time with his young family.

Life continued in a peaceful manner, with no unusual trouble at any of the Things. He was grateful for a country at peace. He hoped his father Halvdan could look down from Gimli and see how setting up the same Code of Laws that brought peace to his eight kingdoms, also brought peace to the thirty one kingdoms of Harald's Norway.

His sixth wife had given him three sons to add to his large family. Ring Haraldson was born in 901and Dag Haraldson followed in 903. They were both named to honor her father Ring and her grandfather Dag. A third son was born in 905 whom Ashild chose to name Gudrod. Because Harald hated the name of his grandfather, Gudrod, she added Skirja as a second name.

After bearing three healthy sons in succession, his wife told him she was content and needed no more children. However, after the passage of four winters, Ashild started dreaming about the girl spirit that Ragnhild was to have chosen for them. She anxiously awaited Harald's next visit, but held her peace until they were lying together in the large bed in their master bedchamber.

"Are you too tired to listen to your wife telling of the dream I have been sent?" she asked hesitantly.

"Does your dream include me?" he asked as he turned toward her. He could see she wore a look of concern on her face.

"Yes, it definitely does."

"And what kind of dream brings that worried look to my wife's face?"

"I have seen your mother in my dream...and she showed me the girl spirit she has planned for us...the one who will bear her name."

"And that is the dream that causes such concern to you?"

"Yes...it is...it has been so long since..."

"So...do you think I have gotten too old to give you the seed for this girl child?" he asked with an edge of irritation in his voice.

"Well..." she replied.

"Yes, you married an old man, a man old enough to be your father. But haven't I given you three fine sons?"

"Yes, but...." Ashild protested, unsure if she should mention that he had not attempted to place a seed in her body in the four years since Gudrod Skirja was in her belly.

"If my mother has told you she has chosen a girl spirit for us, then we had better join together and make a body for her to come to!" he said with more bravado than he felt.

As it turned out, he was too tired to successfully make love to Ashild that night. As he rolled over to seek sleep, he reassured his wife that she did not have to worry. There would be a baby in her belly before he left in the spring.

Sadly, there was no baby in Ashild's belly when the time came for Harald to leave. As it was, Harald was barely able to climb into the saddle as he prepared to begin his journey of travel to visit the many kingdoms and administer justice at the Things.

Erik, Gudrod, Ring and Harald all got seriously ill from exposure to the frozen lake water after a sledding accident on Lake Mjosa. Harald was the worst. He was too sick to even get out of bed for Yuletide. He looked terrible and he felt terrible. Everyone was afraid he might die, especially Ashild. She even worried he would pass away before giving her their girl child.

"Could you not let the jarls handle the Things this summer?" Berdaluke suggested.

"Do you want my people to think I care so little for them that I would stay at home in my bed instead of performing my duty?" asked the King with a look of irritation on his face.

"Nay, and you know I will be by your side wherever you go," the berserker added, determined not to say anything more about Harald foregoing his yearly round of the kingdoms. He knew the people would be shocked to see their King looking so sick and weak, but they might love him all the more to realize he would travel to do his duty despite his poor condition.

"Shall I travel with you this summer instead of sailing to Skagen Manor and the East Sea?" Erik asked his father.

"You traveled the route with me enough when you were young. Now that you have grown, I need you to spend your summer traveling with trade goods. Besides, who is better at collecting skat from the Finns than you?" Harald replied as he gave Erik a hearty slap on the back.

When Harald and his retinue return to Tande Manor the next fall, he could see that Ashild did not have a child in her belly. During the Yule season, his wife declared she wanted no gift except a baby girl. His time of travel in the summer sun had restored Harald's body somewhat and he almost looked like his former healthy self.

As husband and wife were walking through the apple orchard in the spring, Ashild told him that little Ragnhild was growing within her. They were both happy to think they were finally going to have the little spirit who was chosen for them by his mother.

In the fall of 909, Erik arrived at Tande Manor with a surprise...a wife. He had married Gunhild, the daughter of King Gorm the Old from Roskilde. They had met some years earlier in Denmark and she was determined to wed the handsome son of Norway. Knowing he traveled yearly to collect taxes from the Finns, she went there to learn of their magic and used it to capture her prince.

The father now understood why he felt that old tingling on the back of his neck that reminded him of Svase the Finn. He wanted to chastise Erik for marrying a woman who bragged about her ability to practice magic, but his son seemed to be very much in love with this beautiful, dark haired woman. It reminded the King of how he must have looked when he brought Erik's mother to Norway after they had just married.

There was something about Gunhild that Ashild just did not like, though she hadn't had the bad experience with Finns that her husband had. Gunhild could feel the dislike coming from Ashild and decided to put to use some of the magic she had learned. During the time she spent in Finland, she had collected a pouchful of poisonous herbs that became a deadly potion when added to heated water.

The apprentice witch brewed up a cup of herbs and offered them to

Ashild. "I have made a nice herb tea for you that will ease the pains of a swollen belly."

Despite a feeling of apprehension, Ashild decided she would try the tea. This baby in her belly was definitely giving her a lot of pain. Within hours, she became deathly ill and could not rise out of her bed. Harald found her moaning in their bedchamber.

"My dear wife, it is your time? Shall I call in the birthing women?"

"Harald," she whispered, "Something is wrong. I drank some herb tea that Gunhild prepared for me...and now I feel as if I might die! I cannot breathe...!"

"Where is that woman who has practiced her witchcraft on my wife?" Harald shouted as he rose to his feet.

Ashild reached for his hand and tried to pull him down to her.

"Do not leave me!" she whispered with all the strength she could gather.

"And do not leave me!" he whispered to her as he sat down on the edge of the bed.

"Our baby...our little Ragnhild...do not let her die with me!"

"You are not going to die!" he assured her with a conviction he did not feel.

"You have been a good husband to me...your mother was right."

"Yes, many times I have thanked her in my thoughts for asking that I take you to wife. She said I must give you a child to love, but instead I have given you four."

"But, what of our baby Ragnhild? How can we save her when I die?"

"I tell you, you are not going to die. I will pray to Odin and ask a blessing of life for you and Ragnhild!"

"Yes, you must ask a blessing for me and our Ragnhild!" she said in an even quieter whisper.

As Harald knelt by their bed with his head bowed and his eyes closed, he heard his wife's faint whisper, "I love you." At the same time, her limp hand slipped from his.

"No...no...!" he cried as he scooped her lifeless body up into his arms. "You can not take her, not now, not when we were about to have the girl child my mother planned for us! Odin, please help me!"

After his sincere plea for help, he heard the familiar voice in his ear. "Take the child from her belly."

Harald opened his eyes and questioned the message he had just received. A second time the unmistakable message came, "Take the child from her belly."

Unsure of how he was to fulfill this command, Harald slipped the dagger from its sheath on his belt and made a thin slice across the taut skin of his wife's belly. Along with a gush of water and blood came the tiny body of a girl child. As he reached to pick up the slippery baby, a weak cry came forth from the little mouth.

The amazed father, who had never witnessed the birth of a child, cradled the little one to his chest. He pulled a linen shirt from the chest at the bottom of the bed and wrapped the precious bundle. Then he brought her over to the body of her dead mother.

Kneeling on the step of the bed, he bent over and whispered, "Here is our little Ragnhild, my Dear One, here is our gift from my mother. Tell her that the child arrived safely when you meet her in the Spirit World."

He laid the new born babe on her mother's chest and took one lifeless arm and wrapped it around the child. He felt sure Ashild's spirit could feel the warmth of the little body, though her own body was growing cold. Indeed, Ashild's spirit was still in the room, sadly watching over the body she had so recently departed...and the new life it had produced.

With that, he left the room to seek help from the women on his estate who always assisted with the birthings. He was careful to avoid any contact with Gunhild. He did not want her to know what had just happened...and especially, he did not want her to go into the master bedchamber and find little Ragnhild alive.

Harald swore the women to secrecy. He wanted to tell Erik about Ashild's death and Gunhild's part in it before the witch discovered how successful her evil potion had been.

Erik was in the barn with the horses when his father found him.

"I need to talk to you...privately," said Harald, his voice unusually quiet.

"What is it?" the younger man questioned.

"It is a grave matter, and I wish us to be alone. Let us take a walk in the orchard," he answered and began to lead the way.

When they had walked a short distance, Harald began, "Our baby child, Ragnhild, has just been born."

"Does the child live?"

"Yes, the child lives, but the mother does not!" The King kept the tears from his eyes with difficulty.

"I am sad for you, Father," said the son as he reached to put his arm around his father's shoulder.

"You will not be able to comfort me!" Harald retorted as he pushed Erik's arm away from him.

"Why do you treat me so?" questioned Erik.

"You have done a foul deed when you brought Gunhild into our home. She has murdered my wife!" he spat out as anger overcame him.

"I do not believe it! Why would she do that? How could she do that?"

"She gave Ashild a poison tea to drink and now her lifeless body lies in the bed she and I shared!"

"I can not believe Gunhild would do such a thing. I must go and ask her..."

"You knew she had been with the Finns to learn their magic, for that is where you found her! Why you would choose to marry her, I cannot say. The beauty in her face does not erase the evil that is in her heart," Harald shouted.

"Gunhild is not evil! You accuse her falsely!" Erik shouted back.

"You can defend her...despite knowing she has killed the mother of your young brothers?"

Erik stood looking at the ground between them. He knew not what to answer his father.

"You must take your wife and leave Tande Manor. I will not have her under my roof one more night. Go to her family in Roskilde. May be they can influence her to cleanse the evil from her heart!"

As Erik turned to go, Harald grabbed his arm and pulled his son to him in a fatherly embrace.

"You know I love you still, but you have chosen unwisely, and now you must deal with your choice."

Erik returned the embrace, but made no return comment. If what his father said was true, he must indeed deal with an unwise choice.

When Gunhild heard the message that they must leave Tande Manor immediately, she exploded in anger and stormed down the hall to the master bedchamber. Harald was there, sitting by the body of his dead wife and holding their little daughter.

"I demand an apology for your accusations!" she screamed as she burst into the room.

The King stood up calmly and replied in a grim voice, "Leave this room! There is death in this room...death caused by you and your witch's brew!"

Erik had followed quickly behind his wife and now tried to calm her angry explosion, but she shoved him away.

"I will take that baby!" she cried and moved toward where Harald was standing.

"I would put this child in the grave with its mother before I would let you touch it!" he retorted, quickly losing his battle to remain calm.

"But the child needs a mother!" she whined and began to sob.

Harald stared at Erik and a knowing look passed between them.

"Come with me, Gunhild. Let us leave this sad place. We shall have babies of our own for you to comfort. Never fear," he murmured as he took her arm and led her from the room.

Little Ragnild became very sick after Gunhild left and Harald suspected that she had put a curse on the baby. In an attempt to counter the witch's power, he sacrificed Ashild's prized matching team of horses in exchange for the baby's life.

The father had two charms created from the hair of the horse's forelock made into a necklace and bracelet for the child to wear. This was a token from the sacrifice of the horses and was meant to protect the young child.

During the death ceremony for Ashild, Harald was impressed by the kind words spoken about her by her foster brother, Sigurd Rise. He had married Margaret Madsdatter from Aas Manor in Toten just the year before. They looked to be a happy couple. She was a sweet, gentle woman and the King thought how different Erik's life could have been if he had found someone like her.

When the feast was over and the guests were preparing to leave, Harald sought out his son and wife.

"Thank you for the kind words you said of Ashild today."

"We are feeling much sorrow for you and for your young children...especially the baby."

"As I watched you two today, I thought of what good parents you will make. I have a proposal for you. Would you consider moving to Tande Manor and becoming foster parents to Ring, Dag, Gudrod Skirja and baby Ragnhild?"

Sigurd and Margaret looked at each other in amazement. They had been given Stein Manor in Ringerike as a wedding gift, but Stein could hardly compare with Tande Manor in size or beauty.

When they hesitated, Harald suggested, "Even though Stein Manor has fond memories for you, I am sure you could grow to love Tande as I have. It is the place of my birth and I will always want to spend time here, especially Yuletide. You might find a man to care for Stein in your absence and it could be the inheritance for Ashild's sons when they reach manhood. What say you?"

Sigurd spoke first. "We will do whatever we can for both you and Ashild. She was a great friend of Margaret and you have ever been fair with me."

"Then it is settled. You shall be the next master of Tande Manor and your wife shall be its mistress!" Harald proclaimed. He was grateful to this fine couple for helping to solve his problem...and he would have a ready answer in case Erik and Gunhild ever asked for the privilege of moving back to the Ringsaker estate.

CHAPTER 41

PRINCES TO KINGS

The sons he got of many wives,
All twenty they did come.
A blessing from the Gods, you see,
Did fill his soul with glad.
But many a son, of all he got,
Did make their father sad.
They wanted gold, they wanted lands,
And jealous they did feel.
But in the end, as we do know,
One son did win the prize.
For black-haired Erik, favored son,
The fair-haired father's heart had won.

All of Harald's sons came early to strength and manhood, just as their father had. None was made to take over as King at the age of ten, as he had been, but all seemed to want to rule. He called together a large Thing at Eidsvold and made a law that his descendants on the male line should each succeed to the kingly title and dignity. His male descendants on the female line would receive the title of Jarl, but not King.

Though the sons were given the title of King, they all knew they were but petty kings, ruling parts of the large kingdom of Norway that their father had conquered so long ago. For the most part, each was given a chance to rule the district where their mother had lived and where they had been born and reared.

In each of these districts, he gave his sons one half of the yearly revenues, together with the right to sit on a high seat. These seats were a step higher than the jarls, but a step lower then his. Many of his sons wanted to claim Harald's high seat when he died, but he had given an oath to Rani that Erik should be King over all of his brothers.

Gutt, the firstborn of Harald and Asa Hakonsdatter, spent his youth living with his great uncle and namesake in Vingulmark. Much of his adult life was spent helping Guttorm to keep the peace in Gautland to the south as well as Vestfold to the west, to the east and Raumarike to the north. As the oldest of Harald's sons, he was given the title of King when his namesake, Guttorm died.

A less generous man might have demanded his promotion to kingship long before he turned thirty one, but Gutt was content to be second man to the foster father who had devoted his life to raising him. Guttorm had been a great general and Harald never ceased to thank Odin for granting him such an uncle. Without his leadership, Harald knew he might have lost even the eight kingdoms ruled by his father, much less having the power to add twenty three additional ones.

Gutt's youngest brother, Sigrod, as well as his twin brothers, Halvdan the White and Halvdan the Black, were content to rule the great Trondelag area. Halvdan the White ruled north of the Trondelag Fjord while Halvdan the Black chose the areas south. The twins lived together at Lade Manor even after they married at the age of twenty five winters. Halvdan the White married Laure who came from Stiklestad Manor and Halvdan the Black married Ellen from Liaklev Manor.

Sigrod grew up at Lanke Manor with his grandmother, Malfrid and ruled Stjordal, Vaernes, and the entire district to the east of the fjord. He married Anne Siri from Ofsti Manor. Despite being a very small baby and the smallest in stature of the four brothers, he gained the steady and sensible character traits that his mother's mother instilled in him.

For eighteen winters after the death of Guttorm, Gutt had labored in defense of the southern and eastern kingdoms of his father. He became King of of all the country from the Glommen River to Svinasund and Ranrike, as well as all the country to the east. In the year 914, as he was sailing in one of the tributaries of the Gaut River, he was slain by an old enemy, Solve Klofe. There was genuine sorrow for this oldest son of Harald. He had been a faithful son and his brothers swore they would get revenge on their brother's killer.

Halvdan the White and Halvdan the Black went out to find Solve Klofe in the East Sea and there they did battle. Halvdan the White received a death wound, but he succeeded in taking Solve to Valhalla with him. Halvdan the Black returned to Trondelag and built a large mound at Lade to hold his brother's body. He and his brother Sigrod were left to share in the rule of North Trondelag and South Trondelag.

The sons of Harald and Svanhild Eysteinsdatter were Olaf, Bjorn and Ragnar. Olaf received Grenland, Bjorn received Vestfold and Ragnar received Agder as inheritance. Bjorn Farmann was a great trader and had a large fleet of merchant ships he sailed on distant trading expeditions. He lived at Saaheim Manor near Tunsberg and had made a suitable marriage with Evya from Morud. He was a man of good sense and understanding and a fair ruler.

His half-brother Erik came to Tunsberg from a long trading expedition on the East Sea, with ships of war and a great force. He tried to force Bjorn to give him the King's share of the tax that had been collected in Vestfold. Bjorn said he had always delivered the skat to the King himself...and he refused to give it to Erik.

An angry Erik came back that night and surrounded the house where Bjorn and Ragnar were sitting and drinking. Erik called them out and in the fight, Bjorn and many of his men died, as well as his brother Ragnar. Their older brother, Olaf tried to catch Erk and avenge his brothers, but Erik got away and hurried northward to More. This act further alienated the favored son from the rest of his brothers.

When Halvdan the Black heard of the killing, he was determined to help Olaf make Erik pay for the death of Bjorn and Ragnar. He traveled to North More and surrounded the house where Erik slept. The house was burned with many who were in it, but Erik escaped. He sailed immediately to Avaldsnes to demand that his father take his side against Halvdan the Black.

"You must punish Haldan! He tried to kill me!" Erik shouted.

"Would you have me kill one son to please another?"

"Yes," Erik replied, "What if Halvdan tries to kill me again? How will you face my mother in Gimli if you have not protected her only son? And what of your promise to her that I would be your favored son? Halvdan is only the son of Asa, who you did not love as you did my
mother!"

Those words brought Harald to his feet. "You would dare presume to tell me which of my wives I have loved more than the others?"

"You have said in your own words that my mother was your favorite wife! Are you now denying those words?"

Harald's face turned red with anger. "I did love your mother, passionately and completely, and she did exact that oath as her dying words...that I would make you chief over all my other sons...and I have done that. But you have crossed the line with your killing of Bjorn and Ragnar. Had you been any other man, I would have hunted you down and taken revenge on you myself. As it is, Olaf has a right to avenge his brothers. Being less of a warrior than Halvdan, he would naturally ask his help. And now you want me to go against my own flesh and blood? I say, you have lived with Gunhild too long! I think she has cast a spell on you! Can you live with a witch and not become evil yourself?"

"Well, you should know! You married a witch also...and gave her sons!"

Harald crossed to where Erik was standing and struck him a blow across the face. Erik was so stunned at this action by the father who had always taken his side he barely knew how to react. His hand went instinctively to the dagger at his belt.

"Oh, so you would sink your dagger in my chest as you did to Bjorn then?" he asked.

Erik removed his hand and stood before his angry father, saying not a word, but seething from a blow to his face...the ultimate insult.

The blow seemed to have released the pent up anger the father felt for his son and the two stood eye to eye...one with black hair and one with gold...as the candlelight cast shadows across their faces.

"You think to judge me and my choice of wives, but I say to you, you know little of my life before you were born. Yes, I loved your mother best, but I loved Halvdan's mother first, and I loved him before you were born. He carries my blood every bit as much as you do...every bit as much as Bjorn and Ragnar did. I will not take your side against Halvdan or Olaf or any other son."

"I will ask them both, as the right of a father, to cease this revenge, though you deserve it. But you must do something to make amends to Olaf. Einar was fined sixty marks of gold for the death of Halvdan Haleg and I will assign you the same! Sixty marks for Bjorn and sixty marks for Ragnar! But you must be the one to give it to Olaf and ask him to accept it for the life of his brothers. If Olaf accepts your tribute, then I will ask Halvdan to drop his revenge against you."

Olaf reluctantly agreed to the death payment, but demanded that Erik stay out of his kingdoms. Erik looked to his father, who nodded his head. Erik swallowed hard, but agreed. Halvdan required the same. Erik protested but Harald overruled him and forced him to agree.

This should have been the end of Erik's disagreements with his brothers, but it was not. Before the death of their father, Halvdan the Black died from drinking ale which had been poisoned. It was told around that Gunhild had helped Erik get the final revenge against his older brother.

The sons of Harald and Gyda Eiriksdatter were Rorek, Sigtrygg, Frode and Torgils. They were all born after Alov Arbot, the King's first daughter. She was married to Thorer, son of Jarl Ragnvald and older brother to Hrolf. They were given South More as inheritance.

Rorek, as the oldest son, took over Eidsvag Manor and received the kingdom of Hordaland, including the sea port of Bergen. Sigtrygg received the kingdom of Rogaland, to the south of Hordaland, but was not given the Island of Karmr with the great estate of Avaldsnes. His father intended to live out his life in the castle he had built for Rani.

Harald gave ships of war to Thorgils and Frode, with which they went westward to Ireland. They joined the Northmen who made Dublin their home and became the foster sons of King Olaf the White. It is said that Frode got poisoned drink there and died, but Thorgils was a long time King over Dublin. Finally, he was entrapped in a snare set by angry Irishmen and suffered a brutal death.

The sons of Harald and Snofrid Svasesdatter were Halvdan Halegg, Gudrod Ljome, Sigurd Rise and Ragnvald Rettibeine. Einar Ragnvaldson took the life of Halvdan in revenge for starting the fire that killed his father in More. Gudrod died in a storm off the coast of Jadar while on a journey to Rogaland. His foster father, Thjodolf of Hvin had warned him that there was a heavy storm blowing in, but Gudrod refused to listen. All on his ship perished.

Sigurd was given Tande Manor, including all of Hedmark as well as Raumrike when he agreed to raise Ashild's children after her death. Ragnvald, who was stabbed by Halvdan and Sigurd in revenge for ruining their foster sister, got the reward he deserved in Helveti.

Just one son was born to Harald and Ragnild Eriksdatter from Jutland, named Erik after his mother's father. Even though he was to inherit his father's throne at Avaldsnes and the right to rule over all of his brothers, Erik was impatient to begin ruling. He was given North More, Raumsdal and all of Halogaland, but that did not satisfy him and his ambitious wife Gunhild. If any of his brothers tried to challenge his right to rule, he took care of them...one way or another.

The sons of Harald and Ashild Ringsdatter were Ring, Dag, Gudrod Skirja and their younger sister Ragnhild. Ring was given Stein Manor and the kingdom of Ringerike as inheritance. Dag was given Toten and Hadeland as inheritance and Gudrod was given the Gudbrandsdal Valley all the way up through the Dovrefeld.

The daughter who had been cut from her mother's dead body grew up to be a charming and beautiful woman, just like her mother. Harald always felt that his mother must have chosen the best possible spirit to send them. Many suitors were interested in marriage with this youngest daughter of the King, but the man who won her heart was Jarl Knut from Solberg Manor in the southern part of Hedmark.

CHAPTER 42

TORA, THE MAID SERVANT

"A heart that loves is always young." **Greek proverb**

The year was 929 and twenty years had passed since his sweet wife Ashild died. Despite being located in one of the warmest areas of Norway, Harald's stone castle at Avaldsnes was cold and damp. The King was now seventy nine winters old. He had lived a very lengthy and meaningful life, but he wondered how long Odin planned to require him to continue his earth life.

Winter had set in on Karmr Island and Harald was cold. The days were so very short and the nights were so very long. The fire that burned day and night in the great room of his castle was not enough to keep him warm. Neither the bear skin on his high seat nor the wolf pelts on his bed were adequate to warm his old body.

Tora, his maid servant, could see that the King shivered from the cold. She dished up a bowl of steaming meat soup from the large pot that hung over the fire. As she handed him the bowl of soup, their hands touched. She could feel his cold, boney fingers and he could feel her warm, gentle hands.

"Would you let me warm you, My Lord?" she asked.

"You warm me already with this fine soup," Harald replied.

"I could do more," Tora answered hesitantly.

"What do you mean?" he asked as he looked sharply into her flushed, upturned face.

"I could comfort you and give you of the warmth of my body. I could lie with you and help you get through this long, cold winter."

Harald thought for a few moments. What a pleasant thing that would be...to feel the embrace of a young, strong, supple woman in his arms...or to have her warm body wrapped around his sore back. It had been a long while since he had enjoyed the thought of a woman's sweet embrace. May be he had decided his time was so near that he just needed to endure to the end.

"That could be good," he answered with a smile. "Ready yourself and come to me in my chamber this night...and we shall see who gives the greater comfort."

Tora turned back to the fire, a smile on her face. She had grown in admiration for her King in the months since she had first taken a position at his fire on the large estate of Avaldsnes.

During her childhood, Tora had feared the great Lord and King who had fought and won so many battles in his effort to unite all of Norway. His deeds were legendary and his power was great. He had had many wives and by them, a large number of sons. Unfortunately, his wives had all preceded him in death and many of his sons.

She had come from the family of Horda-Kara, a jarl from Moster, who had fought with Harald at Hafrsfjord...his final battle. The jarl loved to tell tales of the brave exploits of the golden haired warrior. The King was generous with all of his jarls and allowed their family members to serve him whenever there was a need.

This great conqueror now just seemed like a tired, lonely old man. He reminded her of her father, who had died a fortnight past. She was happy that she might get the honor and privilege to be of service to the great King Harald Fairhair.

That fair hair had turned from golden to white as Harald's body reached old age. How miraculous that a man could fight with sword and shield, axe and spear, and send so many brave men to Valhalla...and yet be alive and whole. His face still bore the rugged handsomeness of his youth behind the silver of his moustache and beard.

More than that, she could see why so many women had wanted to become his wife. He had a way about him that made you want to be near him, to be with him, to share his thoughts...even to share his bed.

Tora blushed as this last thought crossed her mind. Did she desire the attention of an old man? Even as she thought that thought, she told herself that this was not just any old man. This was an old man like no other. His age did not seem to define him. His person seemed to fill the room whenever he entered.

Of course, he had the respect and allegiance of the countless people who served him as their King. However, Tora felt that Harald possessed something more, something no other man seem to have. There was something about him she could not explain. She finally decided it was his very spirit that set him apart and created the aura that was Harald Fairhair.

After the evening meal was finished and the men were gathered around the fire with their horns of mead, Tora retreated out to her dwelling. There she bathed with warmed water and changed to a fresh linen gown that had dried in the sunlight. The gown smelled of the pine needles she had wrapped it in. The dark blue over gown she had sewn made her blue eyes look even darker.

She released her hair from its thick braid and rubbed it with the bag of fragrant spices she kept in her trunk. Was there anything else she could do to prepare herself to spend the night in the King's bed chamber? No...she felt ready.

Tora crept into the castle as calmly as she could. She did not know if King Harald would remember that he had asked her to come to his bedchamber this night. Maybe he would fall asleep in his high seat surrounded by his men and filled with mead to a state of drunkenness. She did not want others to see her enter the bedchamber.

The large hall was dark, except for the blazing fire. There was no loud laughing or boisterous talk. The men had eaten and drunk their fill and were ready for sleep to overtake them. Tora walked slowly and calmly toward the large bedchamber that filled the end of the hall.

As she was about to open the door, she turned to look at Harald. Some thought must have stirred him, because just at that moment, he lifted his head to see a gown of dark blue with the shine of golden hair standing near the door to his room.

Harald raised himself with difficulty. The legs that in former time had been filled with strong, bulging muscles, now strained to lift his large frame. He stepped carefully down from the high seat and walked to the end of the hall. No one seemed to notice that the King had left the room. He did as he pleased...he always had.

Tora wondered at the flutter in her chest as he entered the bed chamber. She was sitting quietly on the edge of the bed platform, still dressed in her outer gown. King Harald had invited her to share his bed to give him warmth and comfort, nothing more. Or was there more? He looked at her as if there might be something more. She would follow his lead and give just what she had offered.

Why had it been so long since he shared his bed with a soft, warm body, Harald wondered. Had he gotten too old to even think about the pleasures another person could offer? Why would he spend his nights sitting in his high seat filled with mead and surrounded by men when he could spend his nights lying in the soft furs of his bed...wrapped in the arms of a lovely woman? Harald was grateful that Tora had offered and that he had accepted.

Did it matter that he was older than her father? Did he want more than warmth? Were those old stirrings still in there...or had they shriveled along with his other muscles? He no longer felt the need to conquer everything and everybody in his path. That part of his life was now just a memory. He was tired, so very tired, and cold. Harald would take what was offered and accept the comfort and warmth. It was enough.

Tora wrapped her agile arms and legs around the cold, boney back of her King. This had been her intent when she had offered to warm and comfort him. The thought of being in a bedchamber with the great Harald Fairhair had caused her to think there might be more expected of her. Was she ready for more? Did she want more? Was the spirit of a man enough to make up for a deteriorating body? All these thoughts soon ceased as Tora drifted into sleep at the sound of heavy, peaceful breathing from the body next to hers.

What a pleasure it was to wake up to the sight of a beautiful woman lying beside you! Harald felt good. He had slept well. It was still cold in the bedchamber, but it was warm in the bed. Even the thick fur of wolf pelts could not warm him like Tora had. Maybe his life was not going to be a long series of miserable days waiting for the end. There was new hope in his thoughts and in his feelings this day.

The long winter dragged on, but the days seemed less dreary. Harald felt better and he was happier. He had forgotten how it felt to look forward to something pleasant...and nights with Tora were very pleasant. They began to talk about things, things that Harald had been pondering over. When he was busy building his kingdom, he had thought about the future. Now that he felt he was about at the end of his life, he was thinking about the past. His life had been very exciting. Had he accomplished all that he could have? All that he should have?

It was great to have someone to tell his thoughts to. Tora was not someone he had to worry about. After all, she was just a maid servant. Of course, she wasn't a thrall or a slave. She had come from a respected family, even if she wasn't of royal blood. It pleased Harald to find that Tora had some deep thoughts of her own and that she was quite intelligent. He could tell her things that he would not have told any of his wives, his children, or his jarls. He did not have to pretend to be strong and powerful to her, and so they spoke of many things.

One thing that troubled Harald was the fact that he wasn't sure what would happen to his kingdom when he died. He knew that he had sired many sons so that there would be rulers enough to lead all the kingdoms under his control, but some of them had died and there was contention among others.

Erik and his wife Gunhild were a source of a great deal of that contention, but he had promised Rani that he would make Erik chief ruler after him. If only Erik had more of the charm of his mother and less of her stubborn determination. Or maybe it was his determination to rule over all that made Erik so aggressive. That was one of the many things he spoke to Tora about in the long winter nights in the warmth of the king's bedchamber.

Harald was a dreamer. He had dreamed big dreams and he had made his dreams come true. They weren't just his dreams, though. He knew that he was guided by his God, even Odin, through his dreams. Sometimes the dreams came unbidden. Sometimes the dreams came after Harald had prayed and pleaded for help and direction. He had learned about the dreams from his mother, Ragnhild, and he had worked hard to fulfill the dream she had dreamed about him.

Odin had been silent for a long time now, and Harald continued to ask for assurance that he had earned his place in the next life. Why was Odin making him worry and wonder? Hadn't he finished his work here on the earth? Had he done all that he was meant to do? May be not. Is that why he had to continue to sit in this worn out old body that could hardly get up and down and was cold all of the time? Well, not all of the time anymore.

As Harald found solace while confiding in Tora and their relationship grew, Tora decided she could also confide her thoughts to Harald.

"Could I ask a boon of My Lord?" asked Tora quietly.

"A boon...yes," Harald answered. "You have added so much pleasure to my dreary existence that I would gladly grant your wish."

"I want a son. I want a son of Harald Fairhair!" she declared.

Harald turned to face her in bed. "Haven't I already sired enough sons to rule the whole kingdom and to spare?"

"Yes, you have enough sons, but I haven't even one."

"Am I keeping you from marriage to a man of your own age while enjoying your company each night in my bedchamber?"

"No, My Lord. There is no one else I love. I love you. I have loved you from the start. At first I just loved the idea of you and the very essence of the you that is King of Norway. But after these months of knowing the man inside the King, I love that man."

Harald wasn't sure what to answer. He thought of the oath he had given to Rani that he would not take another wife to his bed, but he had no intention of making Tora his wife. Still, sharing his seed was mostly what Rani would object to. Odin and Rani had both approved of his marriage to Ashild, but Tora was a different matter. Could he even physically sire another son if he wanted to? All of these thoughts raced though Harald's mind as he stared into the eyes of his bedmate.

"I shall have to think about it," was Harald's response.

Tora tried not to look downcast. Harald wondered if he should share his concerns with her, but decided not to. She chose to bide her time and wait for another moment to bring up the subject again. Harald was relieved.

Then she thought of a plan. Every night after she heard the even breathing that meant Harald had fallen asleep, she whispered into his ear, "You want to give Tora a son. You want to give Tora a son." This went on for a fortnight.

One night, Harald awoke from his dream and looked over at the beautiful woman sleeping next to him. Her yellow hair was covering most of her face, but he thought he detected a slight smile on her lips.

"Wake up, Tora," he whispered, "this day you shall have a son of Harald Fairhair." Tora's blue eyes opened and began to glisten with tears of joy. Her wish was going to come true.

The dream Harald had was one he had not consciously asked for. Freya, the Godess of love, came to him and told him that he should love Tora enough to give her a son. Odin stood behind the Godess and affirmed that it was his will. Just one more son was required of him and then he would have completed his life's work. This last son, born of Tora, would become a great king after him.

Harald awoke so joyous. Not only was he going to make Tora happy, but he was going to achieve the one last great deed that Odin required before he could be accepted into Gimli...and have his Rani.

The months passed quickly. There was a bit of surprise expressed when Tora announced she was with child. There wasn't much question as to who the father was. Harald seemed almost as pleased as Tora. Erik and his wife Gunhild privately told each other that the King was acting foolish in his old age. The others who lived at Avaldsnes were pleased that the King was happy.

Tora no longer slept with her arms and legs wrapped around Harald's back. Now, Harald slept with his arms cradling her growing belly. How excited they were when the first movements of life stirred within her body. The summer passed quickly and Tora was proud of the child growing inside her.

With the start of a new year came the birth of a new life. Tora was visiting her mother on Moster Island when the pains began. She was determined to have the child born with Harald near and hurriedly boarded a ship. However, the boy would not wait and was delivered on the slate by the gangplank. Jarl Sigurd poured water on the baby and pronounced his name to be Haakon after Asa's father, Jarl of Lade.

The child joined Tora and Harald in the king's bedchamber at night, just as he had before his birth. He was such a good baby and cried very little. He was large for his size and already had the look of Harald in his face. Like his father before him, he had golden curls and a manner that made people love him. As summer came, Harald liked to take Haakon with him outside for a nap on his bench in the warm sun.

The beautiful carved bench that Harald had made for his Rani to sit in under the Yggdrasil tree had been replaced several times over the years. The current bench had a large pillow of feathers to cushion the boney body of the King. The mound he had raised to his black haired wife sat very near to the sacred tree and oftentimes Harald spoke to her when no one was about.

Gunhild and Erik had been living at Avaldsnes for some time now because they assumed Harald was in his last days. At least he had acted that way before he took up with Tora. Erik would never have guessed that his father was capable of siring another child...and why did it have to be a son. Daughters were no threat to him. Actually, none of Erik's brothers or sisters had seemed a threat to him. He had always been confident of his standing as the favored son of his father.

Erik had heard many times the story of how his father had won the heart of his mother, Ragnild the Mighty. He had also heard about the way his father had grieved for the wife that died after just two years of marriage. Erik did not remember anything of his mother, but he knew she was his father's favorite and that favoritism was handed down to him in her absence.

Now it was time for his father to journey to the next world. Erik was ready to take over the kingdom, even if he still had many living brothers. Why had Haakon come to give new life to a dying man? It was not just and Erik was going to tell his father so. Gunhild agreed with him. She had a way of making things happen...things she had learned from the Finns before their marriage. She would help him make a plan.

Harald was holding Haakon on his knee and laughing as the boy pulled on the great silver beard. His father spent much too much time with the child to suit Erik.

"I need to talk to you," Erik said to his father.

"I am listening," responded Harald.

"Give the boy to his mother so we can talk as men," he replied with a frown.

Harald could hear the irritation in Erik's voice and knew of his jealous nature, so he called for Tora.

"Take the boy and give us some quiet," he told her.

Tora was quick to respond. She had seen Erik's jealousy and his irritation with Haakon and she did not want to provoke him. Tora knew all about the wonderful Ragnild the Mighty and the love Harald still harbored for her...even after all these years. She was not jealous for herself, but she knew how much Haakon loved his father and she knew Harald loved him too. This joy in his new son was a point of contention.

"What will be the future for this son of Tora?" Erik asked.

"Do you question that he is also a son of mine?"

"No...but she was not a princess as my mother was."

"Are you saying that Haakon is less my son because his mother was one of my maid servants?"

"That is what people are saying behind your back, Father."

"And would one of those people happen to be your wife?"

"She is only saying what people have said to her."

"I believe her capable of starting the rumor and then repeating it to you when it comes back to her ears."

"You are always blaming Gunhild," he answered defensively.

"That is because she is almost always to blame!" retorted Harald.

Erik felt frustrated by yet another futile conversation with his father concerning Gunhild. He was determined to force his father into facing the issue of Haakon as well as his other brothers and sisters.

"It is time you called all your sons together and set the affairs of the kingdom in order before you leave this world," declared Erik.

Harald looked at his son calmly. He knew Erik was right and he had intended to do just that...at some time. But, it was irritating that Erik should think he must order his father about as if he wasn't still a strong and capable ruler. He was torn between his love for this son and his anger at being treated thus.

His love won out and he answered, "You are right...it is time. Take a message to your brothers and sisters to gather at Avaldsnes in the spring, when the snow has left the ground. Then we will set in order the plan I have made."

Erik was relieved to hear those words and said he would send messages as soon as the weather would allow travel. He did not have to worry about his sisters. His father had ruled that their sons would become jarls and be given large estates, but they would not challenge their kin for the rule of any kingdom.

That night Tora listened as Harald spoke about gathering all of his children to Avaldsnes. "I greatly fear there will be some who will not be happy that I have a new son," said Harald.

"Are you concerned for his safety," Tora asked.

"I am...though there are kingdoms aplenty for all of my sons. May be I am starting to worry like an old woman," he laughed.

Tora laughed too, but she felt uneasy in her heart. She would keep Haakon close to her when his brothers were around.

Though King Harald had fathered twenty sons from six wives plus Tora, by his eightieth year, just ten sons were still alive.

CHAPTER 43

A FATHER'S BLESSING

What a great group of relations gathered at Avaldsnes that spring. Ten sons plus two daughters and their families descended on the King's estate. There was only mild interest in the new brother, Haakon. He was too young to be a threat to Harald's other heirs. They could see that their father's health was failing, despite his determined show of authority.

"My sons and my daughters, I have called you all together to give you a blessing according to the word of Odin, our God. I declare to you that he has watched over and guided me in all my battles, my trials, and my blessings...and you, my children, have been one of my greatest blessings."

"My parents each were given a dream about me before I was even born. I have also been blessed with dreams and many other forms of inspiration as guidance. I haven't always acknowledged Odin as much as he would have me do, but when I have erred, he has chastened me. Those times have taught me to always obey him and praise him."

"In my final days, he has given me the words to say to each of you, so it is both a father's blessing and a blessing from Odin. I challenge you to take these words of advice as those of both your father and your God. Listen well!"

"Eric, you are not my first born, but you will get my blessing and counsel first. You and all your brothers must know that I loved your mother, my Rani, the best of all my wives. That does not mean I did not love the others, but Rani was the beautiful young woman who came into my life when I had passed forty winters."

"She brought new life to both my body and my heart. We loved more passionately than I had ever loved before. Her death all but caused me to take my own life, just for the privilege of joining her in Gimli, but that was not the plan Odin had for my life. My Uncle Guttorm and your grandmother Ragnhild helped me to realize that Odin had not yet finished with me."

"I am not sure when you first heard the words, my son Erik, that I had given an oath to your mother, on her death bed, that I would make you King over all your brothers. I did promise it and I would have promised her anything she asked of me...just to see one more smile on her lovely lips."

"You probably also heard that I promised your mother that I would not take another wife after her death. That is a promise I was not able to keep...not because of any physical desire on my part, but because Odin has asked me to sire additional sons...and I have obeyed."

"I have not always been pleased with your actions, my favored son, and you know that to be true. You have caused the death of more than one of your brothers...no, do not look at me as if you deny that charge...but I have continued to support you for the sake of your mother. I charge you not to rule with a heavy hand, but to allow your brothers free will in the kingdoms I have given them as inheritance. Take no more in scat than the share I have taken and never try to sit in my high seat in their kingdoms. If you follow my will, there might be peace in our land."

"I loved you more when you were a young man and full of adventure. My love for you decreased when you brought into our family a woman who chose to be trained in witchcraft by the wicked Finns."

"Do not bother to look at me with that evil look in your eye, Gunhild, for I know more of your doings than you realize. You must understand that Odin knows everything that happens on this earth, depite having just one eye, and he is not pleased with the work you do. I have not sent you from my sight, though I have wanted to, because of my love for your husband. You both shall continue to live here at Avaldsnes after my death as part of Erik's inheritance, but what kind of reward Odin shall give to you when you reach your death day, I cannot say. Just mark these words...you shall both pass through much tribulation before you leave this earth body behind. Yours shall be an even more difficult trial than shall Erik's...and I shall receive him when he reaches Valhalla...but for you, I give no promise!"

"No, Erik, do not look at me with anger in your eyes. This is my promise to you...as told to me by Odin...and you are as powerless to change his will as am I."

"It saddens my heart to see that you, my son Sigrod, are the only remaining son of my first wife, Asa. It was promised to me, by Odin, that she would bear four sons, and she died giving you life. You have grown to be a steady and sensible man, and much of that credit goes to your grandmother, Malfrid. You have married a gentle woman who reminds me of your mother. I would like to wish you many more years to enjoy her company and that of your children, but Odin has not declared that to me. There will be much sorrow at your death. Live each day as if it were to be your last."

"I have the same regret for you, Olaf, that you have no brothers that yet live. I commend you for your willingness to cease seeking revenge on your brother Erik for the wrongful death of Bjorn and Ragnar. Your mother,

Svanhild, died in sorrow, but she will find her reward in seeing that Odin has planned to send two special spirits through her line, one for you and one for Bjorn. These special spirits will become mighty Kings in their own time and will be the cause of both gladness and sorrow during their reigns."

"To my son, Rorek, first son of my wife Gyda, I bless with a long and prosperous life. You have managed your kingdom of Hordaland with a firm hand, much the same as your grandfather, Halvdan the Black. It is said that you rule in fairness and your people have great respect for you. Your descendants will not choose to rule as kings, but will instead yield a powerful influence on the country of Norway for many generations to come."

"To my son, Sigtrygg, second son of my wife Gyda, I bless with the ability to live life to the fullest. You not only have the red hair of your mother, you have the strong determination to be content, no matter what your circumstances. You are also well loved of your people and treat them fairly. You have accepted your kingdom of Rogaland with no complaint that you did not also receive my estate of Avaldsnes on the Island of Karmr. Despite the fact that you are not collecting the taxes that come from the trade ships traveling through Karmsund, your kingdom has great wealth. Your descendants will reap the profit and benefits of that wealth and they will share it with all those who will live in our land."

"I shall now give words to you, my son Sigurd. You have grown strong and true and weathered life's storms better than I might have expected. Odin has watched over you in your childhood as well as now. You know that your mother was not only a Finn, but also a witch. And even though my body lusted after her and my seed joined with hers to make four sons, I never loved her. If she had not cast a spell on me and used me to accomplish the foul deeds planned by her evil father Svase, I would have taken her life as I took his when I was finally rescued. You would have been left to die in that horrid cave along with your three brothers if your Uncle Guttorm had not rescued you and refused to obey my order to leave you to die along with your Finnish mother and grandfather."

"Fortunately, Odin ordered me to recognize you four as my legal sons and have you fostered in good homes. The fact that you have now become a credit to your heritage shows that you carry less of your mother's blood than you do of mine. I bless you with a large posterity that will be a credit to both you and to me. From your loins will come more Kings than all of your brother's issue together...and they shall all claim the right of kingship through you to me...through the many generations of time."

"To my son, Ring, the first son of my wife, Ashild, I bless you with both happiness and long life. Your mother was the most kind and also the most unselfish person... who may not have married at all, except that she wanted to have children. When you were born, she felt she had fulfilled her purpose in life. You brought her such happiness and she was proud of the good example you always set for your younger brothers. I have continued to be proud of you as well. You have not sought for power or riches, but have been content to rule well the kingdom of Ringerike where your grandfather Ring ruled before you. Yours is the blessing of having a mound raised at Stein to your other grandfather, Halvdan the Black, as well as your great uncle Guttorm. Keep faith with the present, while guarding the past and you shall have no fear of the future."

"To my son, Dag, who was named for your great grandfather, I bless you with peace and understanding. It is not always easy to be the second son and have to try and fill the shoes of your older brother, but you have done it well. You have also been blessed with the fertile lands of Toten and Hadeland, some of the best lands in all of Norway. Your descendants will never starve if they tend the land well. You are blessed to have access to the Lake Mjosa as well as the Randsfjord. These two waterways will provide your people with many advantages and there will be continual prosperity for all the generations who inhabit your lands."

"To my son Gudrod Skirja, the youngest of Ashild's sons, I have a confession to make before your blessing. When your mother told me she would name you Gudrod, we had the most disagreement ever in our marriage. Because my grandfather was named Gudrod the Hunter, and because he had murdered my grandmother's family, I hated that name. To please me, your mother added Skirja to your name, but insisted you must be Gudrod. As you have grown, you have become the greatest hunter I have ever known and thus I gave you Gudbrandsdalir for your inheritance. You have very few people to rule, but you rule over the mountains, the forests, the rivers and the animals...and this brings you great joy. Your other great grandfather, Sigurd Hjort, was also a great hunter and if you live your life as honorably as he did, you will be considered a great man to all who know you. I bless you with that challenge."

"And now to my beautiful daughter Alov Arbot, who has grown to be even more beautiful as her thick red curls have become tinged with silver. I do not know how much more I could give you as a blessing than you already possess. You have married a sober and quiet man who is the best issue of my uncle Ragnvald. He has built you a fine castle in South More overlooking the North Sea and you have five stalwart sons. The only thing I can think that you might lack would be a lovely daughter who possessed your beautiful curls...but alas, it is not in my providence to grant that. You were a joy to your mother and you have been a joy to me. If your sons can bring you an equal amount of joy then that is the blessing I would wish for you."

"Next is my lovely daughter Ragnhild, the sweet spirit that was chosen for us by my mother Ragnhild. Because of the evil designs of others, you have had to grow up without the loving influence of your mother, Ashild. But you have been blessed to have a foster-mother in your aunt Margaret. Both your mother and your foster-mother were possessed of a gentle heart, and thus you have become a gentle hearted woman yourself. Your new husband, Knut, will enjoy a life filled with goodness with you as his wife. I am pleased that I was able to see you matched with a strong jarl who will provide for you well. I would bless you with all the love you can hold and ask you to share that love with your husband and any children you shall be privileged to bear. Love is the greatest gift our God has given us and he expects us to love him and all those we are responsible for...and that is the blessing I leave with you."

"And now for my youngest son, Haakon, I would bless you as well. You have come to me in my old age...when the life seed of my body should have withered and died. But your mother, sweet and strong Tora, pleaded with me to give her a son. She was not content to have any son, but was determined to have a son of Harald Fairhair. Because of her tender, loving assistance, a son has come of joining our seeds, a son who has given this old man new joy and new hope for the future."

"If any of you my children have looked on little Haakon as just the folly of an old man's lust, you are mistaken. It was Odin who sent Tora to me...first to be my hand maiden, then to be a warm body to cover the tired old bones of her King. But, most important of all, he has sent a kind and compassionate young woman to offer me love and to carry the last son that Odin has asked me to sire."

"You may truly ask, 'Another son?' I have already sired more sons than a man might deserve, but who am I to question the will of my God. I said those same words to Tora when she first asked me for my seed, but then I did what I have come to know is the right course for me...I asked Odin what would be his will. And he truly told me that I was to have one more son...that he had saved a special spirit for the last...and that this last son would rule my kingdom in righteousness."

"And what of the mighty sword Frey...that helped you win more than thirty battles when you were putting all the kingdoms of Norway under your rule? You do not intend to give Frey to that boy, do you?" questioned Erik.

Harald turned to face his defiant son. "Do you suppose to tell me what I must do with my prized possessions? Then I will tell you who will receive Frey as their inheritance...none of my sons...least of all you, Erik. You have already been given the sword of your mother's father, King Erik of Jutland. Are you so greedy that you would also demand the right to Frey? Yes, I can see by the look in your eyes that you mean to have it. Your brothers seated in this room might also covet my great sword, but you are the only son selfish enough to ask."

"It was not just the mighty sword Frey that enabled me to win all those battles without losing my life, but it was the will and blessing of our God Odin that protected me and gave power to my body and my sword. I have not been given the inspiration from Odin to bequeath Frey to any of you. I shall have it buried with me in my mound at Avaldsnes. That should keep any of you from feeling slighted that you were not the son who received the reward...and it should answer Erik's question about whether my mighty sword would be given to Haakon."

"It may be hard to think of the young man now seated on my lap as growing to be a great king, but I tell you, he will be great. You look at me with despair, my son Erik, as you see young Haakon cradled here in my bosom, but I tell you that he will succeed you on my throne...and not the sons you have fathered with your wife, Gunhild. I can see that this pronouncement surprises and angers you, but no amount of anger or anguish on your part, or Gunhild's, can change my will nor the will of Odin. You may look down on Tora as Haakon's mother because she is not a princess, but I tell you, I would as soon take a high born Tora to my bosom, as to take a princess who chooses to be a witch!"

"Do not let that hand reach for your dagger, my son, for you are most likely the only person in this room that has any love for Gunhild and to murder your father and your King for her sake would only hasten her sorrow. For Berdaluke and many others would have their daggers at your throat before yours could manage to reach my heart."

"Yes, look around you, my son, and calm your rage. There is much blood on that dagger already and even the blood of your kin. Your enemies, and even your friends, call you Erik Bloodaxe, but I would hate to see your name being changed to Erik Kingkiller!"

With these strong words from his father, Erik looked around him to see Berdaluke and the rest of Harald's bodyguard with their hands also on their dagger handles, waiting for a sign from Harald before they made a move to protect their King.

Erik took another look around the great hall and, glaring at his father sitting in the high seat, grabbed the arm of his wife and stormed out of the room. There was quiet in the hall as those family members still in attendance waited on the response of their leader.

"Erik will rue the day he threatened his father and turned his back on me. His punishment will not come from me or those who guard and protect me, but Odin will see that there is a just consequence for each wrong he has committed!"

"Here Tora, take our good little Haakon from me, but mark my words, and never let him out of your sight...or ill may come to him in a manner and time you least expect."

Tora walked over to the side of her King, the man she had grown to love. He was richly arrayed in his purple pell gown with a jerkin of fine fur covering his bony shoulders. She had to admit that he showed his age with his thick hair now white as snow, but the love she saw in his deep blue eyes as he handed their precious Haakon into her arms was very real.

"And now, my children, it is time for your father to rest. My life has been a long one, eighty three winters, and all of my wives have preceded me in death. I feel Odin will soon tell me I have finished my work here on this earth. It is up to you to carry on with the mission I have begun...to make our country a strong and mighty one with laws that are fair and punishments that are just. It is your duty to know the laws and enforce them with the aid of the lagmen and jarls. You must each attend to the Thing in the kingdoms where you rule and see that justice is done."

"I charge each of you to be honorable men and rule with fairness. Think about the example you are setting for your sons and grandsons. We have been blessed with a country that was founded by Odin when he escaped from the oppressors who would have enslaved him and his people. He was told to come to this North Country by his father and he brought his three youngest sons, Seaming, Yngvi and Skjold with him. As he laid hands on their heads and gave them a father's blessing, he sent them forth and charged them also to rule with justice."

"It is from his example that we have our Code of Laws, the code my father organized in his eight kingdoms and the code I have implemented and enforced in my thirty one kingdoms. We are all of us partakers of the hallowed blood of Odin, and he will bless you, as he has blessed me, if you but ask him and strive to do his will. These blessings I have pronounced on your heads this day are just a sampling of the many blessings he would have for you if you choose the right path."

"At all times, remember who you are, and who you represent. It is not possible to expect worthy acts from the people you rule, if you do not commit worthy acts yourself. Guard your acts of revenge so that they do not overtake you and cause your death or the death of your family. Live your life so that you will be worthy to join with me and the rest of your family in the heaven of our God."

That night, as they lay together in the large master bedchamber at Avaldsnes, Harald told Tora that the time had come for her to give up their joint treasure...for his own safety. They both knew Erik and Gunhild would try to cause little Haakon's death, in spite of Odin's promise. She began to cry softly into the folds of Harald's night shirt as she thought of how her life would change without the love of her Harald and her little Haakon.

The very next day, Berdaluke was instructed to take Prince Haakon and secretly deliver him to King Aethelstan in England, together with the sword Harald had received from the English King years before. Two additional items were sent with his young son...his father's elaborate gold helmet and richly ornamented battle shield. When the time came for Haakon to return and claim his kingdom, he would need to show his countrymen that he did, indeed, possess the blessing of his father in his quest to rule Norway.

The King laid hands on the boy's head and sent his son off with one final blessing...the best blessing he could pronounce...that the boy would always look to his God for guidance.

CHAPTER 44

DEATH AT LAST

"I have fought a good fight, I have finished my course, I have kept the faith." **11 Timothy 4:11**

"Odin, haven't I done enough? Is it not time for me to join my Rani? What more do you want from me?" cried the aged King.

"Yes, your time has come, my son. Return to the Temple you built to my name and I shall be ready for you."

Harald stepped out the door of his castle at Avaldsnes for the last time and walked toward Odin's Temple. The morning sun was streaming in the openings that faced to the east and cast a golden glow on the statue of Odin that filled the center stage of the alter.

This descendant and spirit son of Odin, who had lived eighty three winters and served as King for seventy three of those years, lay down on the rock floor in front of the likeness of his God.

"I am here...I am ready."

"Yes, my son. I have sent a messenger to lead you across the bridge to the eternal world. Do you feel her arms around you?"

At that moment, Harald turned upward to face the gold ceiling of Odin's Temple...and then he saw her and felt her caress.

"Rani...my Rani..."

Those were the last words spoken by the great King Harald Fairhair.

"He that overcometh shall inherit all things; and I will be his God and he shall be my son." **Revalations 21:7**

"Harald Harfagre was, according to the report of men-of- knowledge, of remarkably handsome appearance, great and strong, and very generous and affable to his men. He was a great warrior in his youth; and people think that this was foretold by his mother's dream before his birth, as the lowest part of the tree she dreamt of was red as blood. The stem again was green and beautiful, which betokened his flourishing kingdom; and that the tree was white at the top showed that he should reach a grey-haired old age. The branches and twigs showed forth his posterity, spread over the whole land; for of his race, ever since, have come the Kings of Norway."

Heimskringla

Proof

56013720R00195